IMAGES
of America

HONOLULU TOWN

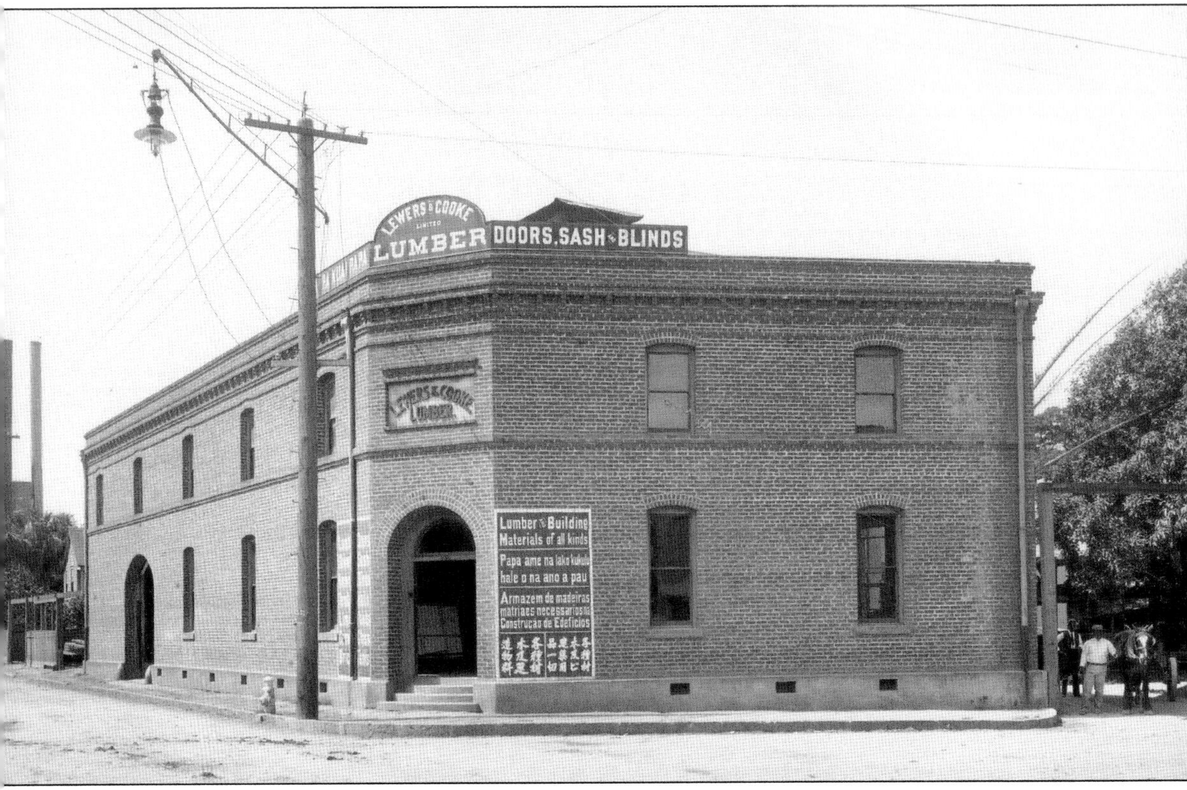

Five Languages. Originally known as Lewers and Dickson, the firm of Lewers and Cooke owned huge lumber stockpiles at the waterfront and in Kakaako and Iwilei. The five languages on the advertisement above—English, Hawaiian, Portuguese, Chinese, and Japanese—suggest the company's readiness to serve a multiethnic community. In the 1920s, the company hired architect Raymond Morris, published booklets of house plans, and gave advice to homeowners if all their building materials were purchased from the company. (Hawaiian Historical Society.)

On the Cover: Joyful Children at the Old Kamamalu Park. Children take advantage of the City Department of Parks and Recreation program that provided sprinklers for them to play in during the summer break around 1956. Old Kamamalu Park was located at the *makai* (toward the sea)-Diamond Head corner of School and Fort Streets. Punchbowl Crater, always within sight, defines one of the gentle boundaries of Honolulu Town. (Anonymous.)

IMAGES
of America

Honolulu Town

Laura Ruby and Ross W. Stephenson

ARCADIA
PUBLISHING

ISBN 978-0-7385-9300-5

Published by Arcadia Publishing
Charleston, South Carolina

Printed in the United States of America

Library of Congress Control Number: 2011935412

For all general information, please contact Arcadia Publishing:
Telephone 843-853-2070
Fax 843-853-0044
E-mail sales@arcadiapublishing.com
For customer service and orders:
Toll-Free 1-888-313-2665

Visit us on the Internet at www.arcadiapublishing.com

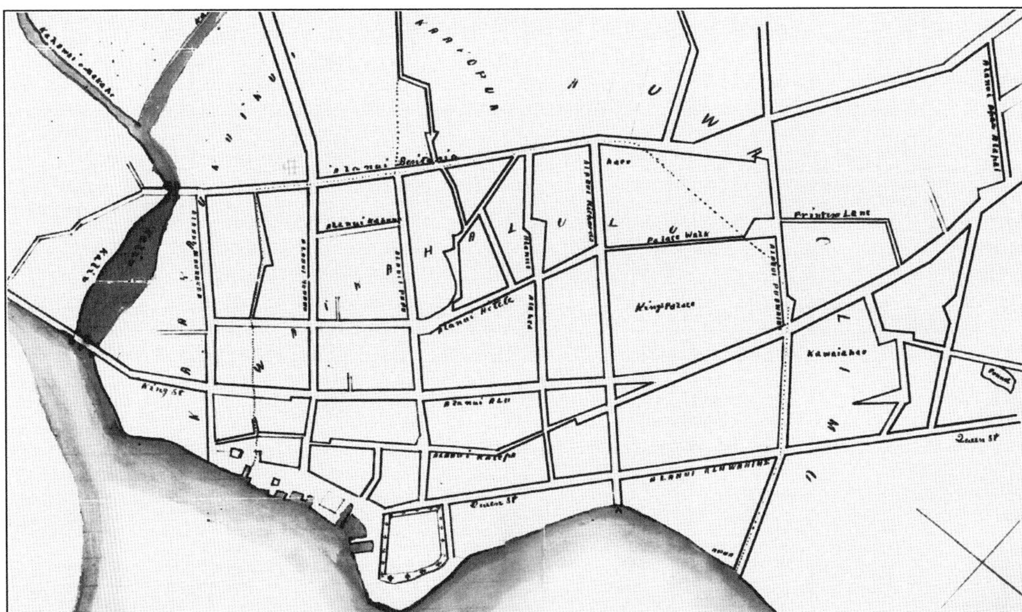

MAP OF HONOLULU TOWN, 1847. A broad open space for loading and unloading ships exists along the waterfront Diamond Head of Nuuanu Stream, while Honolulu Fort is the enclosure on the headland in the lower center. Streets recognizable to a 21st-century reader include the *makai-mauka* (toward the ocean-toward the mountains) Maunakea, Nuuanu, Fort, Alakea, Richards, and Punchbowl. Ewa-Diamond Head streets include Beretania, Hotel, King, Merchant, and Queen. (Surveyor, Metcalf; draftsman, Lydgate, Hawaii Government Survey.)

Hui aku na maka i Kou—the eyes (friends) will meet at Kou
(ʻŌlelo Noʻeau, collected by Mary Kawena Pukui)

Contents

ACKNOWLEDGMENTS

Mahalo nui loa to the following: Charlene Alipio, June Anami, Lowell Angell, Judy Bowman, Desoto Brown, Kanoeokalani Cheek, Stuart Ching, Ron Cox, Barbara Dunn, Nicki Garces, Tom Haar, Suzanne Harter, Rev. Clarence Higa, Joan Hori, Linda Hsu, Jan Kamiya, Rev. Jitsunin Kawanishi, Luella Kurkjian, Kristina Larssen, Candice Lee, William Lowe, Henry Maunakea, Dore Minatodani, Lorraine Minatoshi-Palumbo, Rev. Jun Mitasaka, Daisy Murai, Charlie Myers, Harriet Natsuyama, Victoria Nihi, Brian Niiya, Warren Nishimoto, Eleanor Nordyke, Rev. Akihiro Okada, Nelson Okino, Cynthia Oshiro, Lisa Palm, Tia Reber, Joseph P. Recca, Hanayo Sasaki, Sheldon Seki, Susan Shaner, B.J. Short, Bron Solyom, Donda Spiker, Carol Stephenson, Linda Sueyoshi, Brian Suzuki, Debby Tanaka, Ross Togashi, Wendy Tolleson, Gordon Tomita, Kazue Uyeda, Jessica Von Hauki, Rev. Amy Wake, Carol White, Charles Wong, Kuang-Tien Yao, Father Louis Yim, Debbie Young, Janet Zisk, and Hawai'i Council for the Humanities.

Archives and collections (index located at www.honolulutownbook.com):
Bishop Museum Archives and Library (BM)
Daijingu Temple of Hawaii
Episcopal Church in Hawaii Archives (EC)
Fathers of the Sacred Hearts, Hawaii Province Archives (HP)
First Methodist Church
Harris Methodist Church
Hawaii State Archives (HSA)
Hawaii State Library (HSL)
Hawaii State Historic Preservation Division (SHPD)
Hawaii State Survey Office
Hawaiian Historical Society (HHS)
Historic Hawaii Foundation (HHF)
Hoomana Naauao o Hawaii
Izuma Taishokyo Mission of Hawaii
Japanese Cultural Center of Hawaii (JCCH)
John Young Foundation
Kamehameha Schools Archives
Kaumakapili Church
Kuakini Medical Center
Liliha Shingonji Mission
Mid-Pacific Institute Archives
Mission Houses Museum Library
Palama Settlement (PS)
Scottish Rite Cathedral Archives (SRC)
Sisters of the Sacred Hearts Archives, Pacific Province
University of Hawaii Center for Oral History
University of Hawai'i Libraries, Archives
University of Hawai'i Libraries, Hawaiian Collection
University of Hawai'i Libraries, Jean Charlot Collection (UHL-JCC)
University of Hawai'i Libraries, Map Collection, Magis.manoa.hawaii.edu.index.html
United States Army Museum of Hawaii (USAMH)

Introduction

Before the days of the little higgledy-piggledy Honolulu Town, a small Hawaiian settlement was located at the foot of Nuuanu Valley that provided freshwater and an ideal location for launching canoes. This gathering place was named for the sheltering kou trees whose red-orange blossoms bloomed year-round.

Foreigners arriving in the islands after 1778 became involved in local politics as Hawaii became integrated into the world economy. In 1794, English merchant William Brown located a narrow reef opening, which offered great commercial potential as the only natural harbor in the central North Pacific and a basin large enough to accommodate over 100 ships. As the story goes, the Hawaiian name *Honolulu* means "sheltered harbor or bay."

Hawaii Island ruler Kamehameha the Great united most of the archipelago after defeating Kalanikupule in the Battle of Nuuanu Valley in 1795. This battle was actually fought along a series of defense lines near Kou, beginning at four *heiau* (places of worship) makai of Punchbowl known as Kanelaau (Alapai and Kinau Streets), Mauna (Queen's Hospital near Lusitana Street), Kahehuna (Royal School), and Kaakopua (Central Intermediate School). Kamehameha's troops went through Papakolea and Elekoki/Alekoki (Nuuanu Craigside/Maemae/Ili Kawananakoa) before heading toward the climax at the Pali.

Between 1809 and 1812, Kamehameha resided on Oahu at Pakaka Point. Nearby *alii* (the chiefly class) and retainers occupied the shoreline, with the bulk of the population between Pakaka and Nuuanu Stream.

In 1816, German doctor Georg Scheffer, employed by Imperial Russia, interfered in the internal political affairs of the Kingdom and erected a blockhouse at Pakaka Point. Kamehameha's war leader, Kalanimoku, expelled the Russians and constructed a fort, which was originally known as Kekuanohu there. The main entrance, mauka, became the start of "Fort Street." Another straight path, immediately mauka and at the harbor entrance (today's Richards Street), was used by work gangs to pull ships through the harbor-entrance channel under sights of the Fort's guns.

Haole (foreigners) became entrepreneurs along the waterfront. Spaniard Don Francisco de Paula Marin acted as interpreter for alii and ship captains and planted grapes for winemaking. Ship carpenter James Robinson, after surviving the shipwrecks of the *Pearl* and *Hermes* 1,000 miles northwest of Honolulu, built a schooner from the wreckage. He sailed it to Honolulu and made a profit from the sale of the boat. Robinson began a successful shipbuilding partnership at Pakaka Point.

A different type of foreigner arrived on April 19, 1820. The American Board of Commissioners for Foreign Missions eventually brought 12 groups of religious teachers to the islands. The mission occupied both sides of what is now South King Street, Diamond Head of Punchbowl. Beretania Street and its environs would contain Methodist, Catholic, Episcopalian, Congregationalist, and Lutheran churches.

Public education began in conjunction with Congregationalist churches. Other institutions in town followed, including the Oahu Charity, Fort Street, Honolulu High, and the Territorial Normal schools, and the College of Hawaii, all of which evolved into the present public educational system. Similarly, Kawaiahao Seminary, Mills Institute, Iolani College, St. Andrews Priory, St. Francis School, St. Louis College, and Sacred Hearts outgrew their campuses and resettled elsewhere under the same or different names. By the mid-to-late 19th century, Hawaii would have one of the highest literacy rates in the world.

Within Honolulu Fort, Governor Kekuanaoa conducted court at his home, while prisoners were incarcerated in cells on the opposite, Ewa side. This became increasingly unsatisfactory. In 1851, prisoners were sent to the reefs to cut coral for a new courthouse building adjacent to the Fort. The Court House eventually housed the legislature, supreme court, and other functions, including part of the work of the Land Commission (the Mahele) in 1852, meetings of the Royal Hawaiian Agricultural Society (a forerunner of the Hawaiian Sugar Planters' Association) in 1854, and a ball by Chinese merchants in honor of the king and queen in 1856.

Reminded by an 1851 incident when prisoners rebelled and threatened the town with live cannon fire, authorities had the prison constructed in Iwilei when the Fort was demolished in 1857. Material from the Fort was used to fill portions of the Waikahalulu Reef between the fort site and deep water to create additional wharfage space, known as the Esplanade.

Disasters would periodically close the town. Mosquitoes introduced in 1826 into the stagnant waters behind Honolulu led to waves of malaria. In 1853, a smallpox epidemic forced authorities to dig mass graves at Honuakaha. Fires in 1886 and 1900 gutted the central city. The growing pains of the city were legion, as crowded and unsanitary conditions forced the community to make major investments in water, sewer, and drainage systems; fill in lowlands; and enlarge the harbor.

During the first half of the 19th century, economic activities centered on Queen Street, where sailors from whaling ships sought entertainment in the grog shops. The second half of the 19th and the early 20th centuries were dominated by the effects of agriculture. This included new railroad wharves, pineapple canneries, the rise of sugar factors, and importation of labor. As the laborers' plantation contracts ran out, first the Chinese moved to the city looking for better economic opportunities (and indelibly labeling the Ewa portion of town as Chinatown) before successive ethnic groups followed. The Japanese created Japantown near Aala Park and Nuuanu Stream. These groups in turn founded many temples, shrines, mutual-help societies, and language schools.

Efforts to improve the lives of Honolulu's citizens through social action were undertaken by both government and private parties. Queen Emma, one of Hawaii's great philanthropists, was crucial in the development of Queen's Hospital and St. Andrew's Priory School. After her death, her Nuuanu home became an incubator of the many early ethnic YMCAs that evolved into the all-encompassing Nuuanu YMCA, a free kindergarten, and where planning for the Japanese Charity (Kuakini) Hospital began. Central Union Church founded Palama Settlement on Liliha Street, a facility that provided guidance, athletics, and health care to the underprivileged. Queen Liliuokalani similarly would establish her trust for the benefit of Native Hawaiian children with a facility in nearby Palama.

Meanwhile, the dominant economic classes moved from along Queen and Kaahumanu Streets to Merchant before creating a whole new street, Bishop, where they constructed a district of Mediterranean-, classical-, and Asian-influenced monuments in stone, such as the Alexander Young Hotel and the Alexander and Baldwin Building.

In the 1920s, victory in World War I had brought a fleet of German-built passenger ships under the control of US commercial interests. These ships were too big to be accommodated by the Esplanade. Even larger ships from Matson and other companies led the Territory to demolish the Esplanade and construct new Piers 8–12 terminals, and the iconic Aloha Tower.

After the war, further changes were made to the urban landscape. As Oahu Railway closed, harbor docks went to other uses. Nimitz Highway was developed across other docks, Vineyard Boulevard widened and straightened and land condemned for the Lunalilo Freeway and Pali Highway. Similarly, the Honolulu Redevelopment Agency cleared residents and businesses from multiple acreages in Aala, Kauluwela, Kukui, Pauahi, and Chinatown.

As population left downtown, both retail and social organizations downsized, closed, or relocated. Improvement would have to wait until the mid-1960s, when downtown began to be a much more lively place again.

One

The Edgy Waterfront

The waterfront is edgy because it was the major cusp for all encounters between Native Hawaiians and foreigners. Its character would continually be redefined by these interactions.

Kamehameha I made a crucial choice to locate his business dealings at Kou and to rely on trusted Westerners for his dealings with other foreigners. He lived at Pakaka Point in a compound surrounded by a palisade.

The configuration of the harbor was such that on the inland Ewa side was high ground, freshwater, and the closest in proximity to deep water; and on the Diamond Head side was the narrow channel. The first dock was a sunken hulk near Nuuanu Street (now Avenue), the path used to obtain foodstuffs and sandalwood available inland.

Honolulu Fort, in existence from 1816 to 1857, never fired a shot in anger. Its guns welcomed arriving ships or announced events. The Fort also acted as courthouse, jail, armory, drill center, insane asylum, and riot location. Confrontations there included an 1830 rebellion by Governor Liliha of Oahu, the 1843 cessation of authority to Great Britain, an 1849 ransacking by the French, and an 1852 riot by sailors from whaling ships who also burned the nearby Station House.

The initial growth of the town had been so helter-skelter that in 1837, the alii dismayed many haole by ordering buildings demolished to straighten and widen roads. Notable government institutions first constructed near the shore included the Custom House, Harbor Master's Office, Court House, Post Office, and Police Station. The shoreline moved makai to accommodate harborside businesses, creating the Esplanade. In the 1920s, the Territory removed these 19th-century streets to build Aloha Tower and larger wharves.

New land was also created on both sides of the harbor. Iwilei became known for its slaughterhouses, guano fertilizer storage, Oahu Prison, and pineapple cannery. Kakaako had a military base, graveyards, trash dumps, and sewage pump station. Ironically, Kakaako also contained three generations of immigration facilities through which the composition of the islands' population was permanently changed.

Originally, the easiest method of travel had been by sea. The harbor was the nexus, with land-based pathways makai-mauka for gathering and exchanging island products for the ships and vice versa. The growth in population, limited land between the sea and mountains, and road improvements changed the axis of land-based island travel to Ewa-Diamond Head.

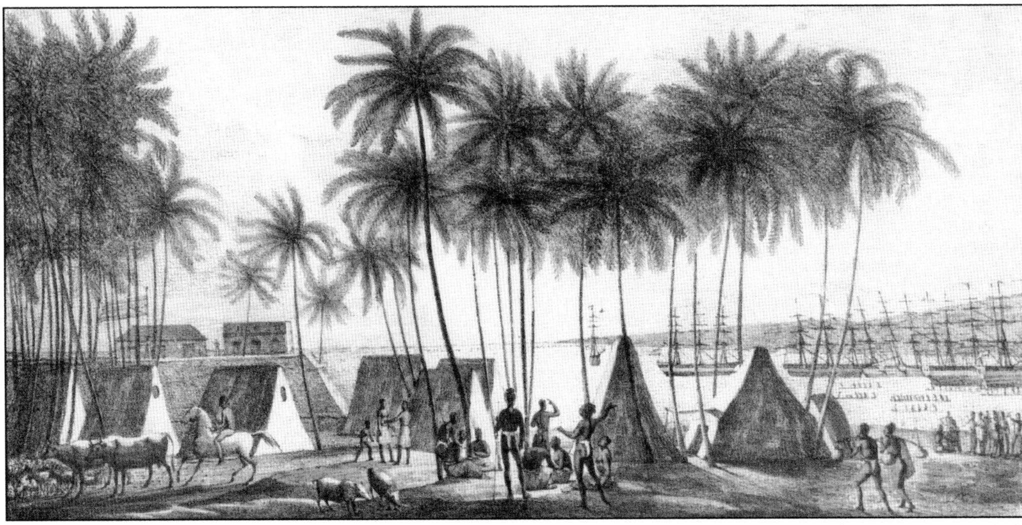

PORT OF HONOLULU. This 1816 Louis Choris artwork (watercolor over pencil) shows Honolulu as a village with grass *hale* (houses) dominant. Cattle and western pigs roam in the compound, and the few foreigners' houses are out of sight. Kamehameha I's Fort stands in the background. Canoes wind their ways between many western ships, suggesting extensive trade at this time. On September 17, 1819, the first whaling ship arrived in Hawaiian waters. (Art by Louis Choris with the Von Koetsebue expedition; HSA.)

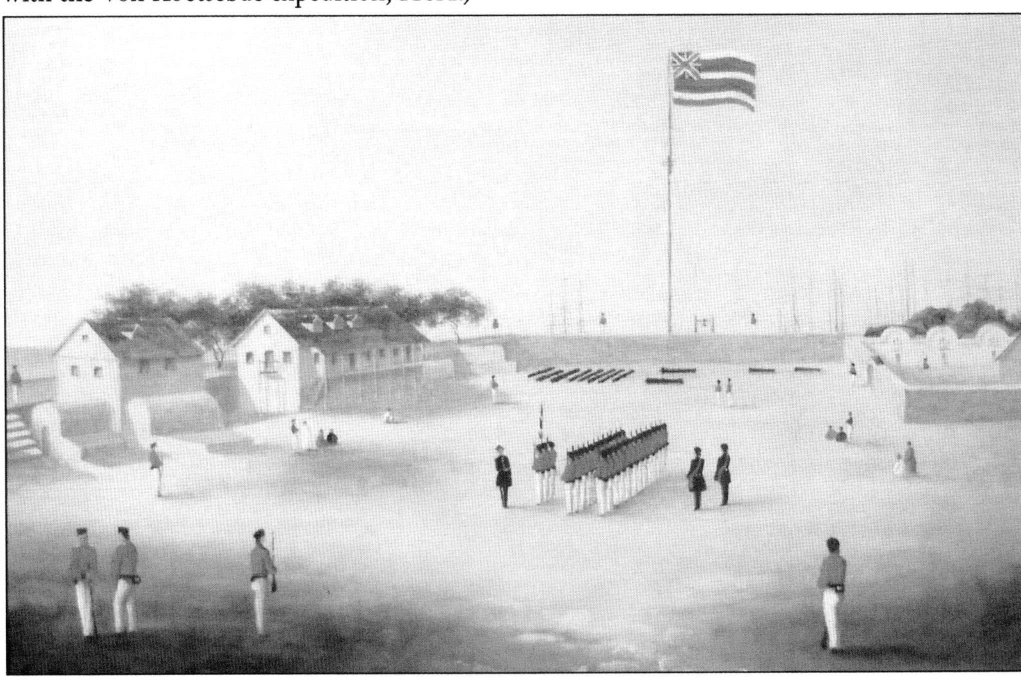

HONOLULU FORT. Paul Emmert painted the inside of the Fort, which was located on the waterfront about 1853. The Hawaiian flag flies proudly over the Fort, which was constructed in 1816 by Kamehameha I. The Fort was so placed because its guns would face the broadside of any ship attempting to enter the harbor. Note the rounded stone powder magazines and Governor Kekuanaoa's long house. The governor's home also acted as a courthouse for prisoners incarcerated in cells on the right. (HHS.)

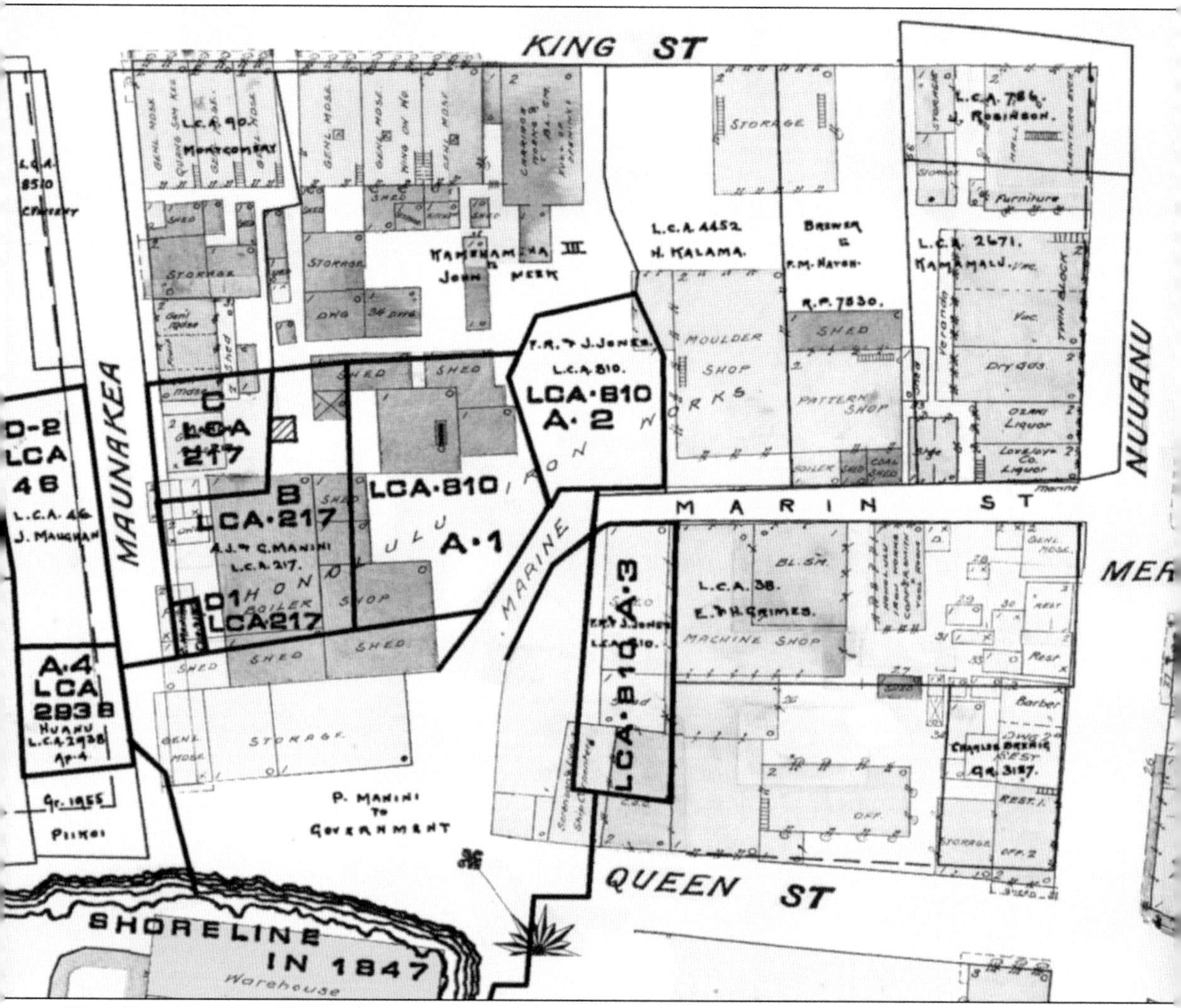

Don Francisco de Paula Marin's Land Commission Awards in Kapuukolo. Marin (1774–1837) arrived in 1793 or 1794 and became a lasting influence in early Honolulu. Known as Manini to Hawaiians and fluent in at least Hawaiian, English, and Spanish, he became an invaluable interpreter for alii and ships' captains. He was also King Kamehameha I's business associate. Marin became an intermediary for the three-way exchange of goods: furs and sandalwood for China, porcelain and other Chinese luxury goods for Hawaii, and fresh produce for the ships traveling to New England carrying Asian goods and Pacific Northwest furs. Such was the mercantile hustle on the bustling Honolulu waterfront. He was also known for his horticulture—his vineyards at the confluence of Nuuanu and Pauoa Streams (River and Kukui Streets intersection today) provided wine for the alii. He cultivated the first citrus, mangos, and tamarind trees in Pauoa Valley and Mokuumeume (Ford Island). According to his journal, Marin, as overseer, began the construction of the first permanent stone buildings in late 1809: the king's house/storehouse and America (Marin's house at Kapuukolo, makai of King between Maunakea and Nuuanu). The hatched square is the approximate location of Marin's stone house and his burial vault. Today, Marin Tower occupies the left-hand side of this map. (Combined 1896 Government Survey, 1899 Dakin, and 1973 Hawaiian Historical Society maps.)

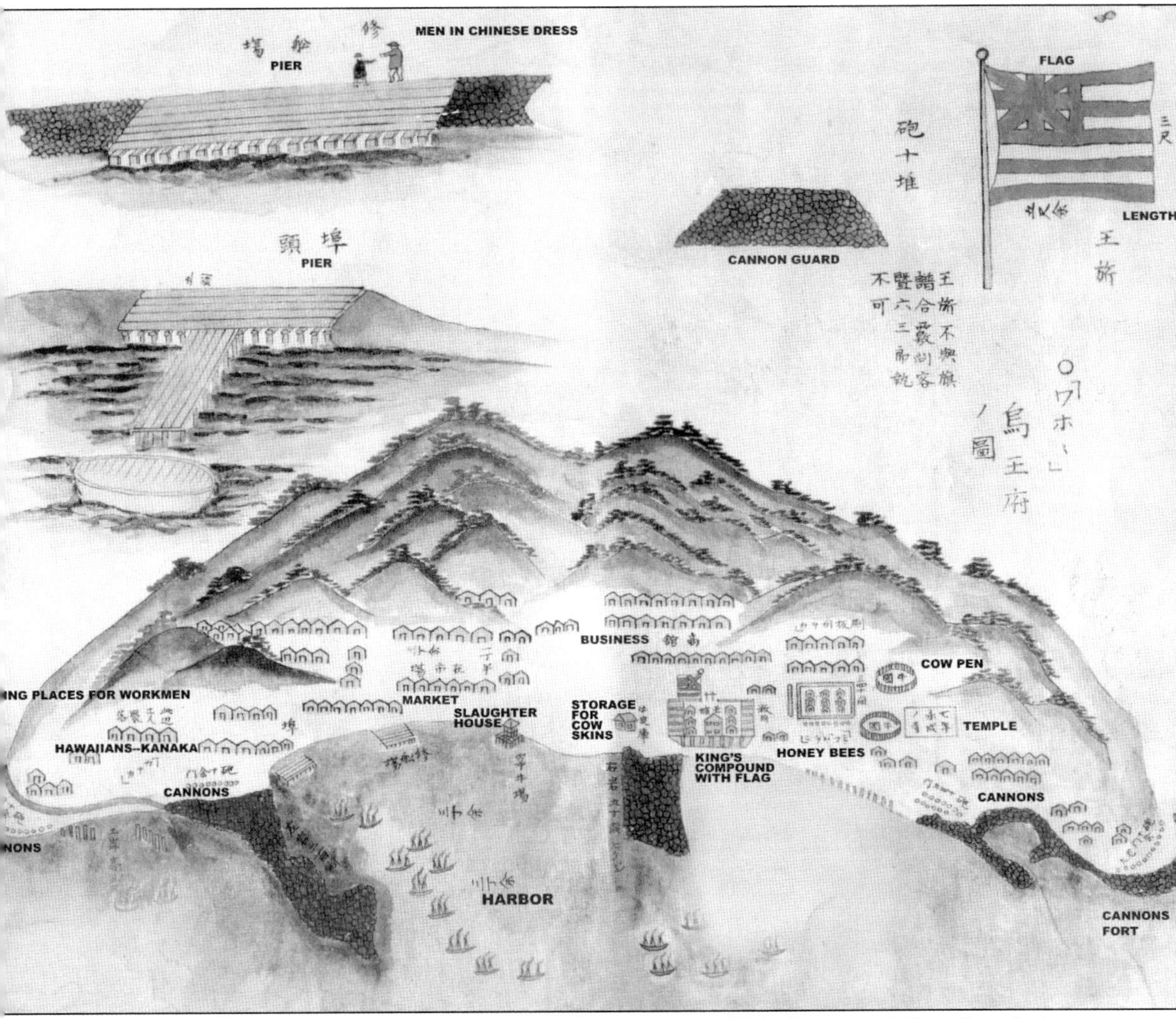

VOYAGE OF DESTINY, c. 1850. Fourteen-year-old Manjiro Nakahama and four friends became castaways while fishing in a time when leaving Japan and returning was punishable by death. They were adrift and shipwrecked for 148 days until a whaler captained by William H. Whitfield rescued them, finally stopping in Honolulu. The four friends stayed, but Manjiro continued on to Fairhaven, Massachusetts, with the captain, received English schooling, returned to Honolulu, and was reunited with his friends. He sketched this Honolulu map and the people he saw. When he and two of his friends returned to Japan, they were questioned at the regional court and absolved of any wrongdoing. To aid the court investigation, Kawada Shoryo was asked to transcribe Manjiro's account and illustrate Manjiro's sketches. The complete account was entitled *Drifting toward the Southeast*. Kawada wrote the map's legends (pictured) in imperial Chinese. Manjiro's skills with foreigners made him the Tokugawa Shogunate interpreter for the 1853 opening of Japan by Commodore Matthew Perry's Black Ships. (HSA.)

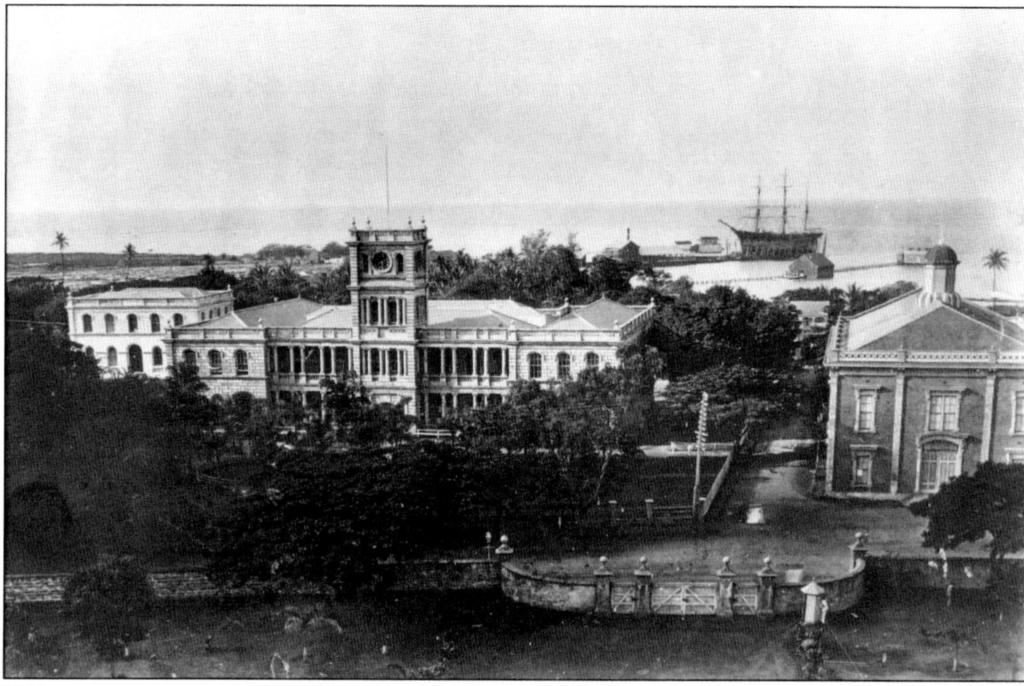

View Makai of the Palace, c. 1884–1887. This photograph was taken from the central tower of Iolani Palace, with the original high palace wall visible in the lower foreground. Aliiolani Hale, the government building (left), and the Music Hall (right) are behind. The coastline stands just makai of Queen Street, and boathouses are in the shallows beyond. The square-rigged ship is in a temporary repair dock in the harbor. (HSA.)

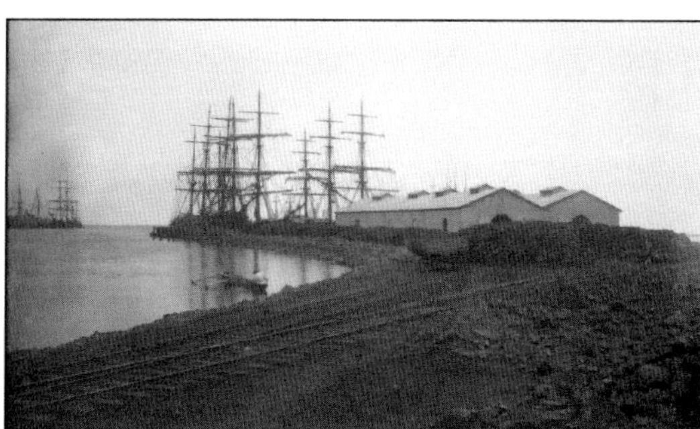

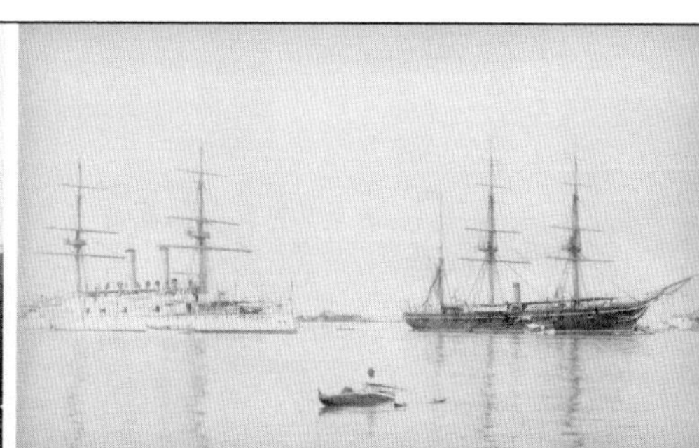

Dynamic Waterfront. Oahu's southeastern shore had extensive shallow reefs. Filling these low areas defined the Honolulu Harbor as it is today. About 1890, portions of Kuwili Pond (left) have been filled for greater access to deep water. A change in technologies (right) is evident as sail is giving way to coal propulsion. The ship on the left is the USS *Boston*, instrumental in the revolution of 1893. (HSA.)

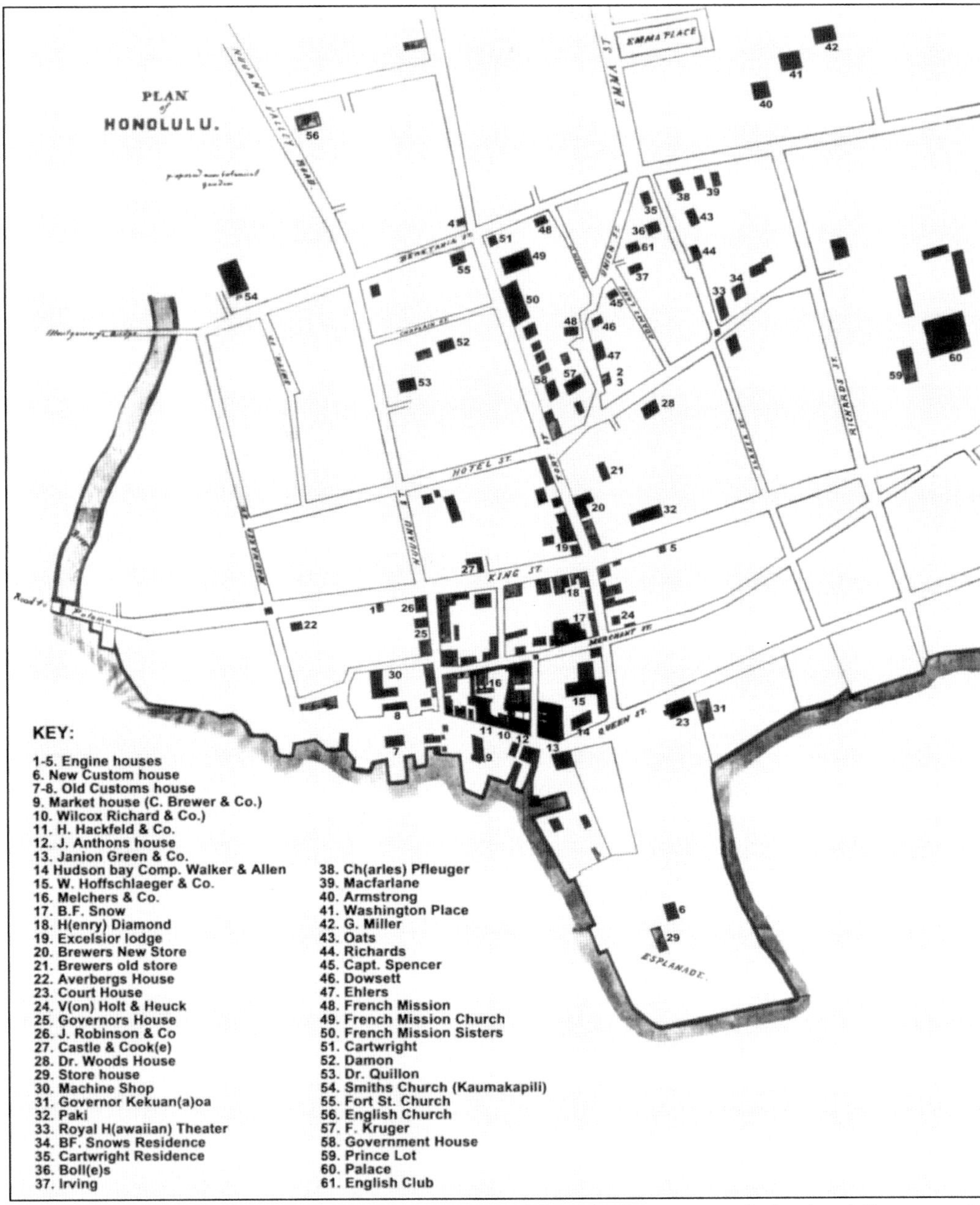

Anthon Estate Map of Honolulu, c. 1862. Notable features include the following: the Kaumakapili Church on the mauka-Ewa side, the open waterfront (Ewa part of Queen Street), concentration of buildings that are mauka of Queen, the Queen Street Court House, the filled peninsula known as the Esplanade, the Our Lady of Peace Cathedral and complex on the mauka end of Fort, and the group of buildings around the original Iolani Palace. (HSA.)

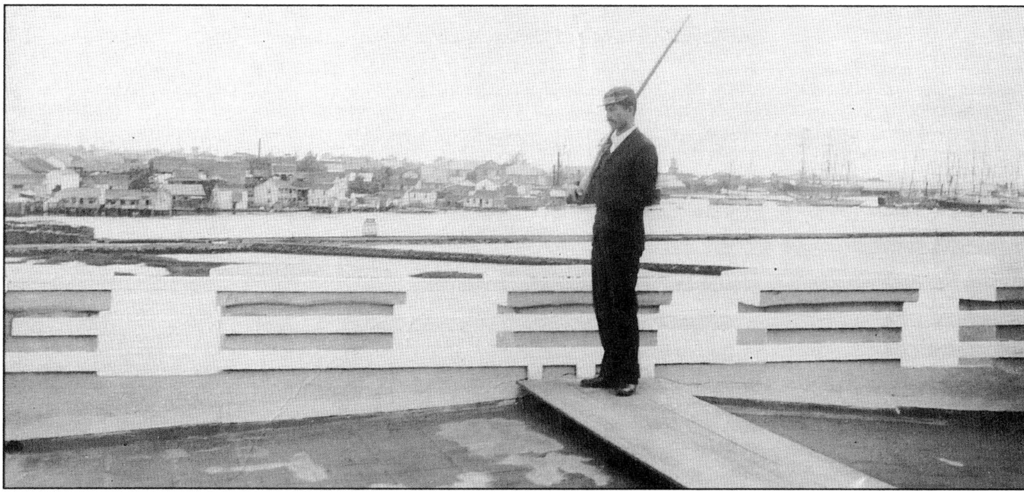

PRISON GUARD AT OAHU PRISON, 1880S–1890S. Oahu Prison was built in 1857 on an isolated high-ground area known as Iwilei ("collarbone" in Hawaiian) that existed on the Ewa side of town. Behind the guard in this photograph are soon-to-be-filled ancient Hawaiian fishponds, the burgeoning waterfront town, and many masted ships at anchorage. Behind the camera were fertilizer works and slaughterhouses. The area later served residential, industrial, and red-light purposes. (HSA.)

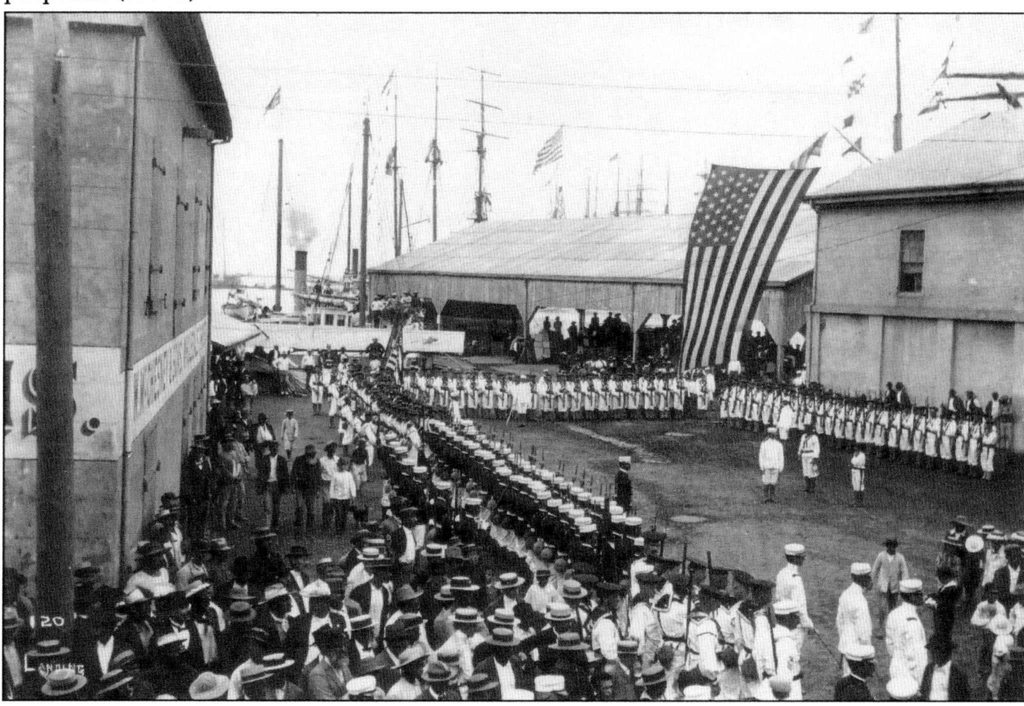

TROOP LANDING. Brewer's Wharf (today's Pier 12) is important in several ways. Off its makai edge are coral blocks from the former Honolulu Fort. It was centrally located along the old waterfront between James Robinson's boat repair works and the Custom House. Most significant, however, was its role as the landing site for American troops of the USS *Boston* in 1893. The photograph shows a US Navy ceremony in 1895. Nimitz Highway covered most of this site in the 1950s. (HSA.).

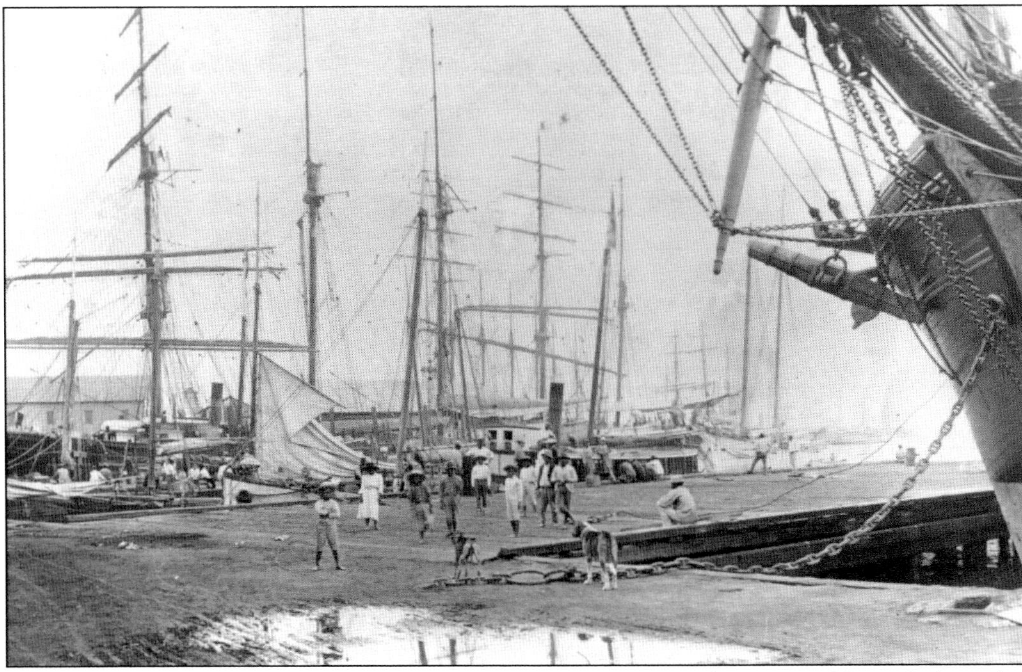

ESPLANADE. The wharves were crowded, dirty, and potentially dangerous. Nevertheless, they were very attractive places because the wharves were where goods, people, and news arrived. This made the area a magnet for merchants, sailors, carpenters, sailmakers, and others. Children, like generations everywhere, hung around the wharves seeking excitement. They were often referred to as "wharf rats." (Photograph by Brother Bertram; HSA.)

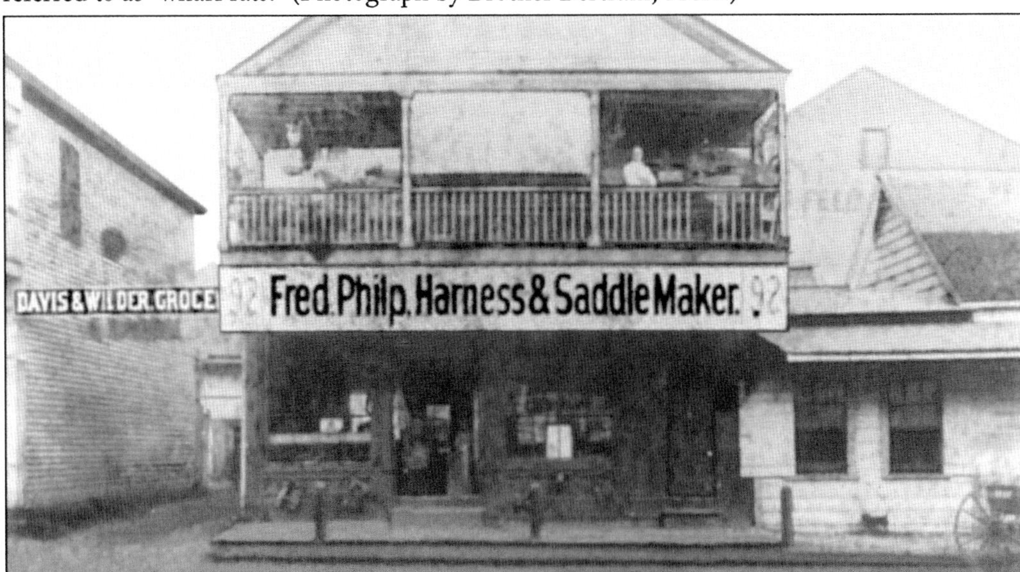

HORSES AT THE WATERFRONT. On June 21, 1803, the first horses arrived in Hawaii aboard the *Leila Byrd*, commanded by Capt. William Shaler. Ownership of a horse became a symbol of both social and economic status, as well as a means to cover more territory quickly. The above Fred Philip Harness and Saddle Maker establishment accommodated those arriving off ships. It was located on the mauka side of King near Fort. (State Historic Preservation Division.)

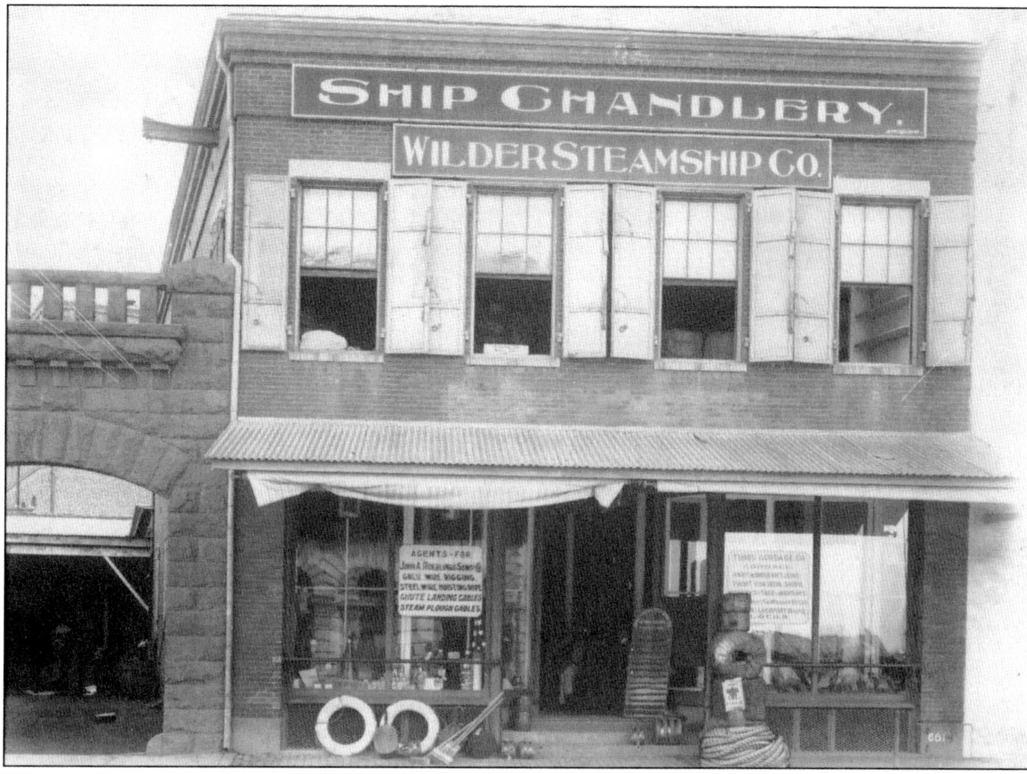

WILDER STEAMSHIP CO. OFFICE AND SHIP CHANDLERY. Samuel Wilder began his Hawaii business career shipping guano for fertilizer to New York. Involved with sugar plantations, land holdings, and railroads, he is best remembered for his shipping activities. The chandlery pictured offered all sorts of maritime goods and worked in conjunction with the Marine Railway (repair yard). Wilder, who initially acted as agent for the government's interisland steamers, eventually operated his own service between Honolulu, Maui, and Hilo. (HSA.)

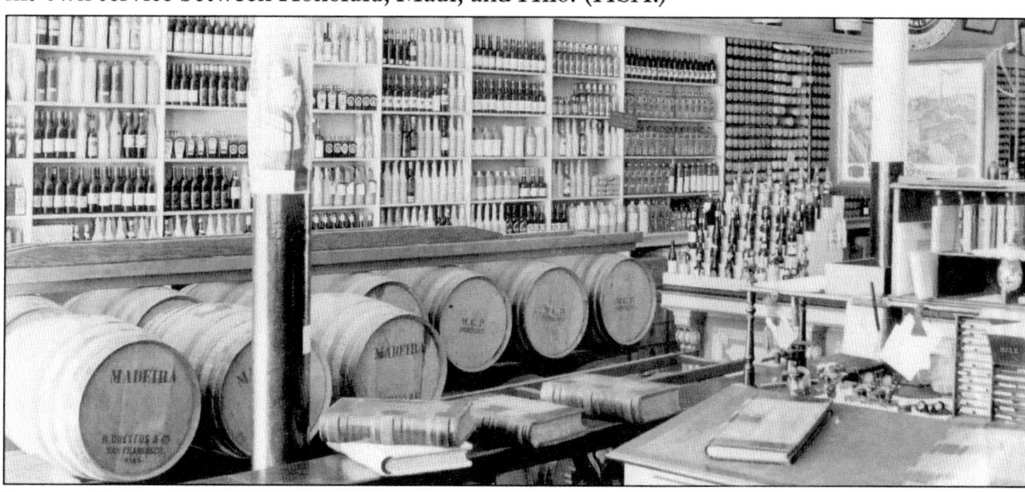

LIQUOR SALES. From the very beginning, Honolulu provided methods for socializing or escape. This well-stocked establishment obviously provided customers more alcohol options than most of its competitors. Liquor and other licenses were a major source of government revenue. Potential opium licenses, however, created a major scandal in the later years of the monarchy. (HHS.)

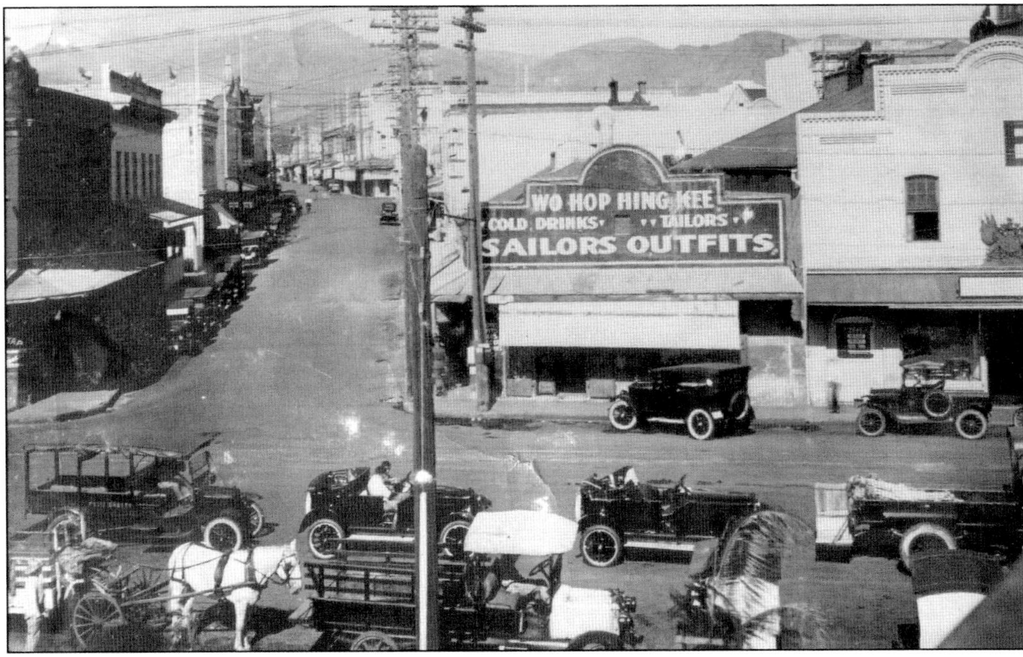

BUSTLE ON THE WATERFRONT. The open space along the waterfront, later occupied by Nimitz Highway, is filled with assembled horses and wagons, trucks, and cars waiting for the arrival of a steamship in order to deliver goods and people throughout the town. A good example of waterfront commerce is Wo Hop Hing Kee, located at the mauka-Ewa side corner of Nuuanu and Queen Streets, where tailors could quickly sew and alter seamen's outfits. (HHS.)

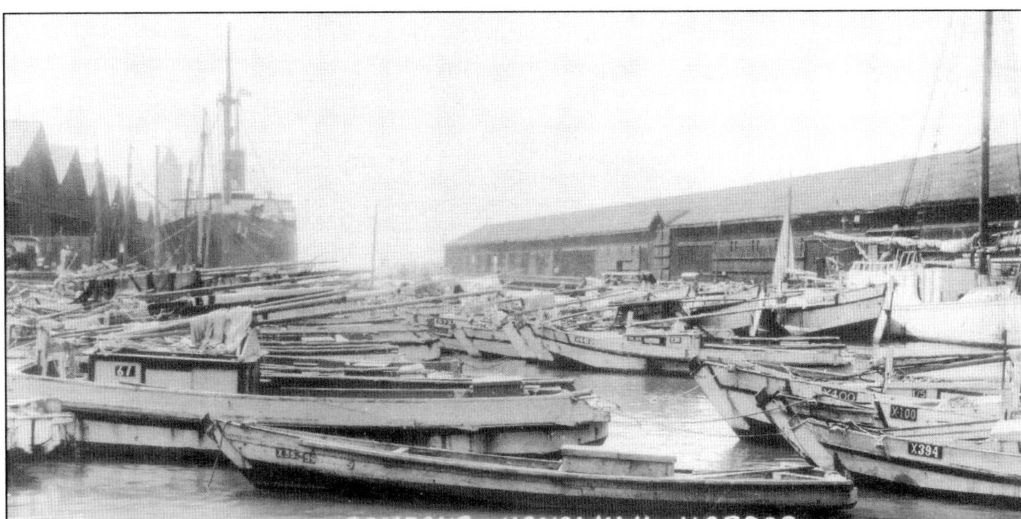

SAMPANS AND FREIGHTER PACK THE HARBOR. Once their plantation labor contracts ended, many Japanese became commercial fishermen. Using methods and craft that they had learned off their home-country islands, the Japanese came to dominate the local fishing industry between the world wars. Their boatbuilding and fishing excursions added to the congestion in the harbor. This view of the crowded docks looks Diamond Head from the railroad yards. Aloha Tower is seen to the left of the freighter. (HSA.)

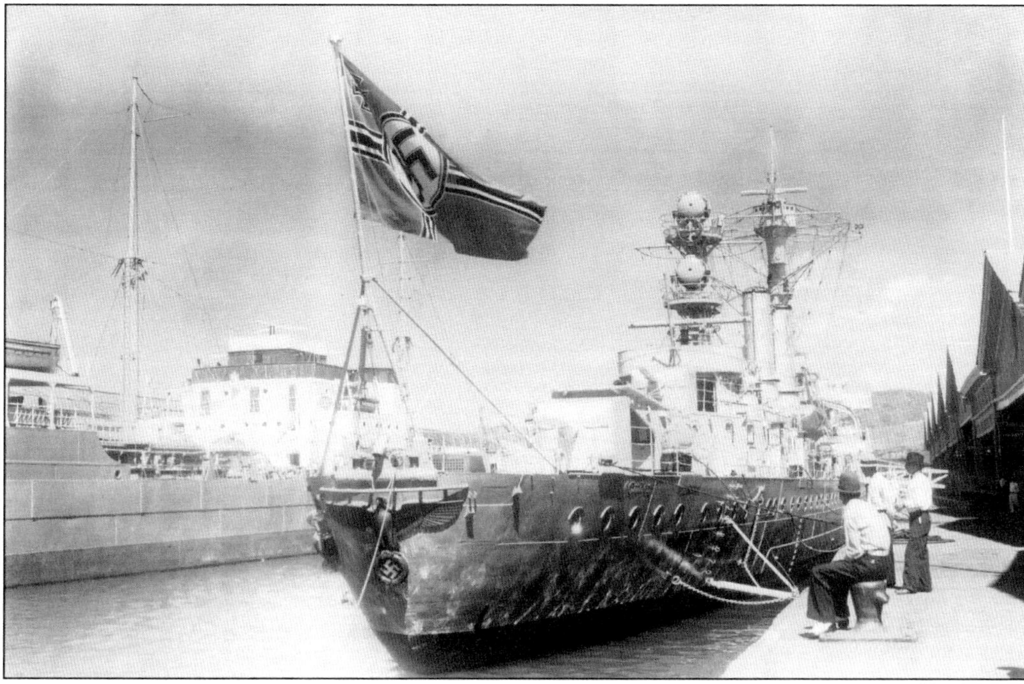

NAZI GERMAN LIGHT CRUISER *EMDEN* DOCKS IN HONOLULU, 1936. Between 1934 and 1935, this German navy training cruiser was commanded by Capt. Karl Donitz, future head of Nazi Germany's World War II submarine Wolfpack fleet. Donitz was the man given control over the Nazi government after the suicide of Adolf Hitler. The *Emden* visited Honolulu in 1936 while on an international tour to show the Nazi flag. (Bishop Museum.)

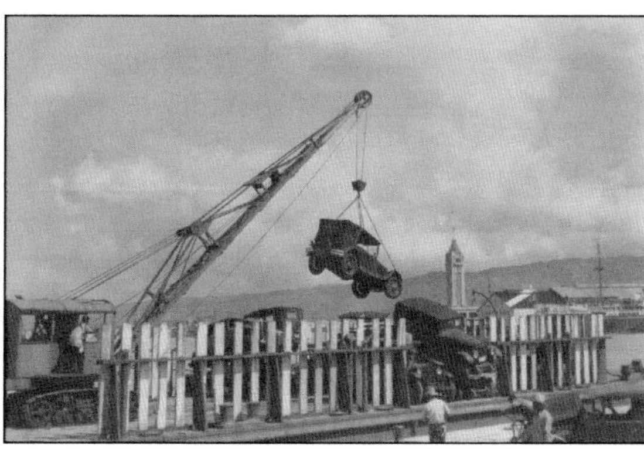

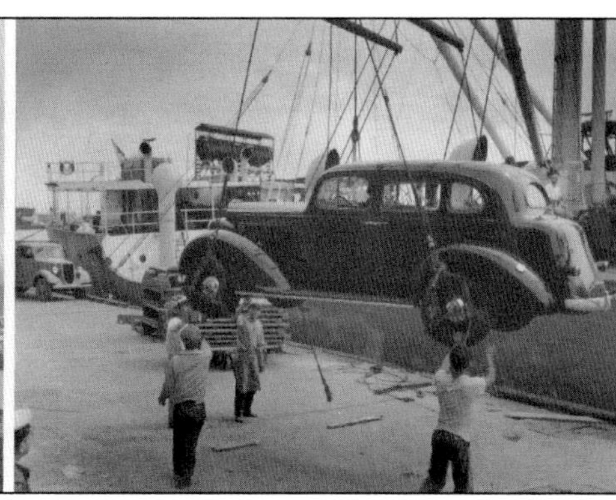

WHAT COMES IN WILL GO OUT. Ocean dumping of waste in Honolulu is an old story. The Kakaako waterfront was used for over a generation for open burning of garbage before incinerators were built, and even then ash and noncombustibles were dumped offshore. A crane operator (left) layers old cars on a barge that will take them to their final resting places in the ocean seabed about 1930. New automobiles arrive and subsequently are unloaded. (HSA.)

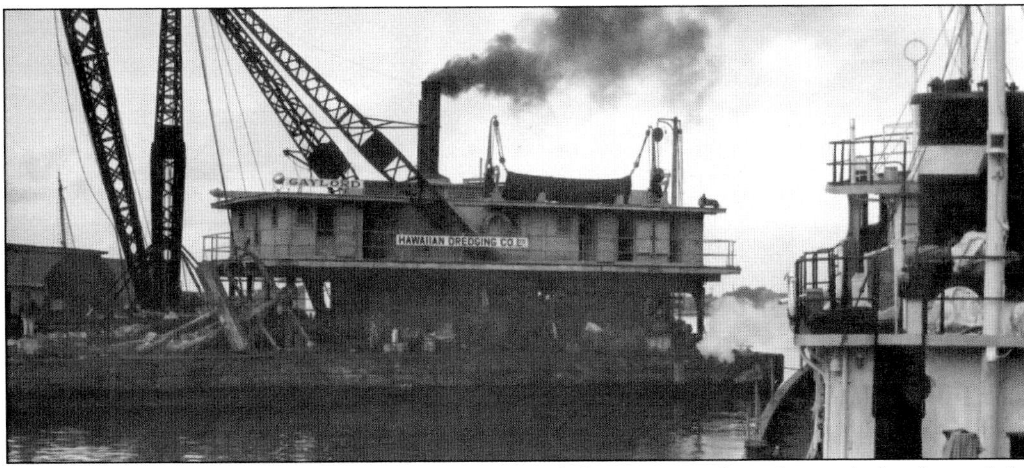

"THE DREDGER." The dredge *Gaylord* was one of the engines that changed the face of the island. Walter F. Dillingham's Hawaiian Dredging, founded in 1902, reworked much of the topography of the city makai of King Street—filling in lowlands, straightening drainage basins, and creating peninsulas that became thousands of buildable acres. The dredgers also widened the channel into Honolulu Harbor, improved the Kalihi Channel, and created the Kalihi Basin. (HSA.)

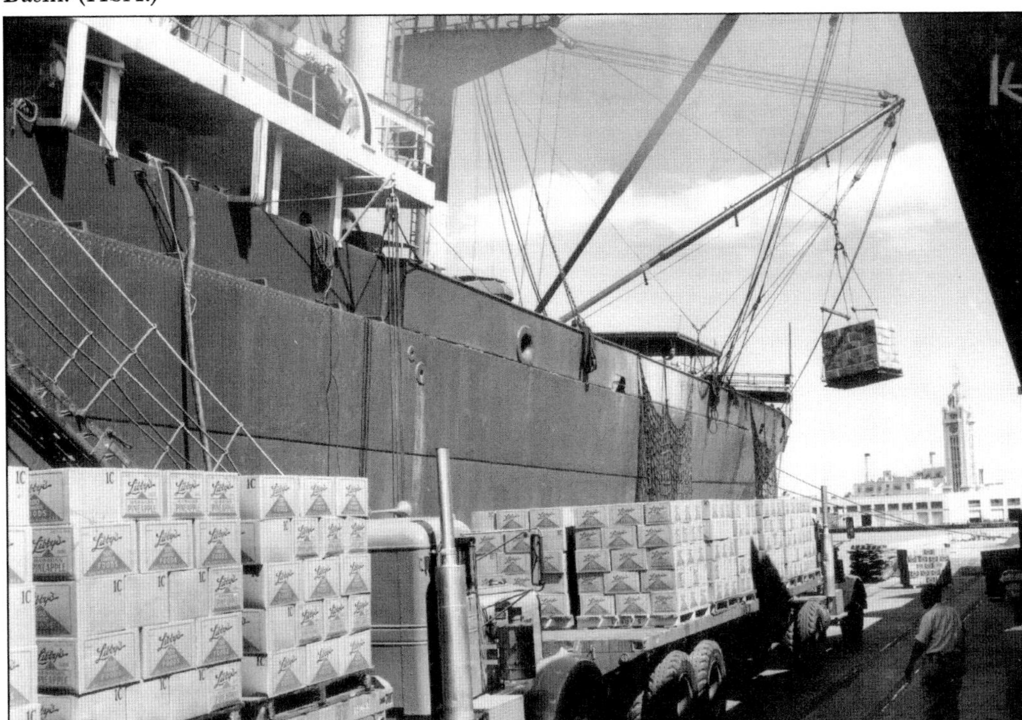

PINEAPPLES FOR THE WORLD. Believe it or not, the original pineapple canneries were near the fields. Those small operations were eventually eclipsed by business consolidation and industrial investment in economies of scale–improvements to roads, use of trucks, creation of the Ginaca pineapple processing machines, and extensive harbor wharf improvements. Industry pioneer James Dole's legendary emphasis on such innovation and quality control gave his products a marketing edge over his competitors. (HSA.)

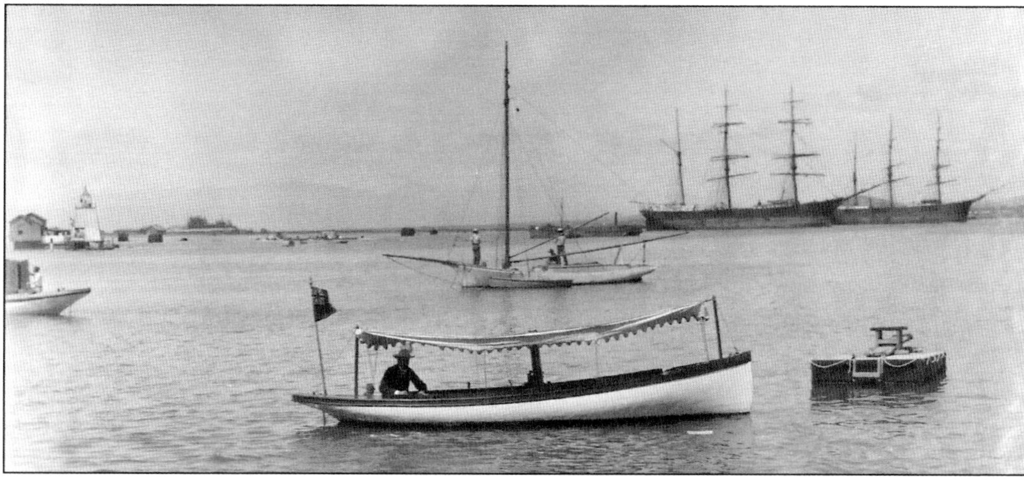

PLEASURE LAUNCH AND HARBOR LIGHT, C. 1890. The Honolulu waterfront was once more extensive than today, with much of Iwilei, Sand Island, and Kakaako covered by shallow water just a few feet deep. As the larger commercial ships concentrated in the deep water along the Queen Street waterfront and Esplanade (right center), pleasure boaters had most of the shallows to themselves. Located in the back left is the 1869 lighthouse, known as the "Harbor Wink." (HSA.)

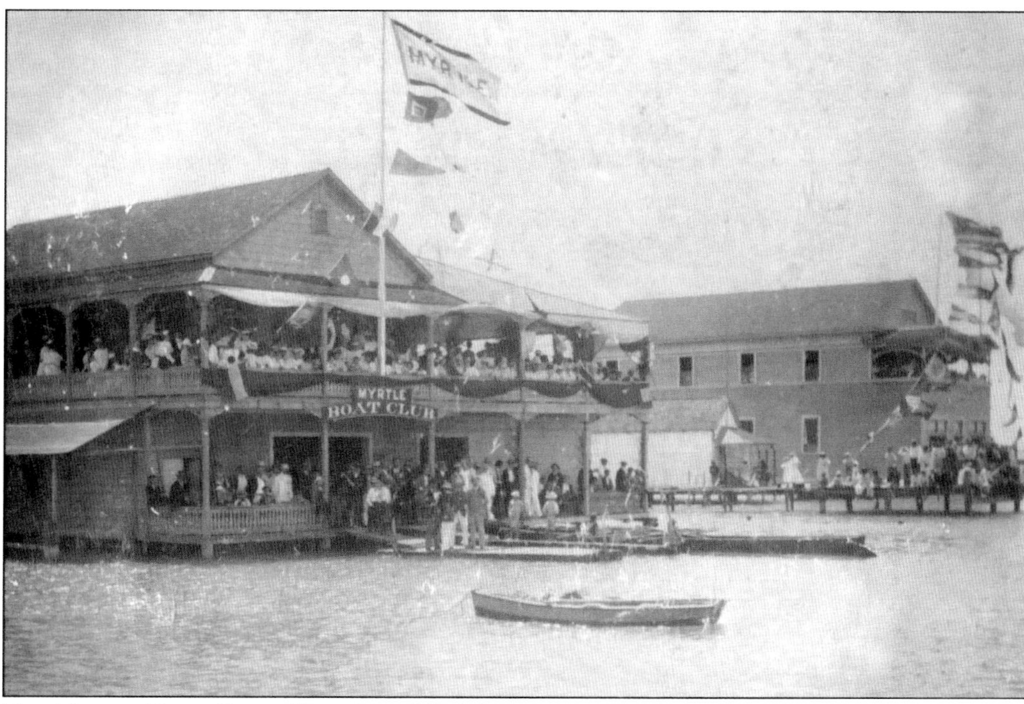

THE MYRTLE BOAT CLUB. King David Kalakaua was a member of the Myrtle Boat Club, often attending social activities and races there. The Myrtle "Reds" practiced daily in the harbor, regularly competing with other local clubs, such as the Healani Boat and Rowing Club's "Blues." These clubs were located in the shallows adjacent to what is now Pier 2. (HSA.)

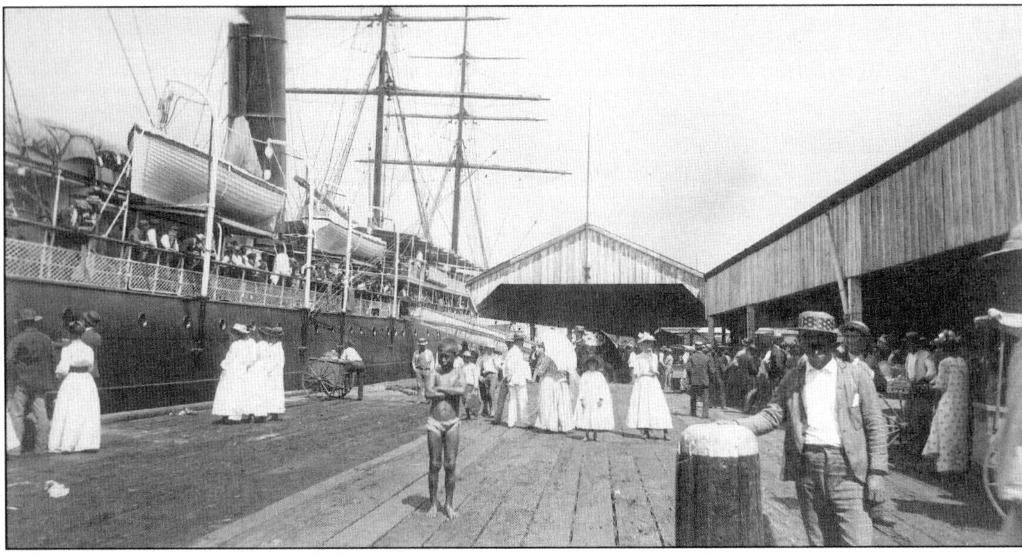

HARBOR IMPROVEMENTS. The history of Honolulu Harbor is one of continually updating wharves to accommodate greater numbers of passengers and cargo on bigger ships. This photograph shows people on a wooden wharf greeting the SS *Australia* around 1885. Note that both nautical steam and wind propulsion are employed. Both the length and height of the ships would increase further in the next few years, leading to construction of multiple-story docks. (HSA.)

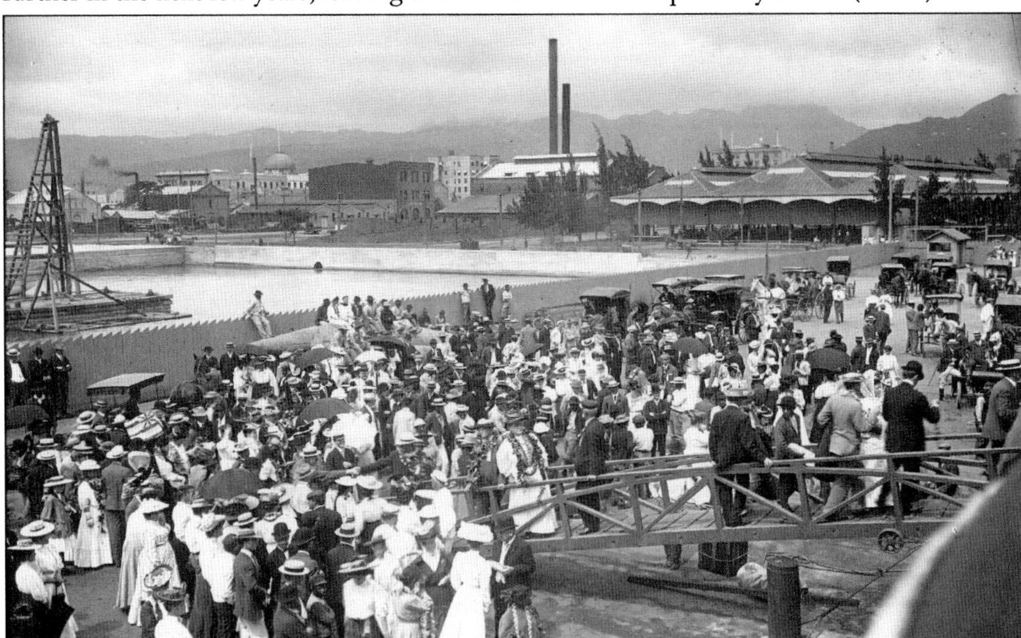

PIER 2, 1907. The folks in the foreground from Los Angeles probably stayed at the original Royal Hawaiian Hotel and had taken a volcano tour via steamship. Behind, at Alakea and Halekauwila Streets, is the new high-vaulted iron marketplace, open to the air with concrete floors for hosing down the day's scraps and fish-dressing remnants, which replaced the earlier government-controlled fish market on Nuuanu Street. Further behind, the stacks of the Hawaiian Electric Company point skyward. (Bishop Museum.)

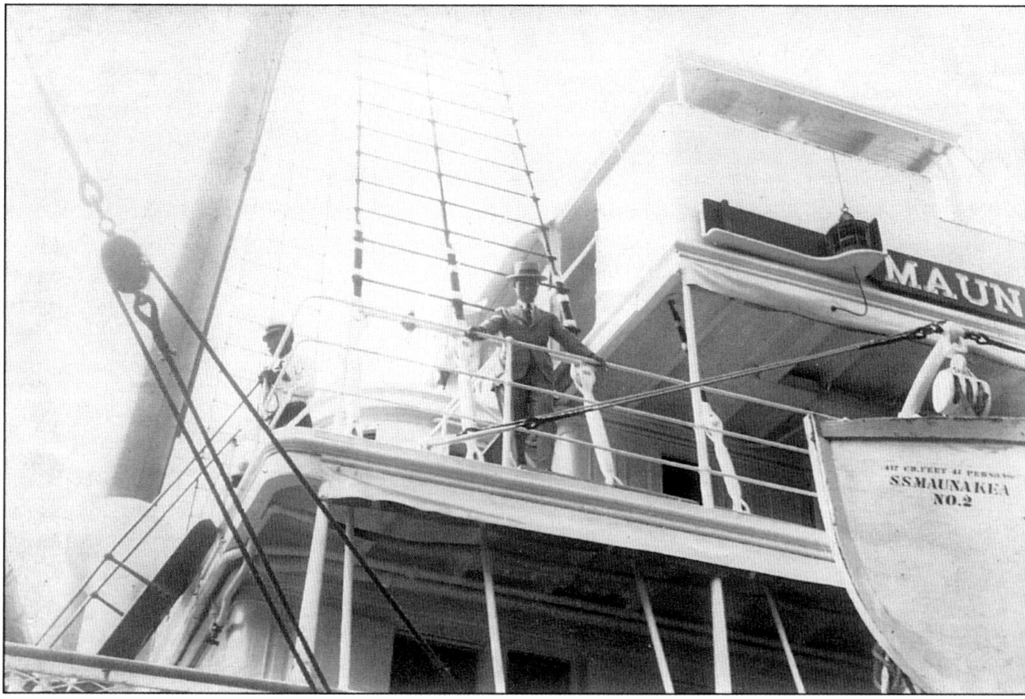

TRAVELING TO THE NEIGHBOR ISLANDS IN STYLE IN SUIT AND TIE. This man is possibly a businessman going to another island to sell packaged food items or wares from his distributor in Honolulu or a neighbor island merchant who has just completed his purchases in town. The *Maunakea* steamship was a freighter that was run by the Inter-island Steam Navigation Company. (Japanese Cultural Center of Hawaii.)

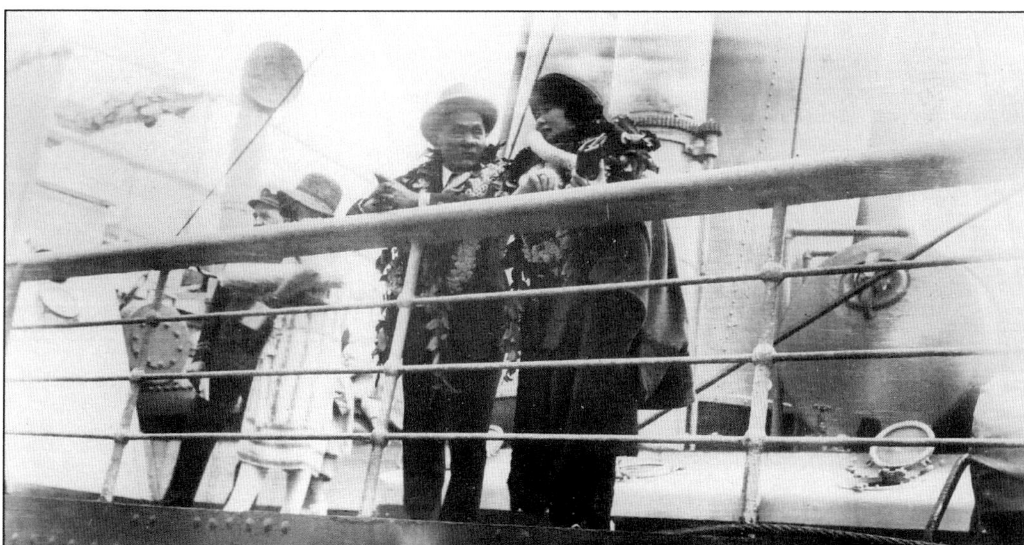

HAWAIIAN STYLE. A local couple, identified only as Mr. and Mrs. Yamanaka, were photographed about to depart for the mainland with many lei from well-wishers. The dress of those on board and the women's cloche hats date this photograph to the 1920s. (Yamanaka/Angeles Collection.)

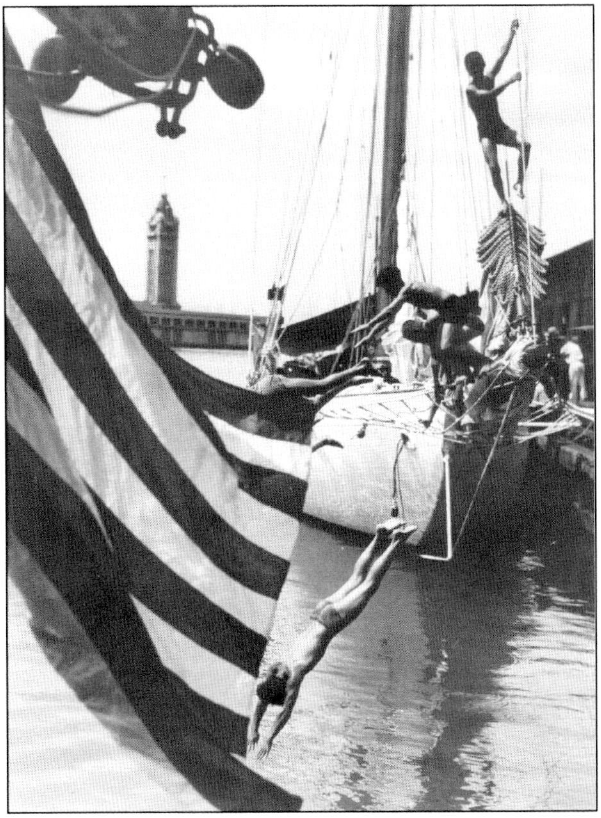

Boys Diving in Honolulu Harbor. There was always adventure at the harbor—climbing the rigging of a sloop and plunging into the clear waters of Honolulu Harbor, whether for fun or for coins (or for both). Perhaps these boys were members of the Coin Diving Club of Kakaako. (HSA.)

Redeveloping the Esplanade, June 1924. The use of former German cruise ships in the tourist trade encouraged the construction of new Piers 8–12. Temporarily remaining were the old customs buildings in the center and the beginnings of Irwin Park, visible in the upper right. The major ship in the foreground, the British battle cruiser *Repulse*, would be sunk by Japanese aircraft north of Singapore on December 10, 1941, within days of the Pearl Harbor attack. (HSA.)

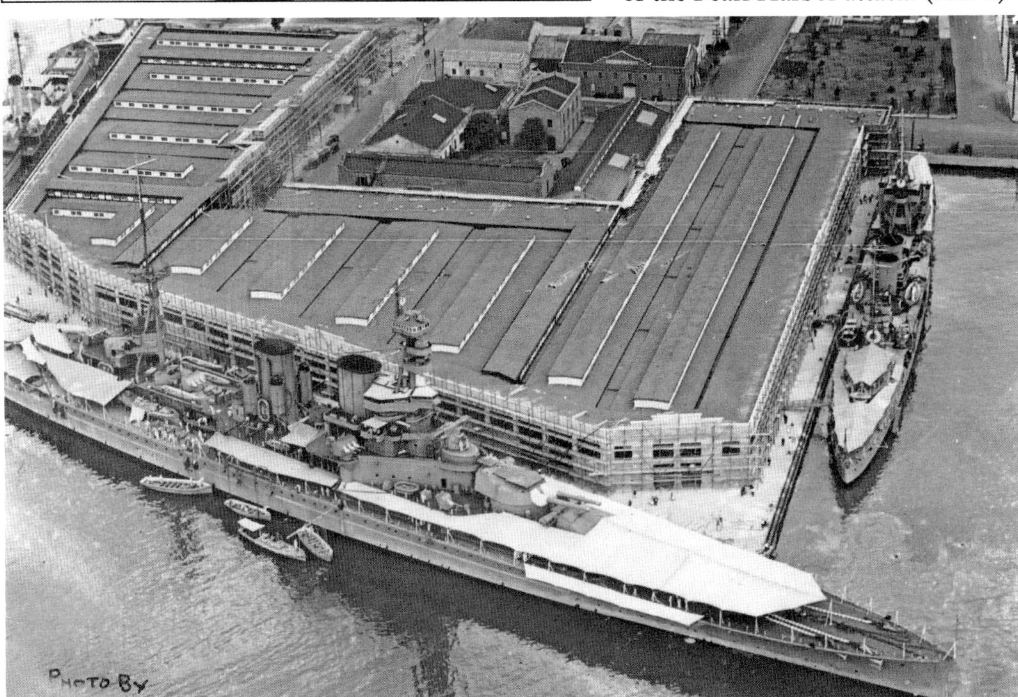

Two

SCHOOLS FOR *KAMAAINA*

In the Hawaiian method of learning, a young person requested permission to learn from an elder, paid strict attention to every word of the narrative, and recited it back correctly (or repeated it again correctly if need be). Mary Kawena Pukui, *kamaaina* (child of the land) and esteemed *kumu* (teacher), imparted her knowledge this way. She went on to learn *a wahi pana* (the places of interest) and the legends connected with those places.

But after 1820, inculcation of knowledge changed with the missionary emphasis on the preeminence of the Bible. The printing press in 1822 produced the word of God, and thereby enabled all to read the Word. Hawaii in the mid-19th century achieved one of the highest levels of literacy in the world in its own vernacular, a product of a system that attached schools to missionary churches throughout the islands.

The missionary-focused schools evolved into the public school system. After 1893, authorities sought to Americanize an increasingly diverse ethnic population. American-specific values, such as American patriotism, were taught, and in 1896, English became the preferred vehicle of instruction. A separate, dual-path education program, known as the English Standard Schools, was subsequently instituted only for those who passed an English fluency examination.

Interestingly enough, "school days, good old golden rule days," originally promulgated by the Congregationalists, were basically the same as the Chinese Confucian precept and the Buddhist teaching of "Do unto others as you would have them do unto you." The methodology was strikingly the same—lots of rote learning, oration, chalk-slate penmanship, and brush-and-ink *kanji* (Chinese characters) literati practice in grid-and-stroke order. The schools taught what it was to be civilized in a civilized culture.

In preparation for the public schools and the future work force, kindergartens, supported by the Castle family, were also founded downtown on South King Street, and the Free Kindergarten and Children's Aid Association was established in many town neighborhoods. Public recreational grounds focusing on children existed on both Beretania and School Streets.

Language schools, including Chinese, Japanese, German, and Korean, were active on major streets—such as Nuuanu, Beretania, and Punchbowl—and on small lanes in the Kauluwela, Aala, and Kukui neighborhoods.

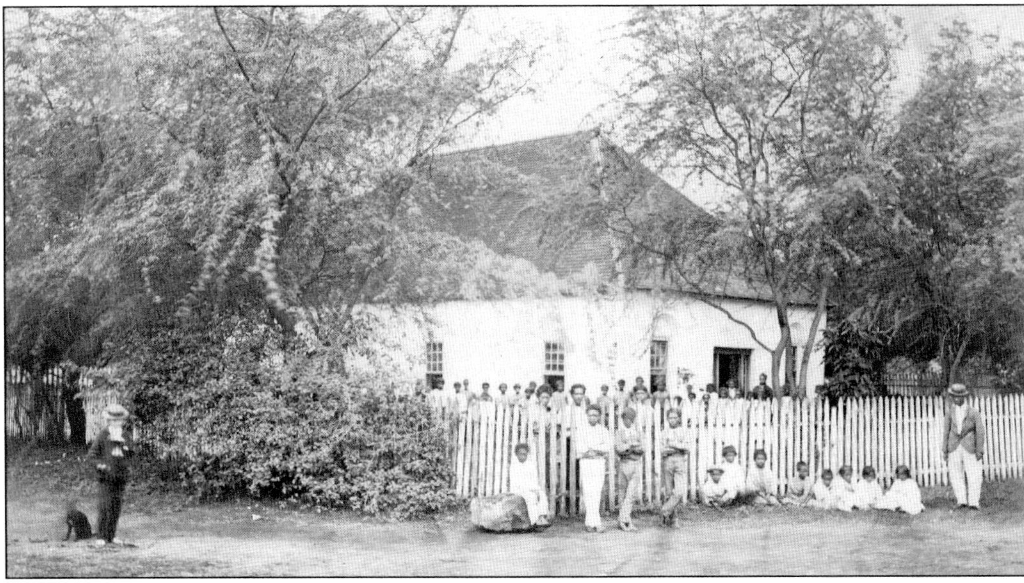

ADOBE SCHOOLHOUSE. Originally constructed of air-dried bricks and lumber between 1833 and 1835, it replaced an earlier thatched school and meetinghouse. The building has been used as a school and social hall, and for the annual Congregationalist General Meeting of the Mission (from throughout the islands), Thursday daytime meetings of Kawaiahao Church (hence the nickname/informal name Hale Poaha), and in 1852 was the location for the founding of the Hawaiian Mission Children's Society. (HSA.)

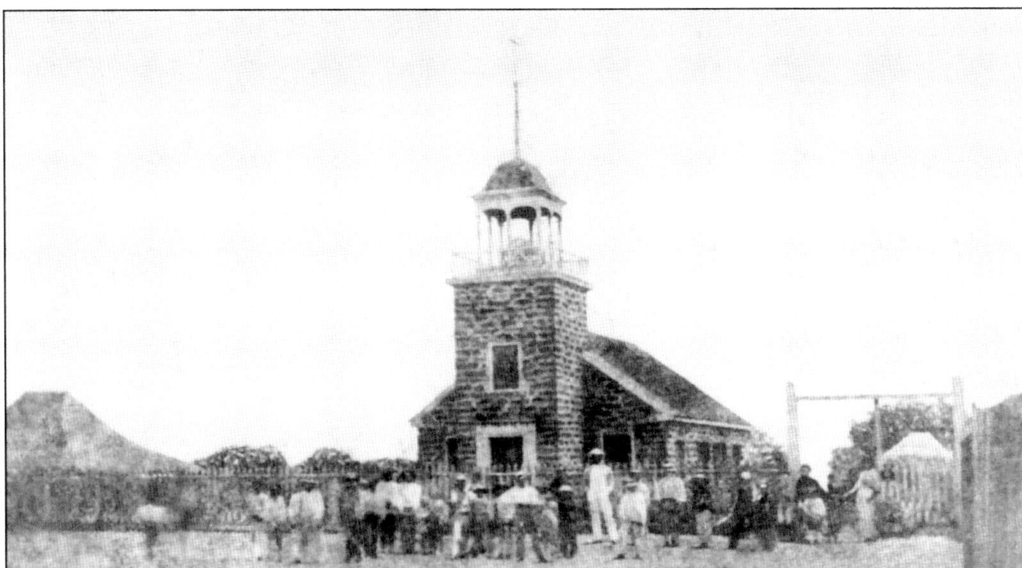

OAHU CHARITY SCHOOL, 1853. It was started in 1835 by Mr. and Mrs. Andrew Johnstone as an English-language school for the children of foreign residents, some of whom came from as far away as Kamchatka and Russian America. In 1851, the name was changed to Town Free School. In 1865, the sexes were separated, and it became the Mililani School for Girls. A land exchange in 1874 allowed the government to erect Aliiolani Hale just Ewa of here. (HHS.)

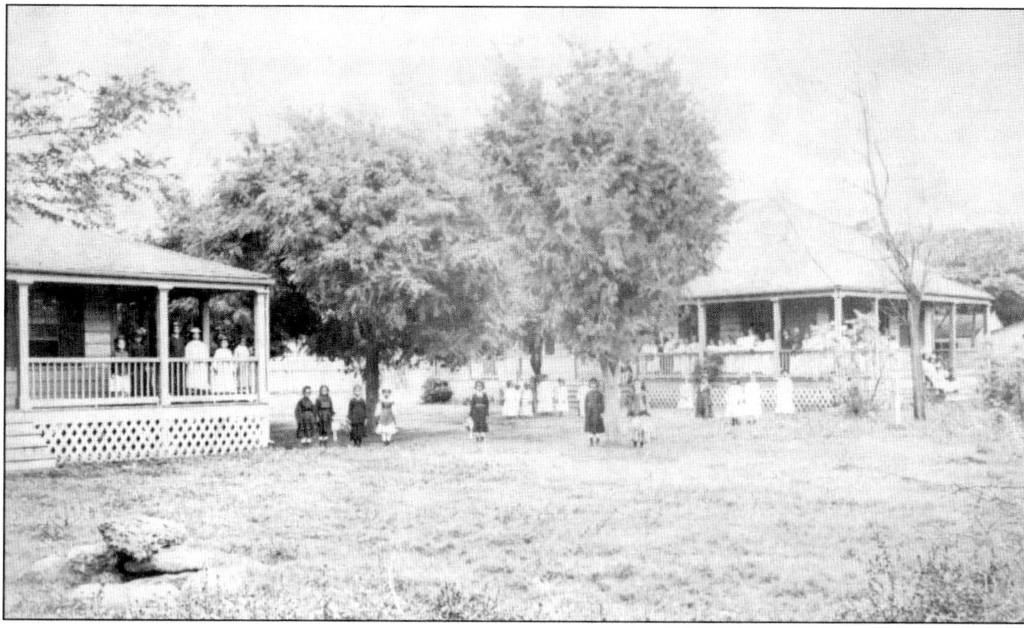

POHUKAINA SCHOOL. Given the Native Hawaiian name for the site of Iolani Palace, Pohukaina School was located nearby in the middle of the block between Likelike and Punchbowl Streets from 1874 to 1913. Its two main buildings are shown here, looking in the mauka-Ewa direction from Punchbowl Street. The school was moved to Kakaako, between Keawe and Coral Streets, by Gov. Walter F. Frear to make room for the new Library of Hawaii. (HSA.)

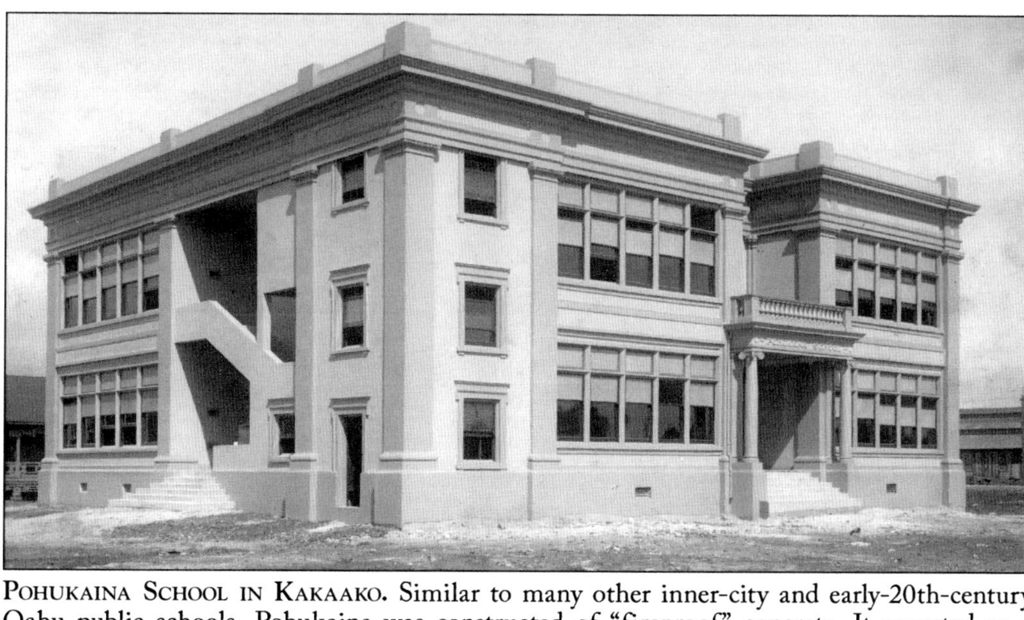

POHUKAINA SCHOOL IN KAKAAKO. Similar to many other inner-city and early-20th-century Oahu public schools, Pohukaina was constructed of "fireproof" concrete. It operated as a regular public school in conjunction with the adjacent Mother Waldron and Atkinson Parks before becoming a special-education facility in 1966. The building was demolished in the 1980s after its functions were moved to the campus of Kaimuki Intermediate School. The site today is used by the Friends of the Library of Hawaii. (HSA.)

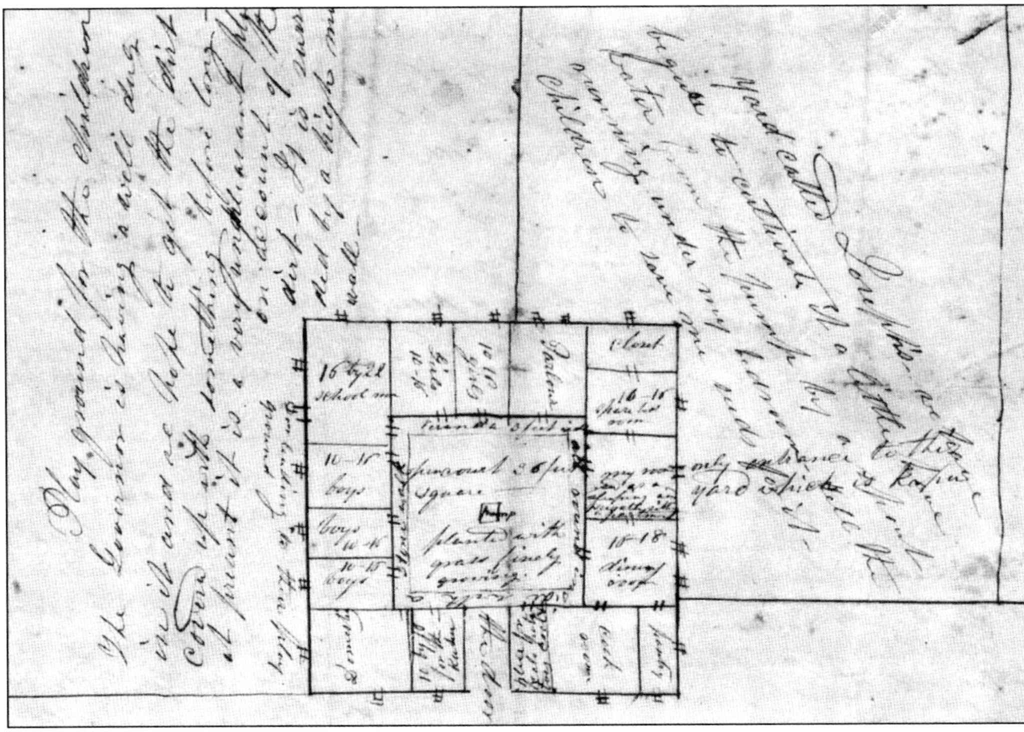

MAP OF CHIEFS' CHILDREN'S SCHOOL. Located at the present makai-Diamond Head side of the Hawaii State Capitol, the Chiefs' Children's School was organized in 1839 to give alii children a western education under the missionary Amos Starr Cookes. Every ruling monarch after Kamehameha III attended. Renamed Royal School in 1846, it closed in 1850. Here, Lydia Kamakaeha (Queen Liliuokalani) met John Owen Dominis, and Bernice Pauahi Paki met (and later married) Charles Reed Bishop. (Scottish Rite Cathedral.)

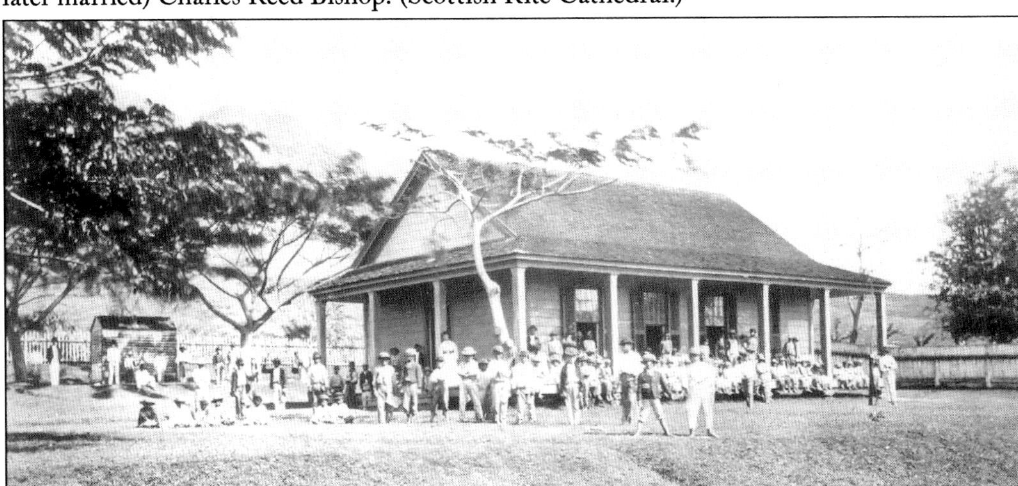

ROYAL SCHOOL. The second Royal School began in 1850 at Kahehuna. It was reached from town by walking first along Union Street, crossing Beretania, and proceeding along a path through the "King's Garden" (later to be known as Queen Emma Street). Though it opened to the general public as a coeducational school, a change in public policy in 1865 temporarily separated the sexes, with Royal School for boys and Mililani School for Girls. (HHS.)

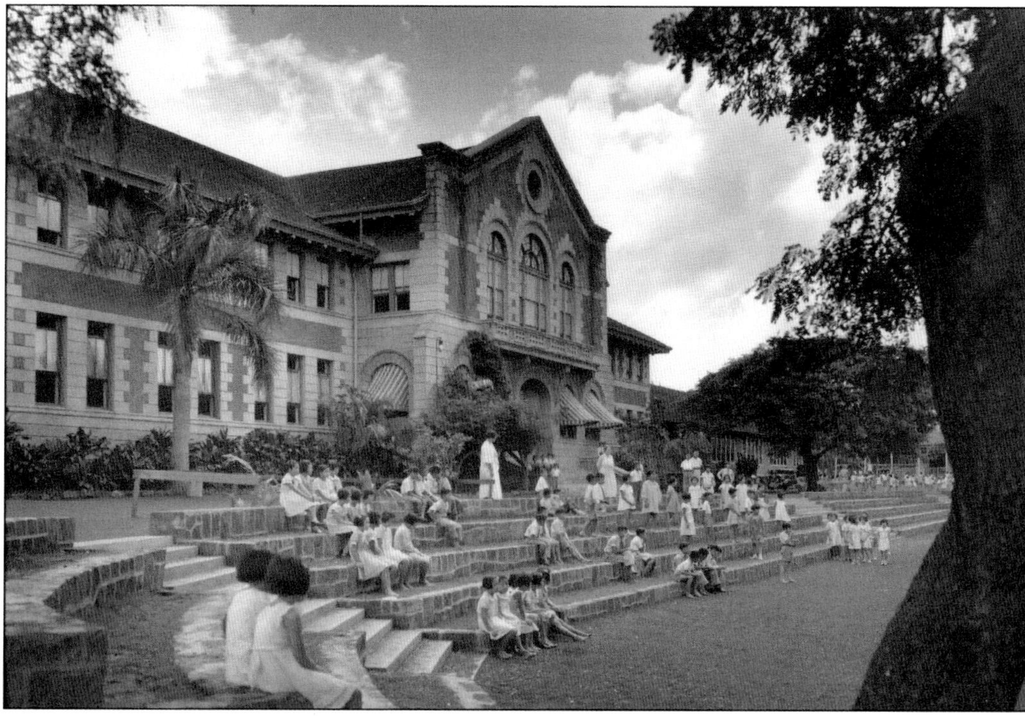

ROYAL SCHOOL IN THE TERRITORIAL PERIOD. Designed by C.W. Dickey, this fireproof structure was dedicated on March 3, 1905, and reflected mainland educational buildings. This was deliberate, as the school sought to Americanize its enrollment of Japanese, Chinese, Hawaiian, part-Hawaiian, Puerto Ricans, Filipinos, Spanish, and Anglo-Saxon students. The iconic two-story concrete edifice, located on Queen Emma near Luisitana Street, was demolished for construction of the Lunalilo Freeway; it served as the model for the present administration building. (HSA.)

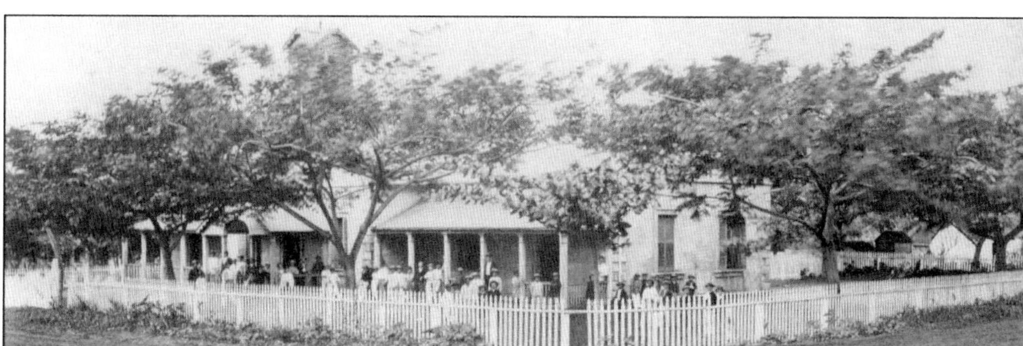

FORT STREET SCHOOL. Founded in 1865 by Maurice Beckwith in the Fort Street Church basement as the private Fort Street English Day School, in 1869 it became public and operated from this new building at Fort and School Streets. It became Honolulu High School in 1895 when moved to Princess Ruth's old Queen Emma Street home and later McKinley High School at Beretania and Victoria Streets in 1907. (HSA.)

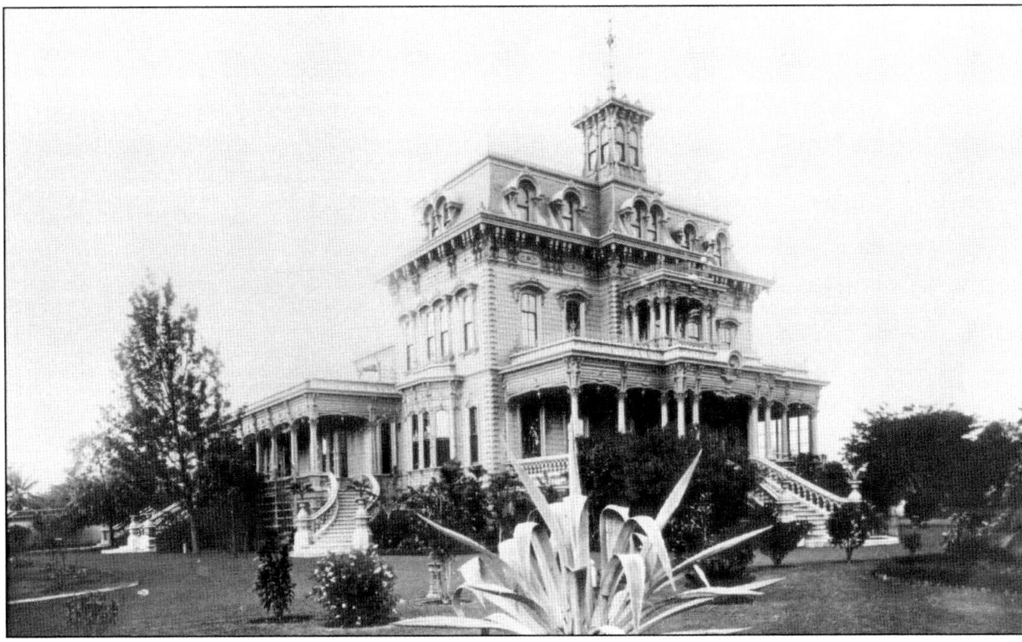

KEOUA HALE. This home was completed by Ruth Keelikolani, of the Kamehameha line, in February 1883 soon after King Kalakaua's second Iolani Palace (1882). Bernice Pauahi Bishop died here of cancer on October 16, 1884. The building was used for Honolulu High School before becoming Central Grammar School in 1907. In 1922, the school pioneered oral examinations for admissions as an English Standard School. The three present buildings date from 1927, making Central Intermediate the only secondary school in Honolulu using its original buildings. (SRC.)

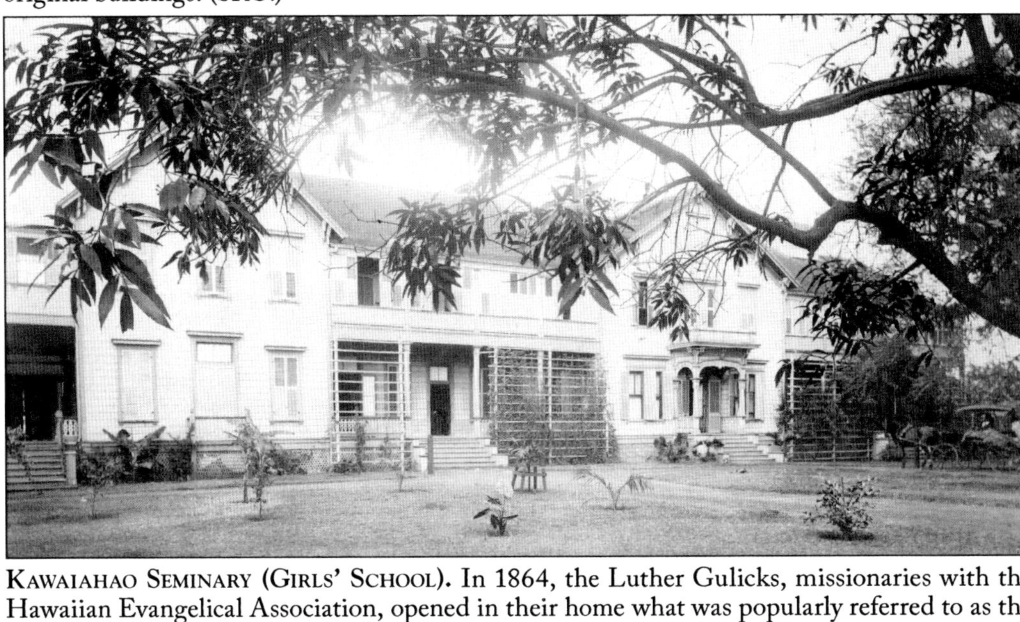

KAWAIAHAO SEMINARY (GIRLS' SCHOOL). In 1864, the Luther Gulicks, missionaries with the Hawaiian Evangelical Association, opened in their home what was popularly referred to as the "Ragged School." The first non-Hawaiian students were admitted in the 1870s. By 1905, the school included kindergarten through eighth grade. Kawaiahao moved with Mills Institute to Manoa in 1908. (HSA.)

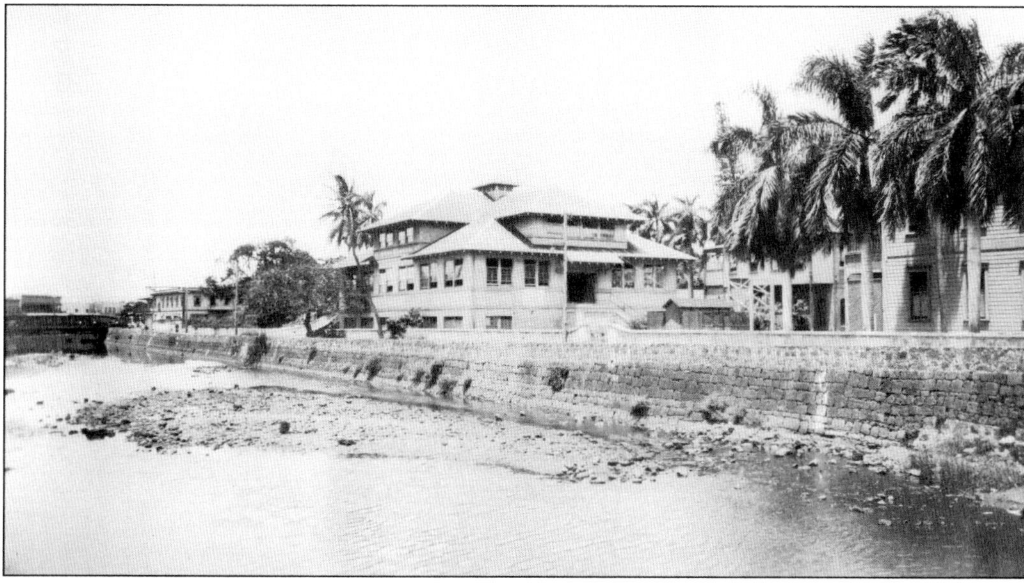

St. Louis College at College Walk, c. 1927. Emma Nakuina, curator of the Hawaii National Museum and noted judge of the water court, began championing a park proposal for Aala in 1896 at the site of shanties and Chinese laundries. By 1898, the area had been filled and walled-in to restrain floods from Nuuanu Stream. This allowed St. Louis to greatly improve its campus, as noted by the buildings pictured. College Walk, named for St. Louis College, lies immediately behind the wall. (Bishop Museum.)

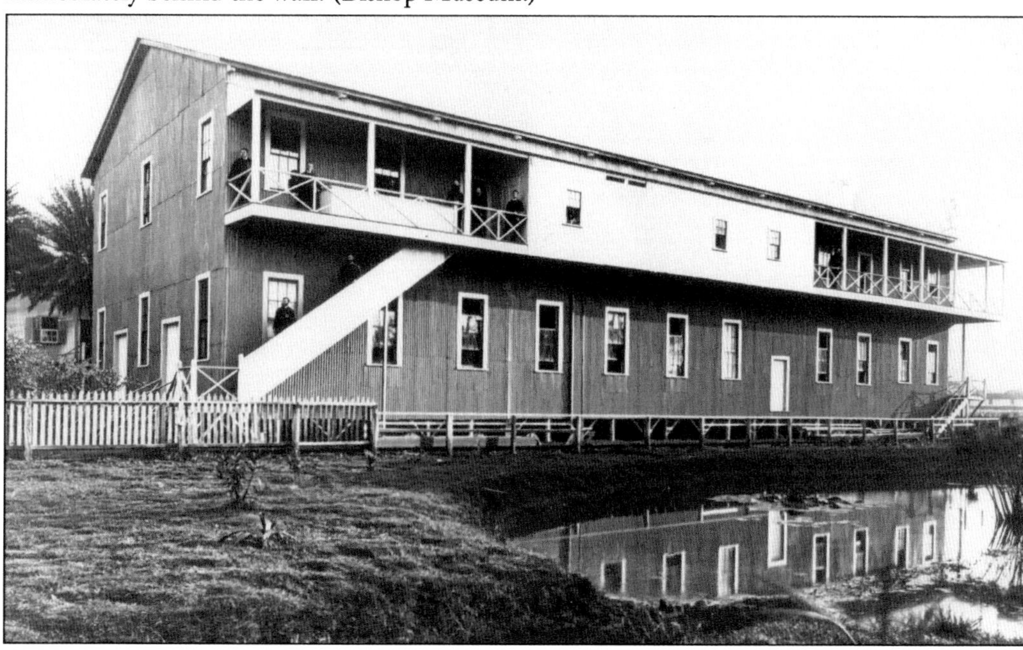

St. Louis College in Aala. The school already had two previous locations (windward Oahu as the College of Ahuimanu in 1846 and Beretania near Richards as the College of St. Louis in 1880) before moving to four acres of lowlands at Kamakela. The school was located on the Ewa bank of Nuuanu Stream, makai of Kukui Street at Aala in 1883. Note the *totan* (corrugated tin) clad siding on this inexpensive building. (HSA.)

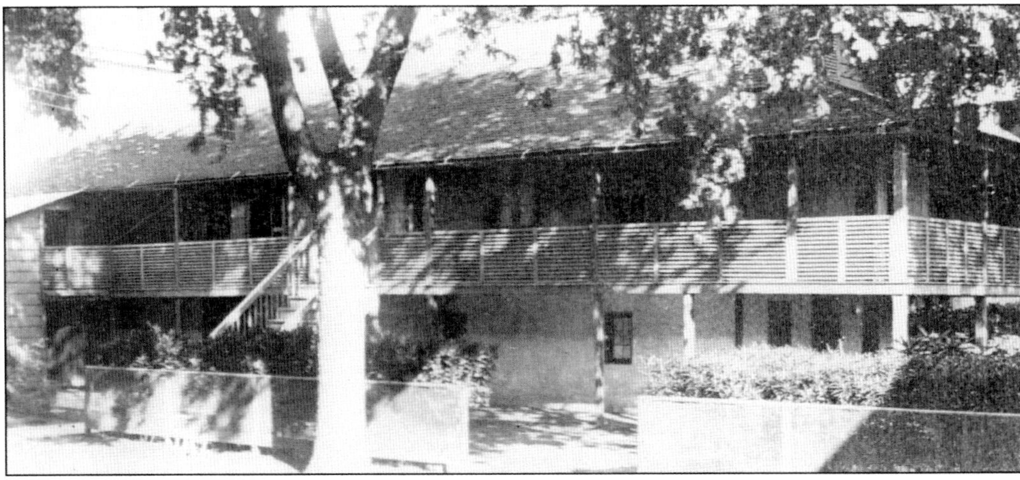

SACRED HEARTS FORT STREET CONVENT, 1859. Following the loss at sea of 25 Catholic missionaries, a second group of 10 sisters left Le Havre, France, in 1858, determined to assist Bishop Louis Maigret in starting a girls' school in Honolulu. Arriving in 1859, the sisters opened the doors of a boarding school on July 9. Mother Maria Josepha George soon began purchasing property adjacent to Our Lady of Peace in order to expand the Sacred Hearts Convent and School. (Hawaii Province.)

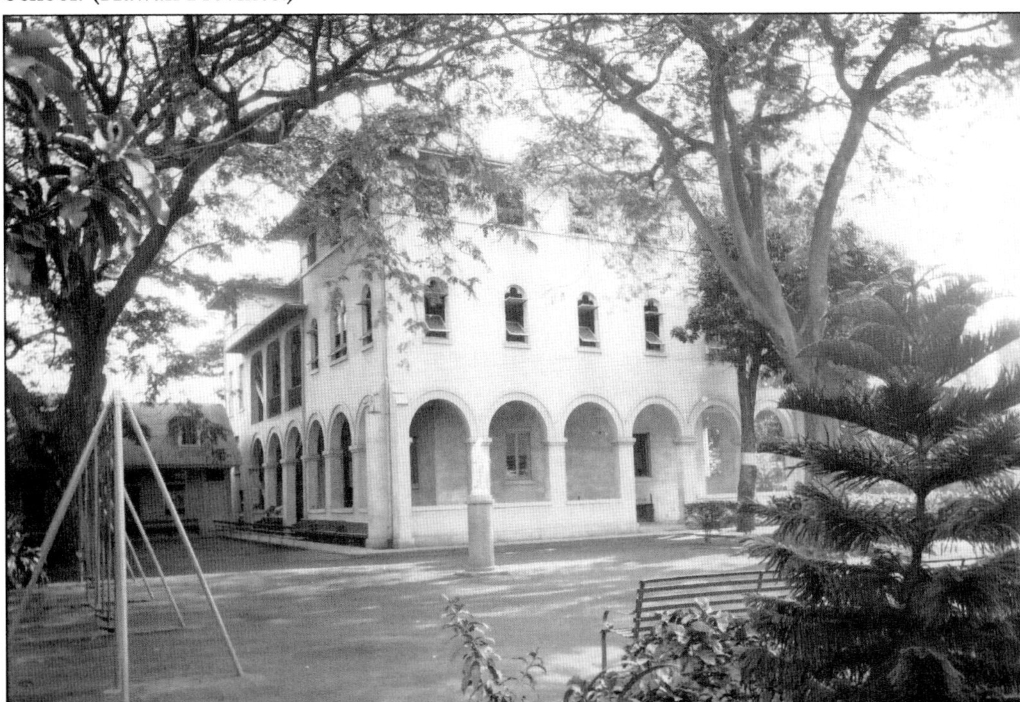

OASIS. By the first part of the 20th century, the Sisters of the Sacred Hearts had constructed an educational oasis in the center of town. This photograph was taken from the back of the main building along Fort Street. It shows the central play area and actual convent building for the sisters, known as St. Joseph's Hall. The photograph was taken before 1925, after which another classroom building was erected on the left and a cafeteria on the right. (HP.)

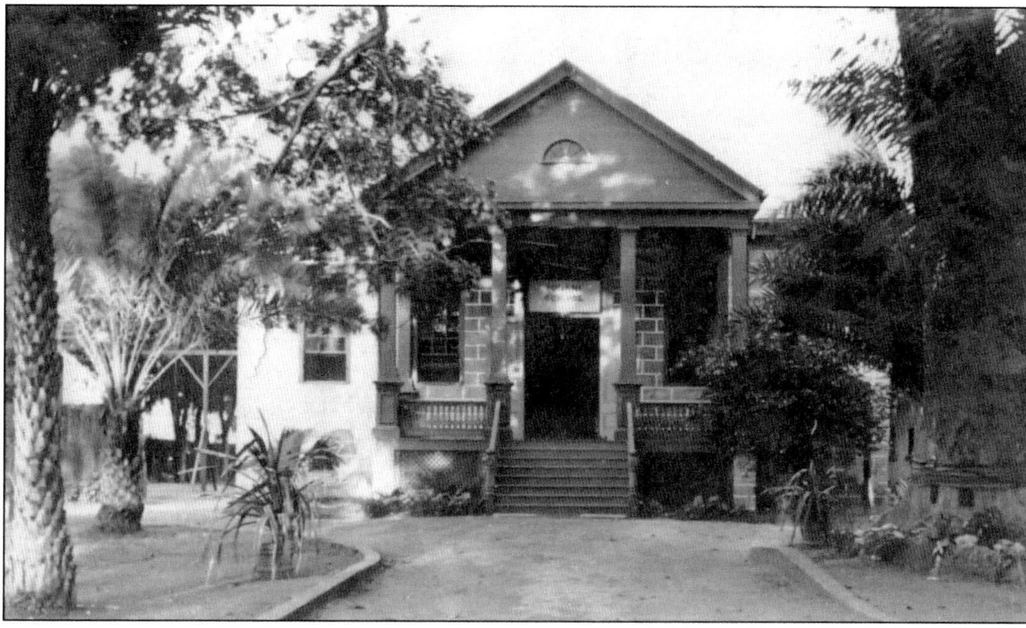

STONE HOUSE. Located at the top of Richards Street, this residence was named to honor British Adm. Richard Thomas, who restored Hawaiian independence in 1843. Samuel Chapman Armstrong (a Union Civil War general who fought at Gettysburg and founded Hampton Institute in Virginia) grew up here. It was purchased by Punahou School for a preparatory academy in 1881 and used by the Episcopal Church in 1905 for Iolani School. The building was torn down in 1931 despite public efforts to save it. (Episcopal Church in Hawaii.)

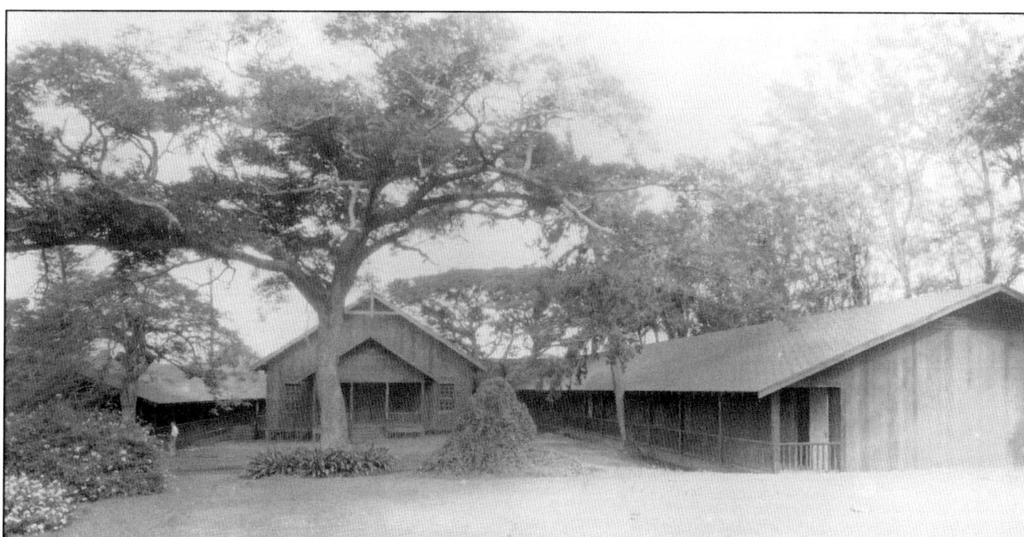

IOLANI SCHOOL JUDD STREET CAMPUS. Iolani raised $50,000 to purchase the old 5.4-acre Davies property at the mauka-Diamond Head corner of Nuuanu and Judd. The 1927 campus included wooden classrooms and chapel, a headmaster's residence, and dormitories on the higher land near Nuuanu Avenue, and a practice field below where legendary sports figure Father Bray taught his players. The last class graduated at Nuuanu in 1953; however, the central tree in the photograph is still growing in 2012. (HSA.)

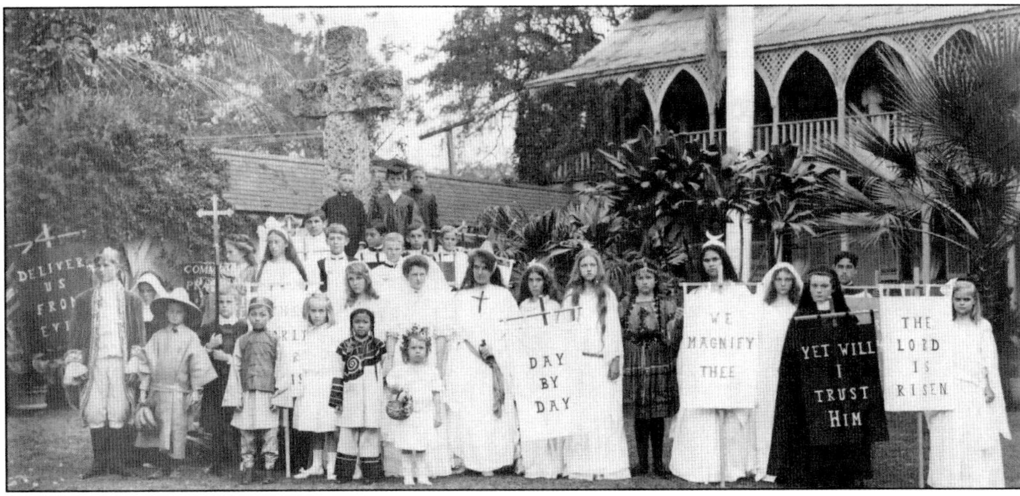

PRIORY PAGEANT. The buildings pictured were extant when, as legend has it, school patron Queen Emma sought refuge here on the grounds of St. Andrew's Priory from rioters after losing the legislative vote in her bid to succeed King Lunalilo in 1874. The coral cross in the background has witnessed two succeeding generations of buildings on the site, numerous school functions (such as this pageant), and is traditionally included in photographs of each year's Priory graduating class. (EC.)

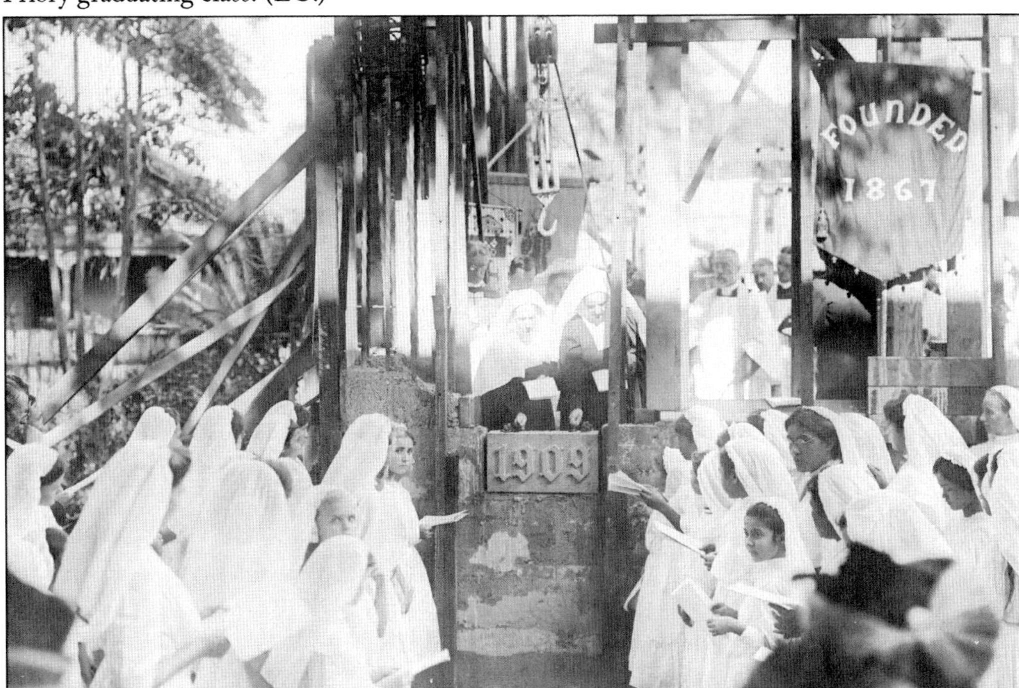

LAYING A CORNERSTONE AT ST. ANDREW'S PRIORY, 1909. Founded on Ascension Day, May 30, 1867, by King Kamehameha IV, Queen Emma, and Mother Priscilla Lydia Sellon of the English Society of the Most Holy Trinity, the school was designed to provide females with the same education offered to males. After annexation, nuns came from the American Order of the Transfiguration. The photograph shows Sisters Beatrice and Albertina in the center assisting in the cornerstone ceremony. (EC.)

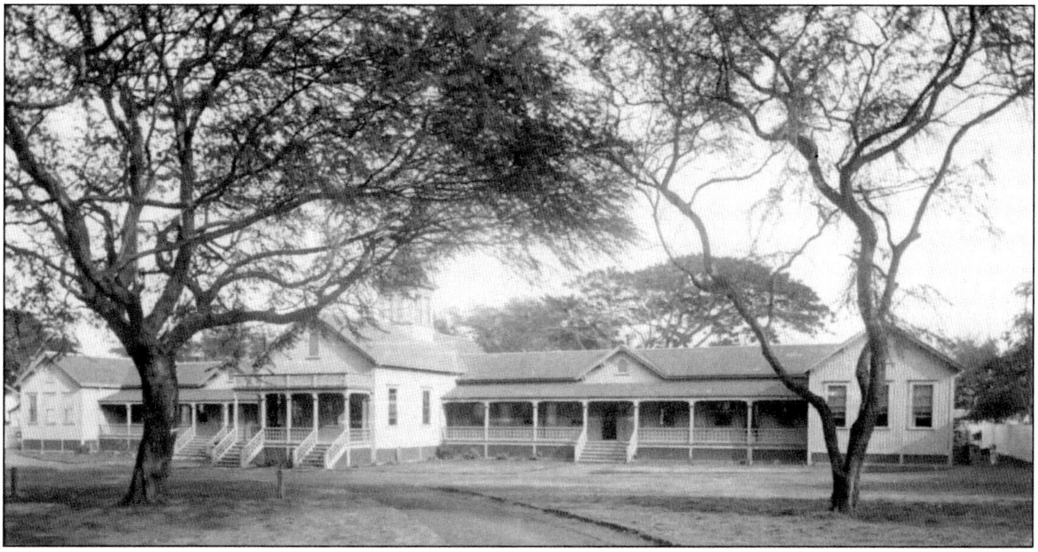

KOREAN METHODIST EPISCOPAL CHURCH AND SCHOOL. Located on Hawaiian Board of Missions land at Punchbowl and Beretania from 1905, the church began a coeducational elementary school that was recognized by the Board of Education in 1907. In conjunction with the school, a boys' dormitory was established, while girls lived at Susannah Wesley Home. After graduation, many students attended Mills Institute or Kawaiahao Seminary to complete their educations. A new Korean Methodist Episcopal Center was erected on Fort Street in 1922. (HSA.)

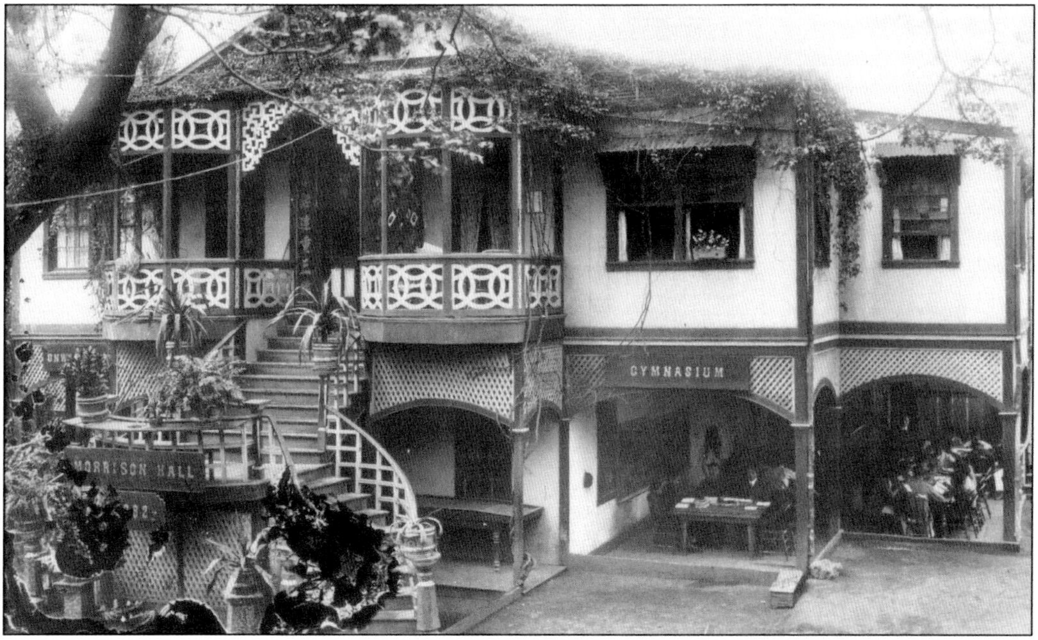

MONTAGUE HALL, MILLS INSTITUTE. Mills Institute's original student composition and location meant that it was involved in Chinese political, social, and economic affairs, and this view reflects Chinese architecture in its fenestration. At an 1894 meeting on nearby Queen Emma Street, Sun Yat Sen helped found the Hsing Chung Hui (Revive China Society), a revolutionary group (which included C.K. Ai, founder of City Mill) that pledged to overthrow the Manchus. The group utilized the Mills Institute playfield for military training. (HHS.)

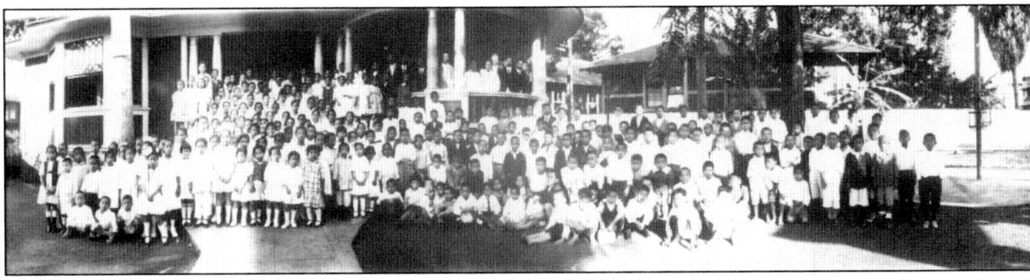

WAH MUN SCHOOL, 1920. Young Kum Hoy was brought from Sun Ming Ting Village of Zhongshan in 1916, when he was 60 years old, to teach at Wah Mun School. He had earned the high degree of *sau choy* at the age of 17 through examinations in Peking. The school, located on South Kukui between Nuuanu and Fort, was founded on February 4, 1911, and taught the culture and language of the ancestral Chinese land. (HSA.)

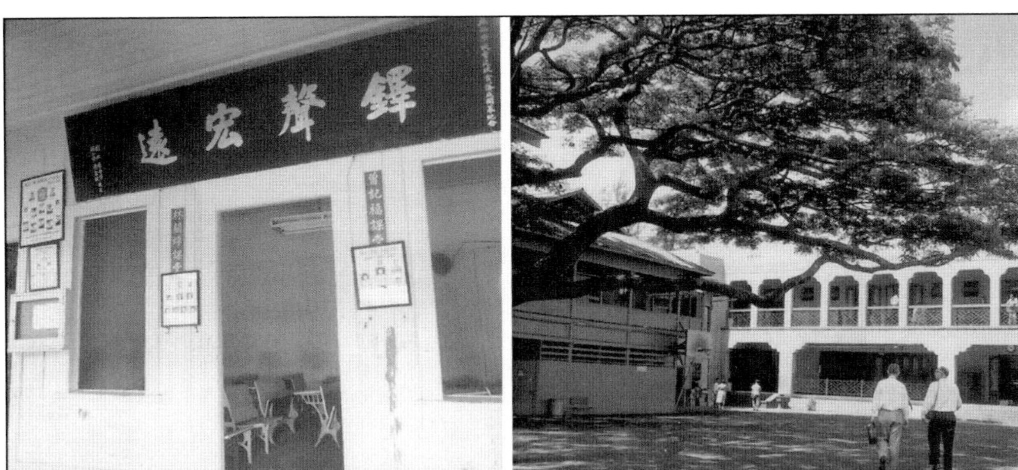

SMALL KAULUWELA CHINESE SCHOOL (LEFT) AND MUN LUN SCHOOL (RIGHT). This small Kauluwela neighborhood Chinese school's banner reads, "The sound of [children] reading can be heard loud and far." Founded on February 4, 1911, the Mun Lun School intended to teach the Chinese language and culture to Chinese youth. The 1931 building shown here, located near Smith and Kapena Streets, had long graceful corridors of a southern China design and was razed as part of the Kukui Redevelopment Project. (Photograph by Nancy Bannick; HSA.)

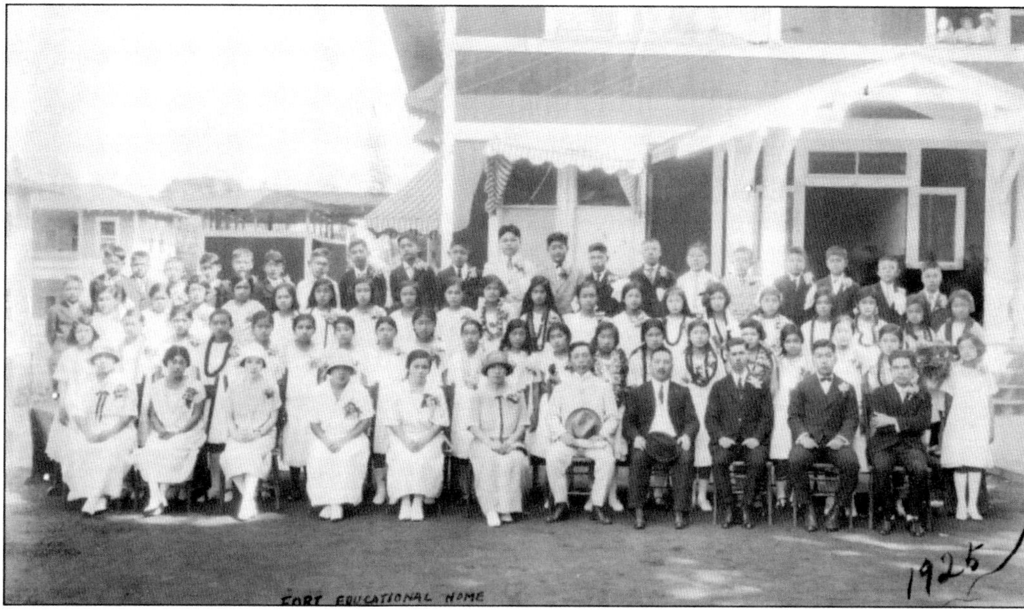

FORT STREET GAKUIN. When the Honpa Hongwanji opened its elementary school, its mission was to prepare children for a return to Japan and entrance to Japanese schools. These children already attended public English-speaking schools during regular school hours and then Japanese school afterwards. When it became apparent that there would be no return, the parents urged that the school continue to support Japanese language and culture. (Photograph by Toshiharu Murai.)

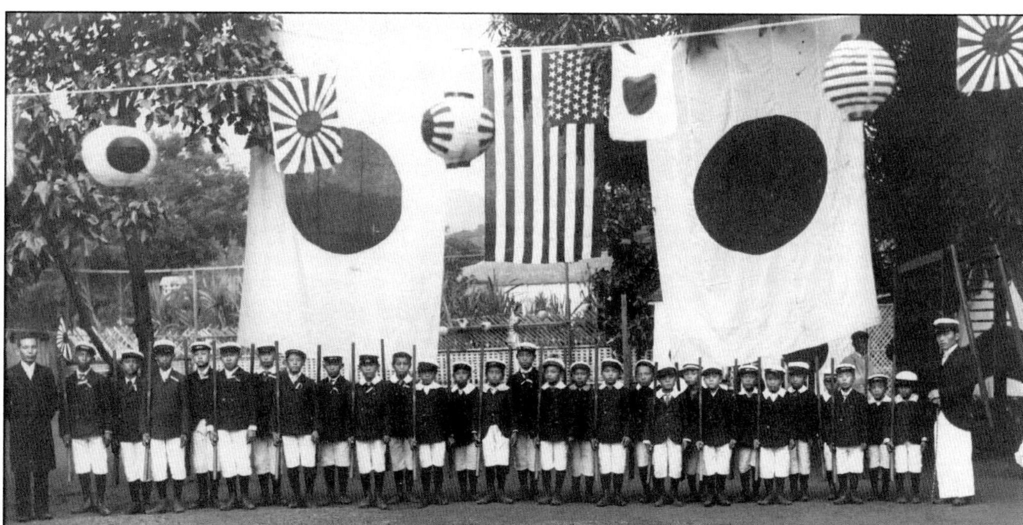

JAPANESE CHRISTIAN BOARDING SCHOOL ON NUUANU, 1901. In *The Friend*, published on August 1, 1906, Rev. T. Okumura (the man in the suit on the left) says: "The boys who stay with us during the summer are busy every day cleaning the houses and yards. We had 62 children before vacation, and we hope they will all come back bringing new ones with them when the vacation is over. We are very glad to state that the school had made good progress during the past six months, and the financial difficulties have been relieved by the generosity of kind-hearted friends." (Bishop Museum.)

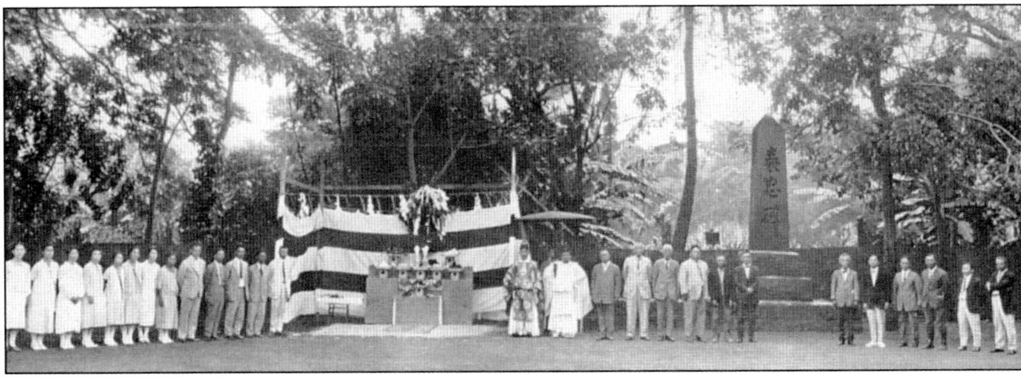

CHUO GAKUIN–JAPANESE CENTRAL INSTITUTE OF HAWAII AND THE HYO CHU HI OBELISK, 1927. It is not known why Admiral Togo, a Japanese national hero and Hawaii Shinto *kami* (spirit), was honored in 1907 with a monument. His words, "*Hyo* (symbol) *Chu* (patriotism) *Hi* (inscription)," were engraved on the obelisk that stood on the Christian school grounds. Rev. Takie Okumura distanced his school from the predominant Buddhist Jodo (Pure Land) sect in nisei (second generation) education. However, mindful of tradition, Shinto priests (Reverend Miao, from Isumo Taisha in patterned clothing, and Reverend Kawasaki, from Daijingu, in white clothing) officiated in this "secular" school's blessing. During World War II, all identifiable Japanese symbols, including the Hyo Chu Hi obelisk, were hidden or given away. The obelisk was toppled from its base, and the obelisk and its two pedestal stones, amazingly, were taken to the Kaheka Street Buddhist Shinshu Kyokai Mission by the reverend's wife, Sumiko Tatsuguchi. The stone was covered with concrete and buried for the duration of the war. Today, the obelisk is at the relocated temple on Beretania Street. The earlier 1923 photograph of the Japanese Central Institute (JCI) indoor baseball (softball) team below shows the ballplayers sitting around the monument for their team photograph. (Both, JCCH.)

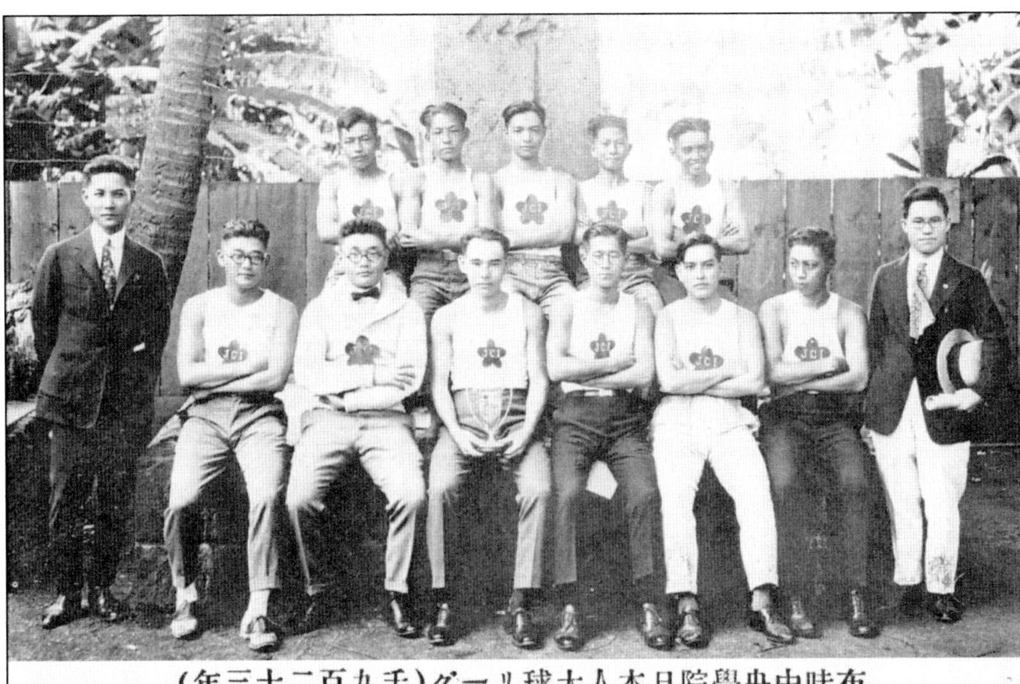

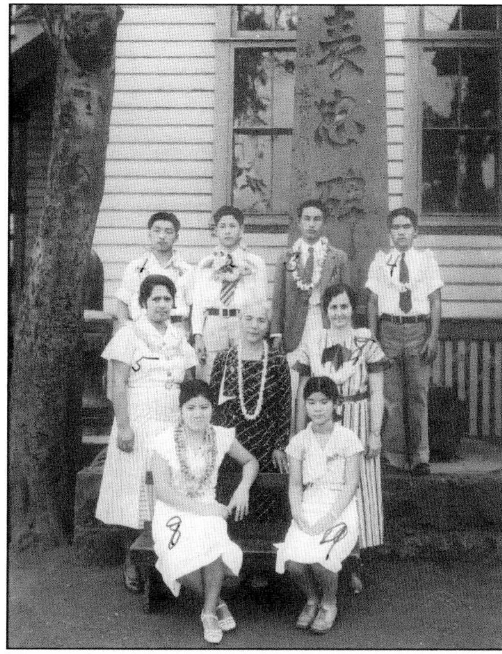

NUUANU DAY SCHOOL, 1934. Hannah Suehiro (center) taught English to immigrant Japanese students at the Nuuanu Day School. It was located at the Nuuanu Japanese Central Institute. There was also a Nuuanu Night School for adults. Class photographs over the years show wood and stucco-clad buildings in the backgrounds, meaning that there were funds from donors to erect a substantial school. (HSA.)

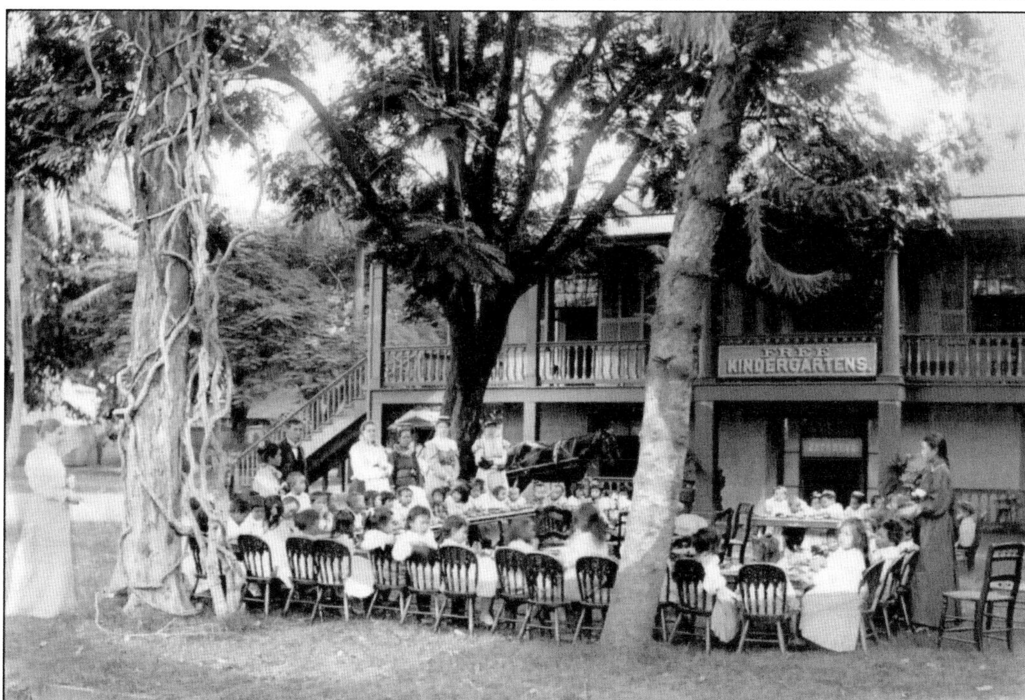

FREE KINDERGARTENS, EMMA HALL, NUUANU STREET AND CHAPLAIN LANE, C. 1895. The former home of Queen Emma also served as a Free Kindergarten and Children's Aid Association (FKCAA) site. Proponents of kindergartens wished to prepare children for formal schooling. The first kindergarten in Honolulu was established by Francis M. Damon in 1892 as part of his Chinese Mission. As the "Japanese" sign implies, initial classes were ethnically separated, a policy that was reversed after 1900. (HSA.)

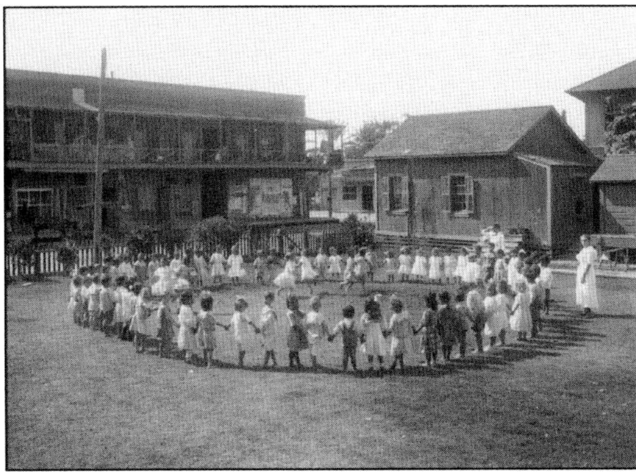
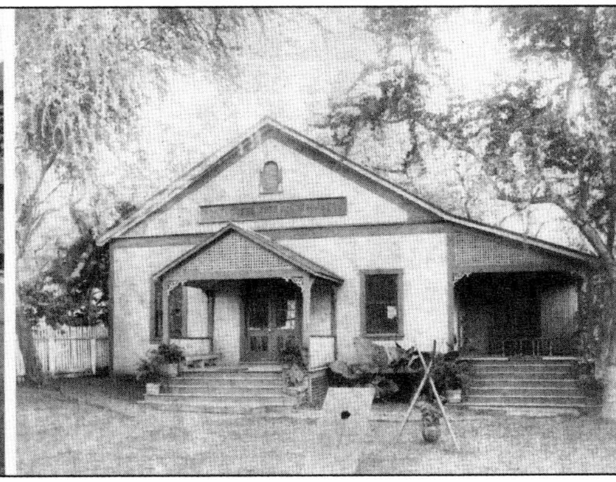

FKCAA. The Beretania Settlement kindergarten (left), located on the mauka side of Beretania Street between Smith and Maunakea, was established to provide medical care, recreational activities, and especially preschool child education. (Note the movie posters on the far building announcing *The Virginian*, which was possibly playing at the nearby Beretania Theater.) The Portuguese Kindergarten (right) was located on Miller Street near Queen's Hospital (1913). (Photographs by L.E. Edgworth; left, Bishop Museum and right, HSA.)

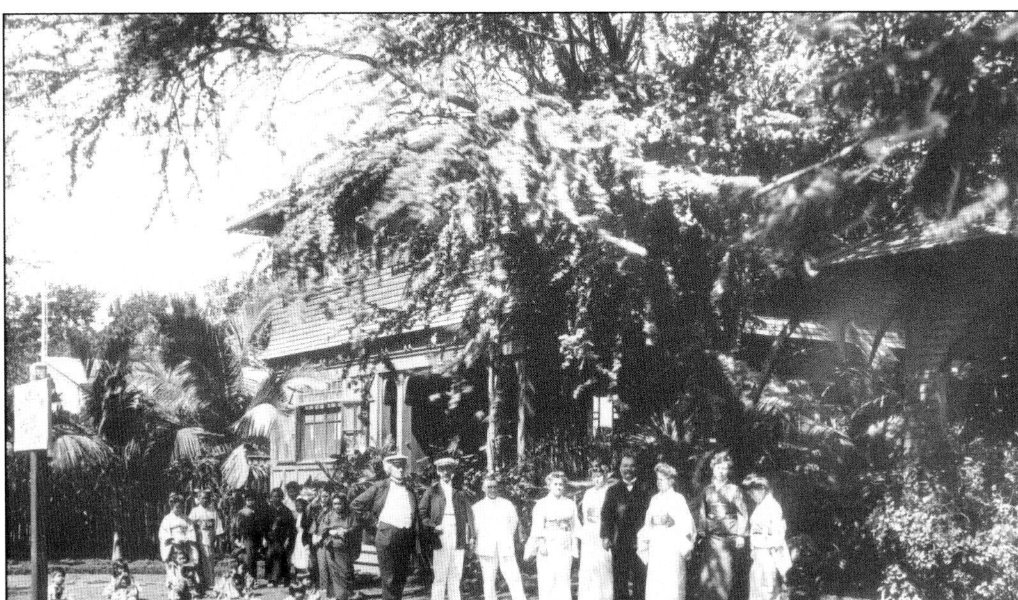

HAOLE DRESSED IN KIMONO. In Waipahu in 1899, the Women's Home Missionary Society of the Methodist Episcopal Church began to teach Japanese and Korean immigrants sewing, English, and the Bible. A girls' orphanage was established in 1919. A sign in Japanese, English, and Korean above the entrance to the Susannah Wesley Home, which reads "Home and Training School for Japanese and Korean Women and Children," is still preserved at the center today. (HHS.)

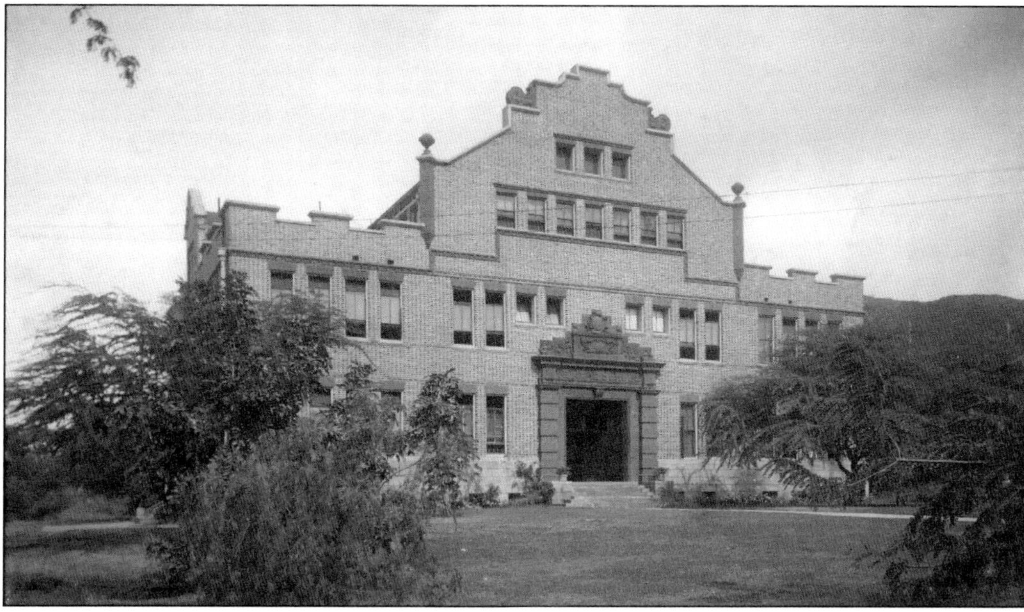

TERRITORIAL NORMAL SCHOOL. In the latter half of the 19th century, most people reached, at best, the eighth grade. Public schoolteachers often had little more education than their students. Formal teacher training began in Hawaii in 1888 at the Fort Street School. The Honolulu Normal and Training School was finally established in 1896 and built on the mauka-Ewa corner of Magellan and Hackfeld (Emerson) Streets. The Normal School later was merged into the UH College of Education. (HSA.)

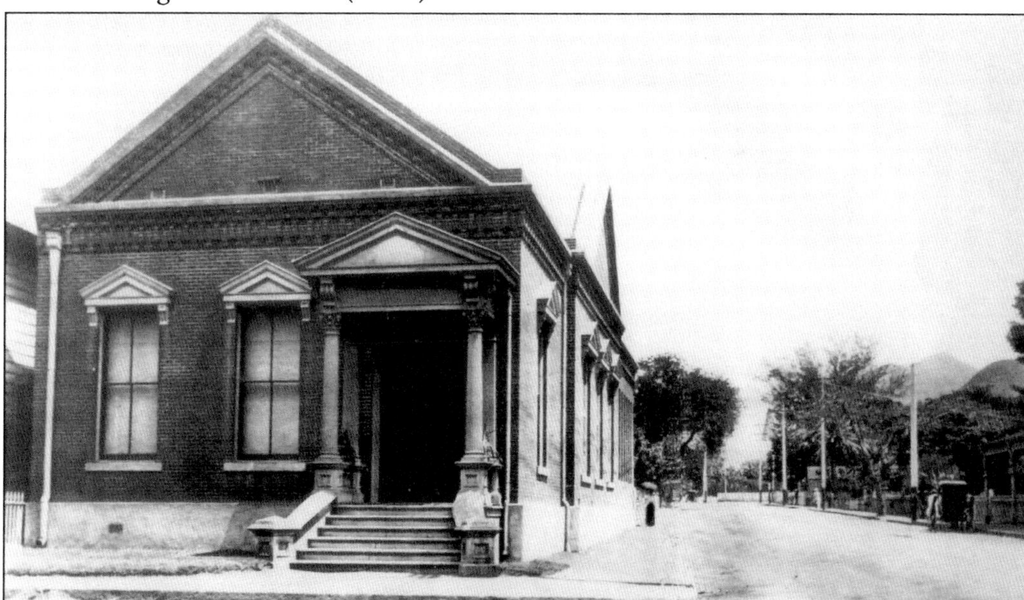

LIBRARY. Libraries had been attempted in 1850 and 1855. The Honolulu Library and Reading Room Association was initially located above the C.E. Williams's furniture store on the Ewa side of Fort Street in 1879. Books and furniture were donated. This subscription library was able to purchase property on the mauka-Ewa corner of Hotel and Alakea Streets, opening this brick building in 1884, and a mauka addition to the building was constructed in 1895. (HSA.)

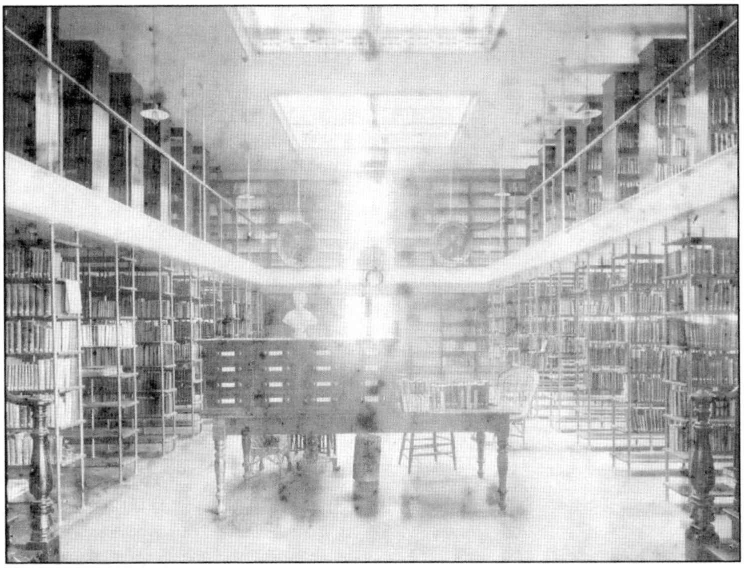

LIBRARY INTERIOR. The library had ceilings that were 16 feet high. There was natural light from above and two levels of bookstacks. The original building had room for 20,000 volumes but initially had only 4,000 books. Major contributors to the library included Alexander J. Cartwright, Queen Emma, Bernice Pauahi Bishop, Charles R. Bishop, Auguste Marques, and Samuel N. Castle. (HHS.)

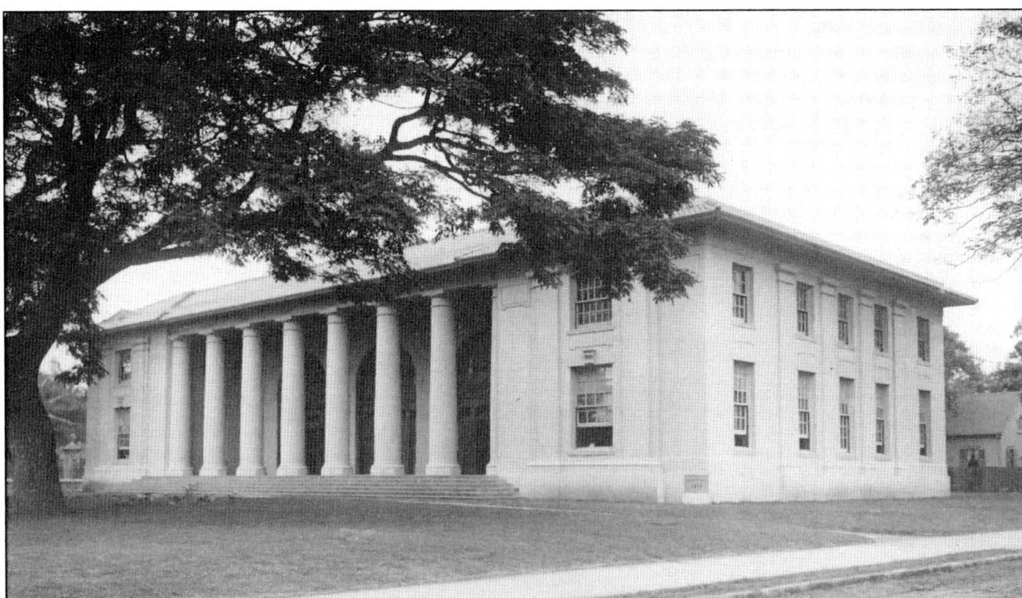

LIBRARY OF HAWAII. Andrew Carnegie was a Scottish immigrant who became a multimillionaire steel magnate and funded 3,000 libraries in the United States and Britain. Gov. Walter J. Frear obtained an agreement for a $100,000 library grant from Carnegie in 1909. The legislature committed to $10,000 a year for expenses, and the Honolulu Library and Reading Room Association and the Hawaiian Historical Society agreed to join the project. (SHPD.)

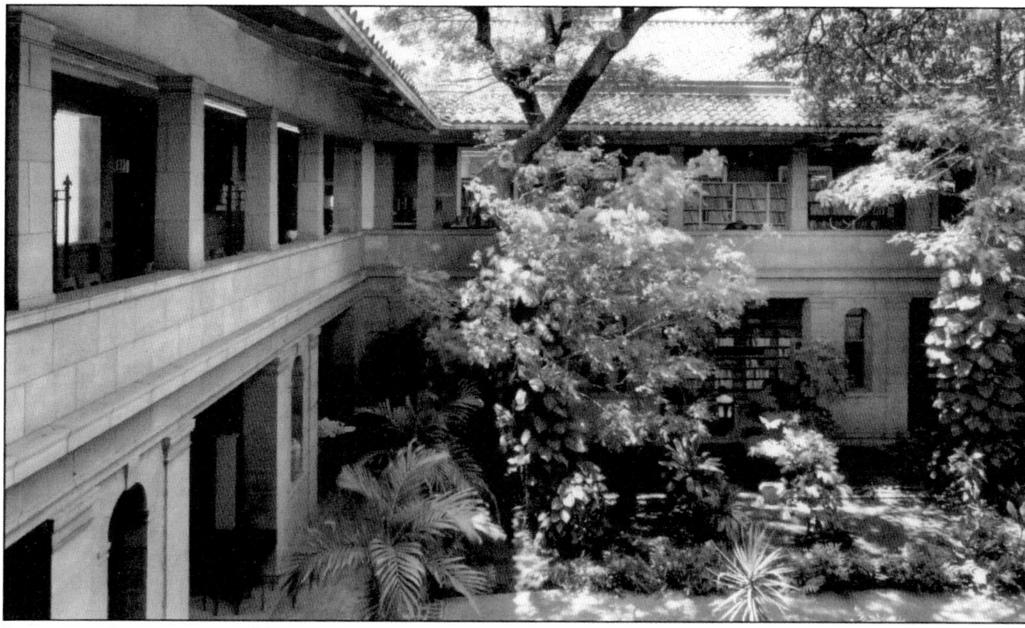

LIBRARY COURTYARD. The cornerstone of the King Street frontage was laid in 1911, and the building opened on February 11, 1913. The design, by architects Henry D. Whitfield and H.L. Kerr, featured classic Doric columns. Makai and mauka additions were made in 1930, creating a courtyard with covered lanai (veranda) and space for the children's reading room and its Juliette May Fraser murals of Hawaiian legends. Another two-story addition on the mauka side enclosed the courtyard in 1992. (SHPD.)

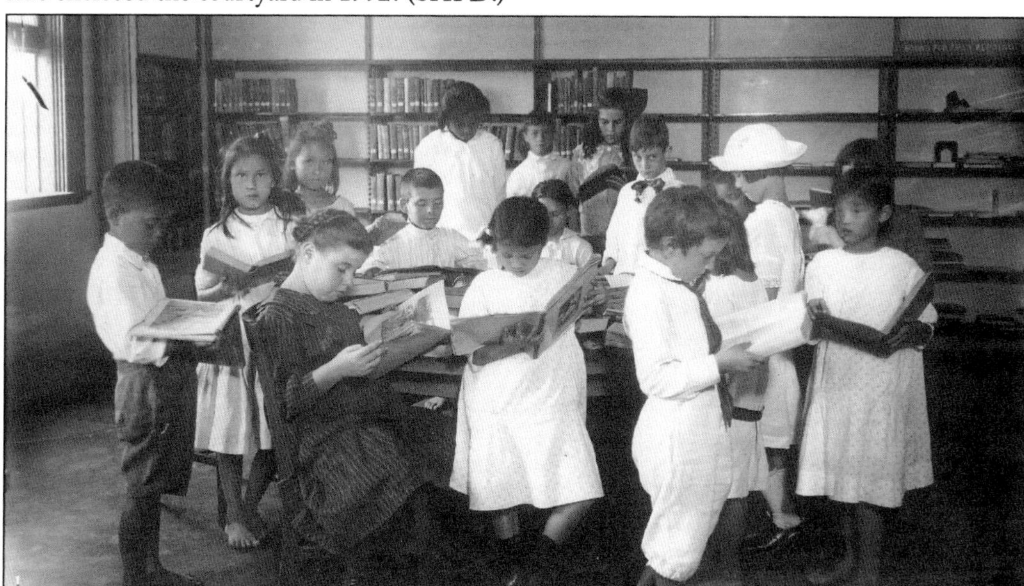

NEW LIBRARY PATRONS, 1913. Kindergarteners, in what appear to be homemade cotton clothing, read picture books in the new library. The shelves were yet to be stocked with books. Edna Allyn was the first librarian at the Honolulu Library and Reading Room. Today, the children's books are housed in the Edna Allyn Room at the Hawaii State Library, and a bust of Andrew Carnegie is located in the building lobby. (HSA.)

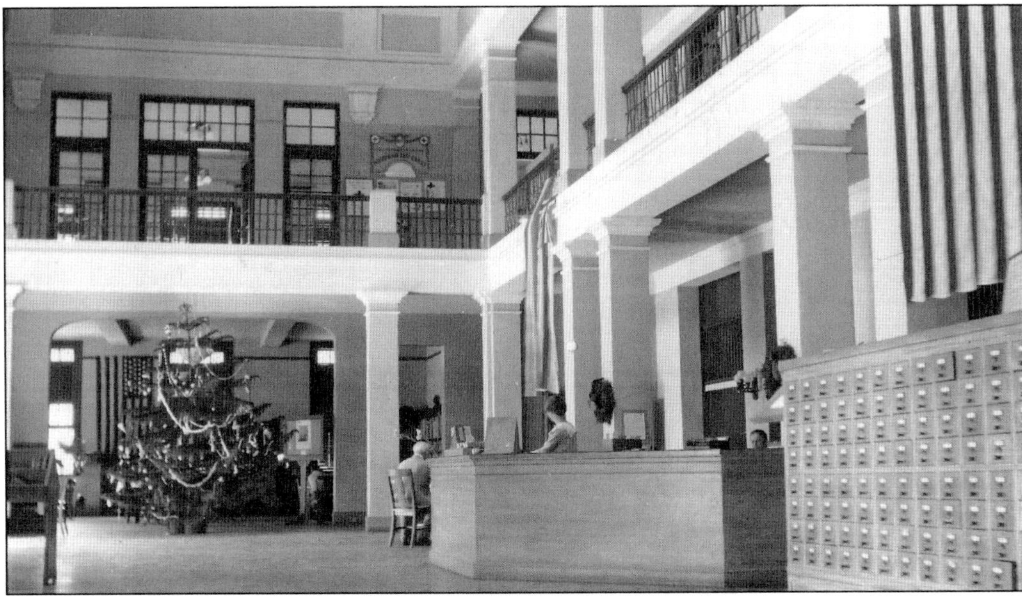

ORIGINAL LIBRARY FOYER. This photograph was taken within a decade of completion of the first phase of the library. It shows the simple classical architecture based on the government's Americanization effort of the period. Note the Christmas tree on the left, the openness of the room behind (without steel shelving), the circulation desk dominating the room, the extensive (pre-computer) card catalog on the right, and the prominent display of flags. (HSA.)

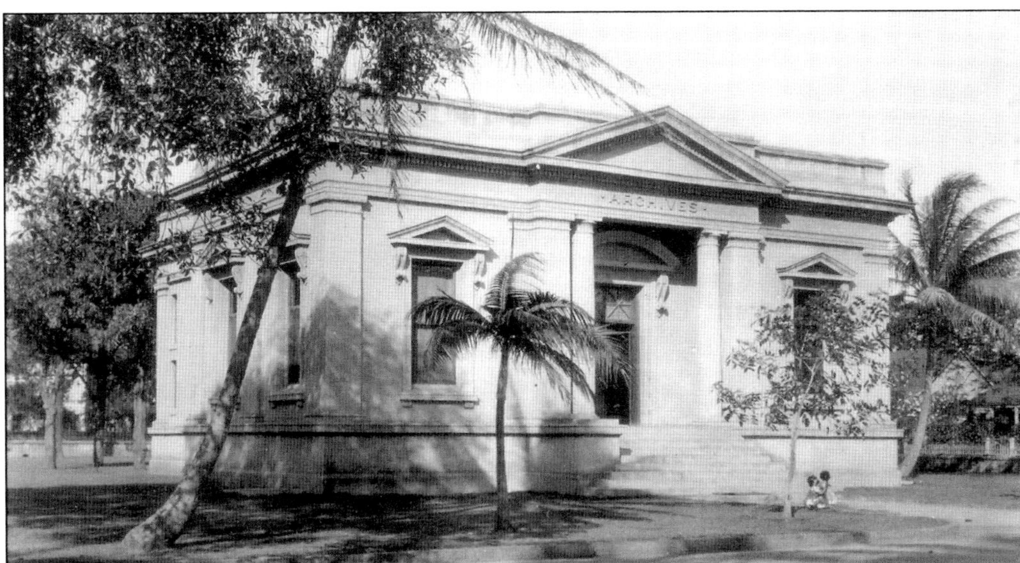

ARCHIVES. During the monarchy, government records and a national museum were housed inside Aliiolani Hale. After the 1893 overthrow, many materials ended up in Bishop Museum or private hands. Annexation held the possibility of mainland relocation of documents and artifacts. The Territory prevented this by constructing the first fireproof structure specifically designed as an archive. The original 1906 building, by local architect Oliver Traphagan, was expanded on both sides, and a wing was placed at the back in 1930. (HSA.)

Three

Spiritual Homes

When the Congregationalist missionaries arrived in 1820, they entered a Hawaiian religious void. The *kapu* system (rules of prohibition) had been overthrown by Kamehameha II (Liholiho), symbolically breaking the *aikapu* by eating with women. Missionaries approached the alii to acquire land and establish the first Congregational church, homes, and printing press. From this time forward, almost everything written by *kamaaina* and foreigners alike was couched in Christian moral terms.

The missionaries proselytized throughout Honolulu Town and on all islands as converts helped build the *apana* (branch) churches. *Makaainana* (commoners or those living on the land) from the "village" wished for their own town church as they felt a difference between themselves and the alii congregation at Kawaihao. They organized their own congregation, acquired land, and raised money to build the Kamakapili Church, which was located just mauka of the intersection at Beretania and Smith Streets.

In the late 19th century, Honolulu was known as a city of churches and church institutions. Beretania Street, for example, was a "church row." Traveling Ewa on Beretania, one could find the German Lutheran Church and home located near Miller; the Anglican St. Andrew's Cathedral, Priory School, and St. Peter's near Queen Emma; the Catholic bishop's residence on Garden Lane and Our Lady of Peace nearby on Fort; the Congregationalist Fort Street Church at Fort; the Hawaiian Evangelical Association Chinese Church mauka on Fort; the Japanese Congregationalist Church mauka on Nuuanu; Kaumakapili Church near Smith; and the Japanese Methodist Episcopal Church makai on River.

Though Christian outreach seemed to dominate the town, Honolulu neighborhoods included a wealth of temples and shrines. This was largely a story of recent arrivals looking for solace in community. People gathered together, oftentimes from their home villages or regions, raised money (in the case of the Japanese issei [first generation] often by *tanimoshi* [mutual financing associations]), and built structures that looked like their homelands' religious buildings. In the early part of the 20th century, extremely large congregations gathered for celebrations. But later generations moved away from the town center, and membership dwindled or disappeared partly because of World War II and mid-century urban renewal. When compared to the austere Calvinist churches, these temples and shrines brought pizzazz to the town with festivals, processions, elaborate costuming, and firecrackers.

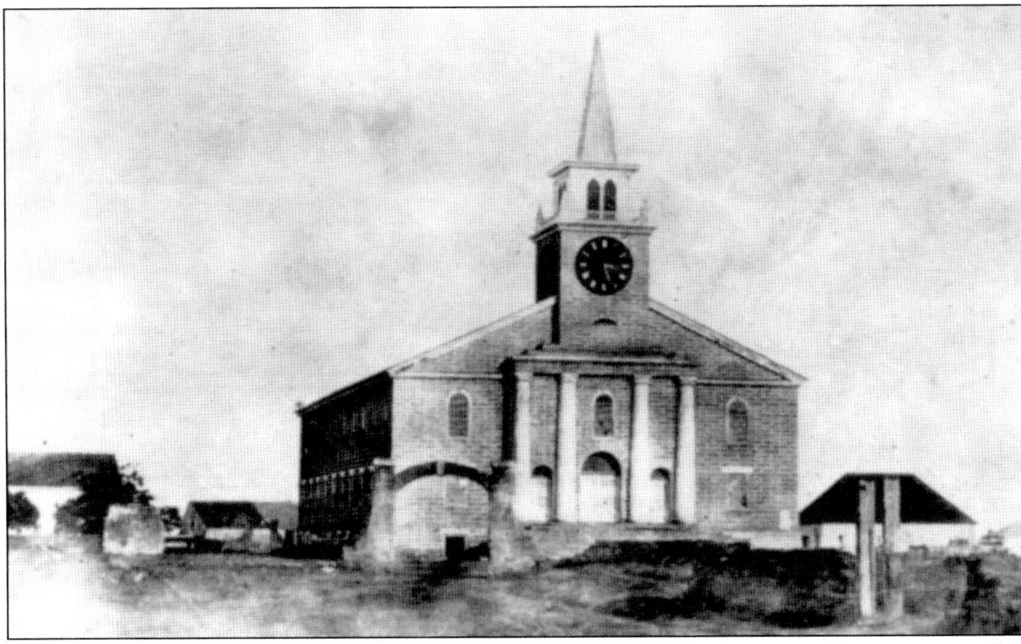

KAWAIAHAO CHURCH. The church name is correctly spelled *Ka Wai a Hao*, meaning "the freshwater of Hao." Four thatched churches had successively stood here in the present graveyard. A six-foot foundation was dug, and previously buried bodies were removed. The cornerstone came from Waianae, the blocks from the Mamala reefs, lime from Waikiki, and wood from the mountains between Waikiki and Moanalua. Children were in awe of the great fire pits burning lime, which, when mixed with sand, became mortar for 14,000 building blocks. It was dedicated in 1842. (Mission Children's Society.)

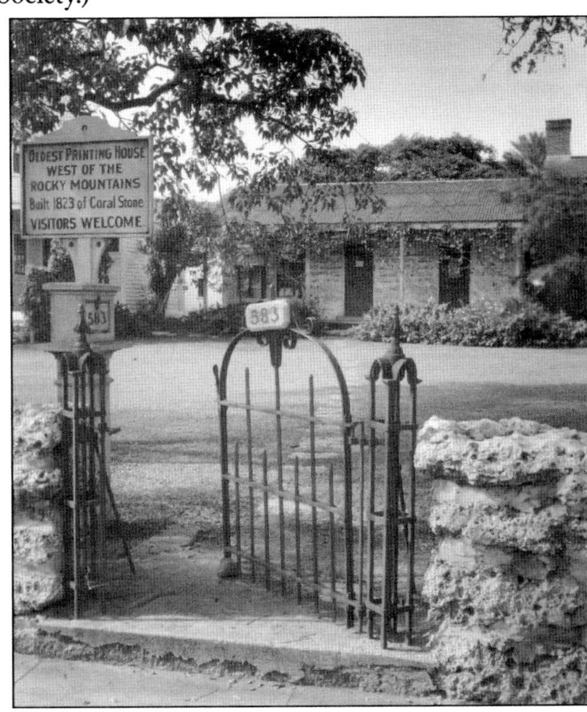

PRINTING HOUSE. The missionaries carried on their first ship, the *Thaddeus*, a used Ramage press to print Bibles in the Hawaiian language. The missionaries constructed this 28-by-17-foot print shop in December 1823. Besides Bibles, hymnals and bills of lading were soon produced. By approximately 1828, the demand for printed material was so great that printing operations had moved to a larger two-story coral structure across South King, located on what later became Printer's Lane. (HSA.)

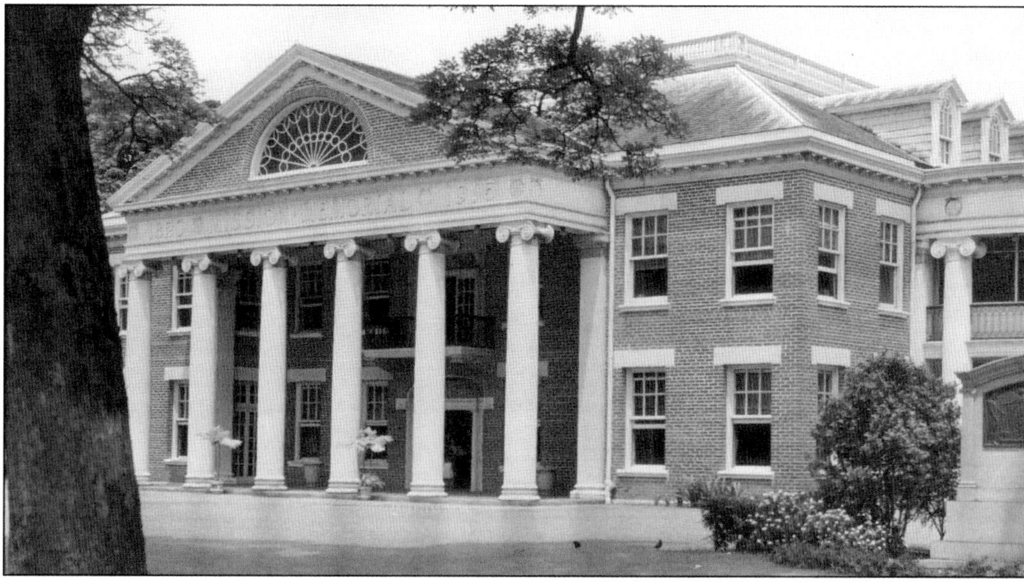

MISSION MEMORIAL COMPLEX. The complex contains three buildings. Two were designed by local architect H.L. Kerr for the Hawaiian Evangelical Association (dedicated 1916) and commemorated the anniversary of the first missionary arrival. The third building, the Annex, was designed by architect Mark Potter (dedicated 1930). The city government acquired the Mission Memorial Complex for additional office space in 1945. If one looks over to the entrance of the Annex, the words *Christian Education* are still visible. (HSA.)

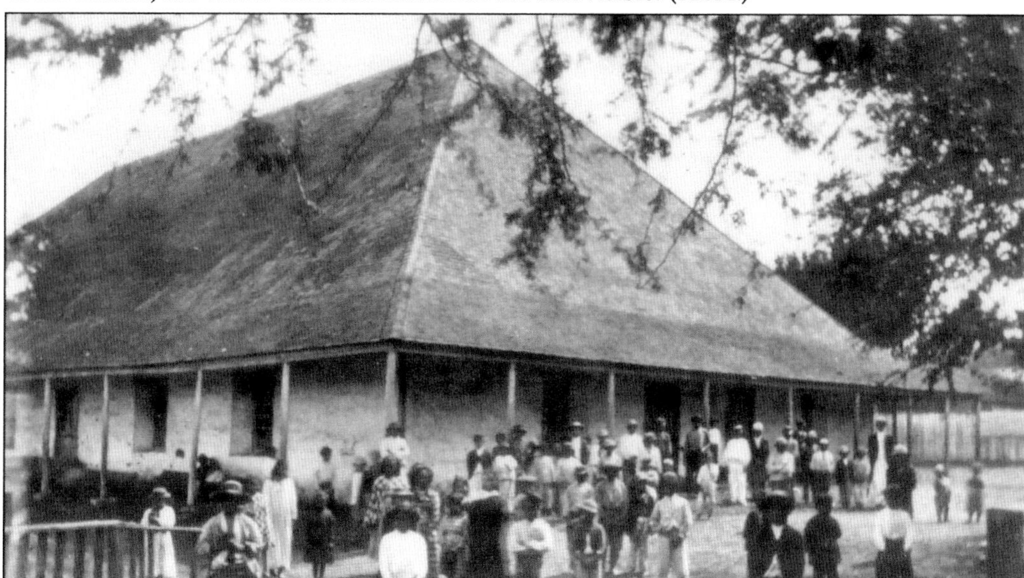

ORIGINAL KAUMAKAPILI CHURCH. In 1838, religious revival and competition for souls with Catholics in Honolulu led to establishment of Kaumakapili Church. Chief Abner Paki and his wife, Konia, provided land on the mauka side of Beretania at Kaumakapili (meaning "perch with closed eyes"). The adobe building with steep, thatched *pili* (long grass) roof accommodated 2,500 people. The cornerstone was dedicated on August 29, 1839. Rev. Lowell Smith lived on the makai side of Beretania, near today's Smith Street. (HSA.)

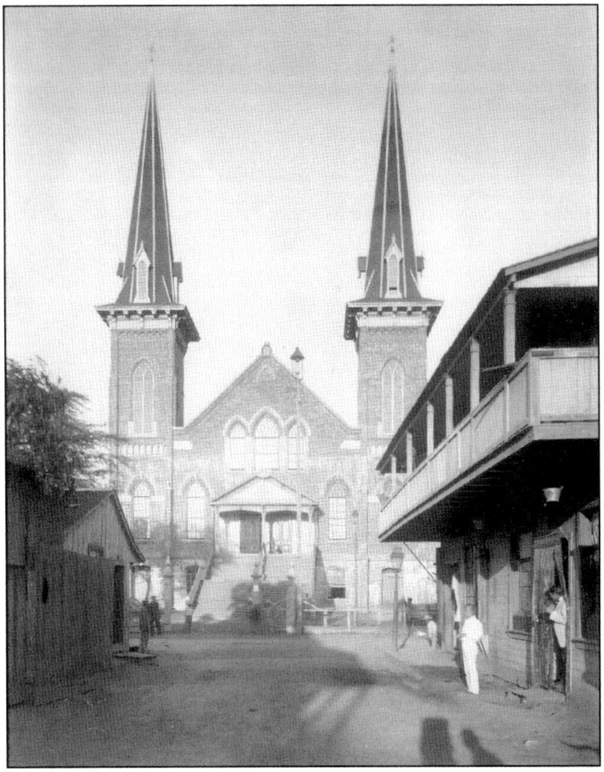

SECOND KAUMAKAPILI CHURCH. In 1881, the old adobe church was torn down. The new cornerstone was dedicated by Princess Liliuokalani. While members of the building committee had planned a one-story structure, King Kalakaua wanted a more imposing edifice with two steeples. After seven years of construction at a cost of $65,000, the imposing brick structure did have two towers. Note that the sanctuary on the main floor of the building was reached by an impressive large set of stairs. The organ, built by Bevington and Sons of London, arrived in 1888, and St. Andrew's Cathedral organist F. Wray Taylor (shown below) celebrated with a program that included *Hawaii Ponoi* and *Kaumakapili March*. The organ was destroyed along with the rest of the building in the 1900 fire. (Left, HSA; below, Bishop Museum.)

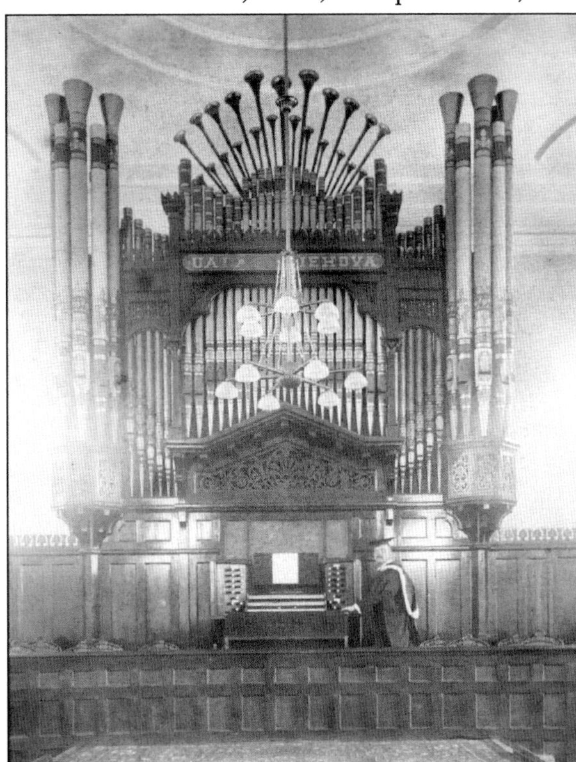

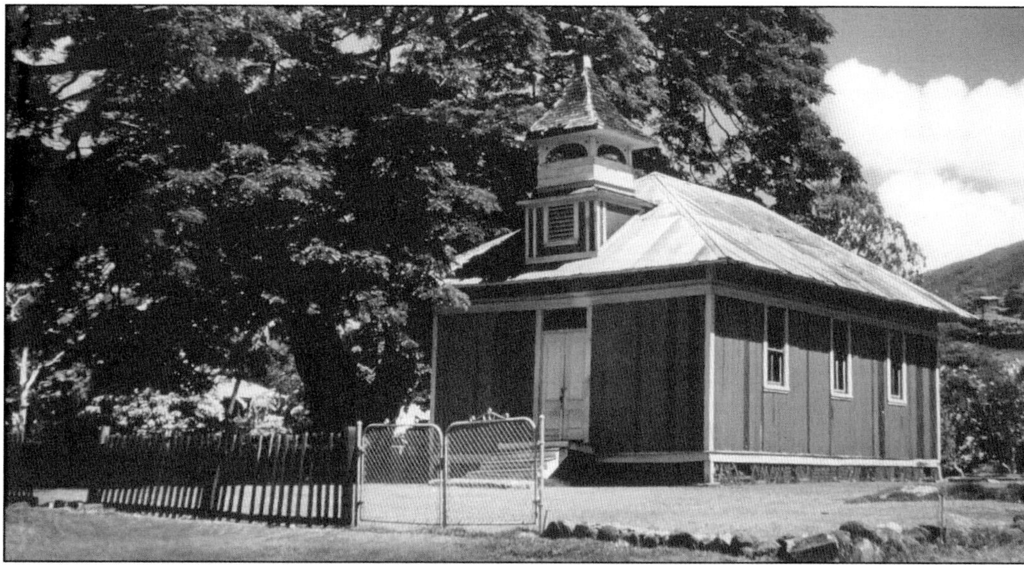

KAUMAKAPILI CHURCH O PAUOA OR AUWAIOLIMU PAUOA CHAPEL. The red-painted Pauoa Chapel was an *apana* (branch) church of Kaumakapili. In 1931, the Territory gave the land for the cemetery, and the church was built shortly after. The cemetery had two sides—Kawaiahao Church members were buried on the left, and Kamakapili Church members interred on the right. In the 1960s, the deteriorated building was deconsecrated and demolished. The tree in the photograph remains in 2012 but is much larger. (Kaumakapili Church Archives.)

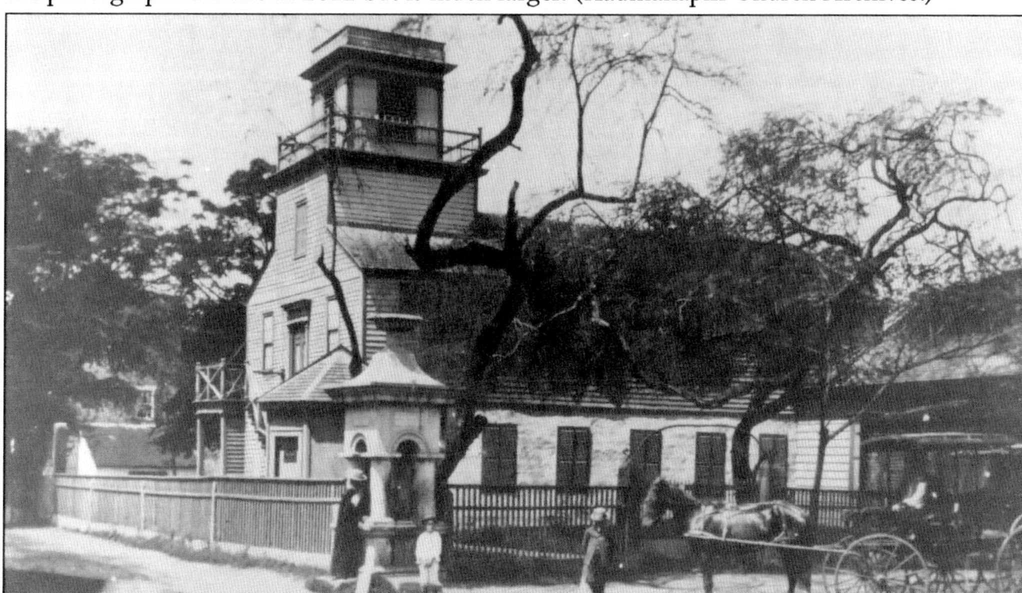

THE SEAMEN'S BETHEL. The American Seamen's Friend Society (ASFS) was established to supply religious reading materials to whaling and trading ship crews overseas. Materials for the building were contributed by Connecticut shipowners and carried free in the holds of whaling vessels. The Reverend Samuel C. Damon served here for 42 years while editing and publishing the periodical *The Friend*. The church, popular for its pillared fountain, burned in the 1886 fire. (HSA.)

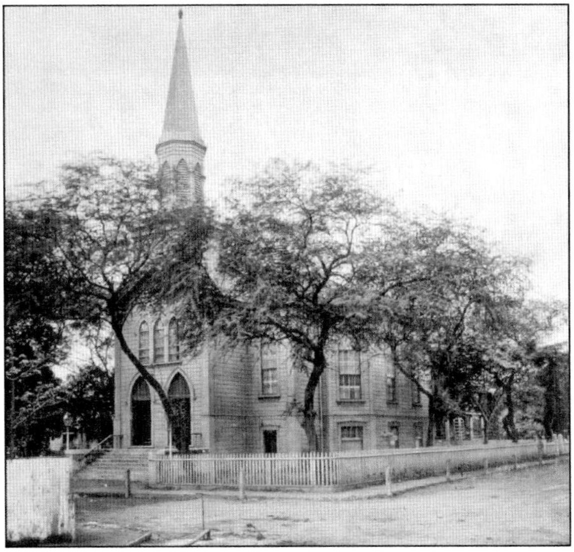

FORT STREET CHURCH, C. 1890. In 1853, the Second Foreign Church of Honolulu was formed from among the members of the Oahu Bethel Church. Erected in 1856 at the makai-Ewa corner of Fort and Beretania, the wooden church cost $15,000 and included a steeple financed by the sale of parishioner livestock. Membership included the Afong, Judd, Lishman, and Waterhouse families, who had their own pews. The building was popularly known as the Fort Street Church. (HSA.)

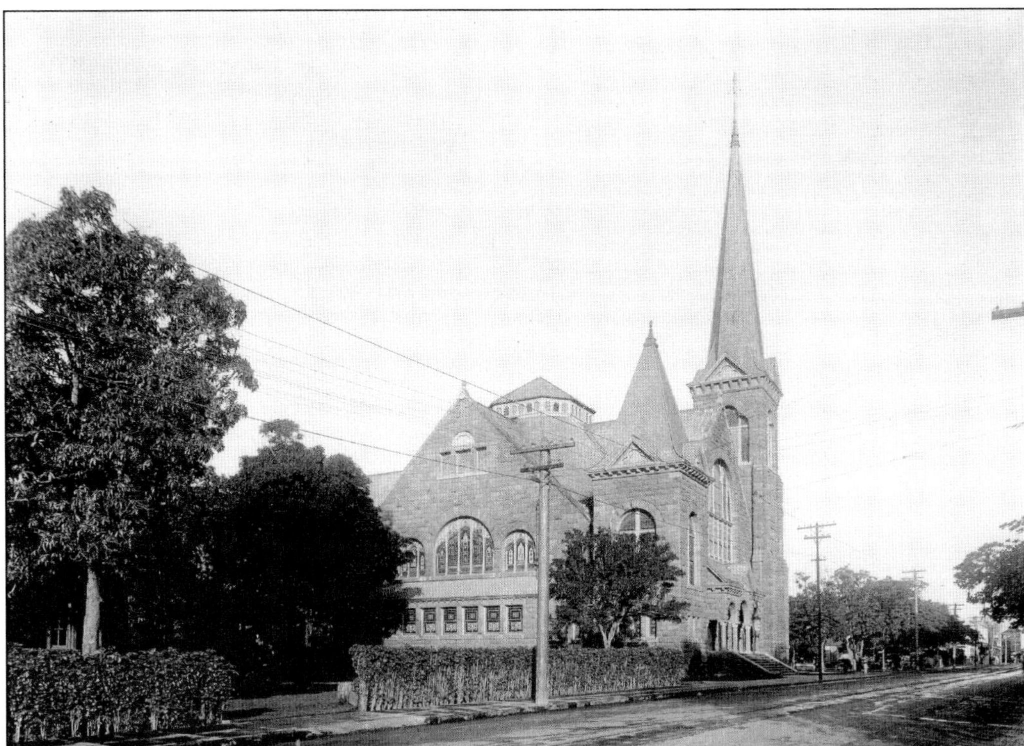

CENTRAL UNION CHURCH. After the 1886 fire destroyed the Bethel Union Church, the congregation decided to purchase a new lot. However, the next year the Union and Fort Street congregations merged, creating Central Union Church. It decided to build on Bethel Union's Beretania Street parcel. To accommodate crowds, walls were placed close to the property lines and both ventilation and the number of fire exits provided were maximized. The church was opened on December 4, 1892, with over 1,000 people attending. (HHS.)

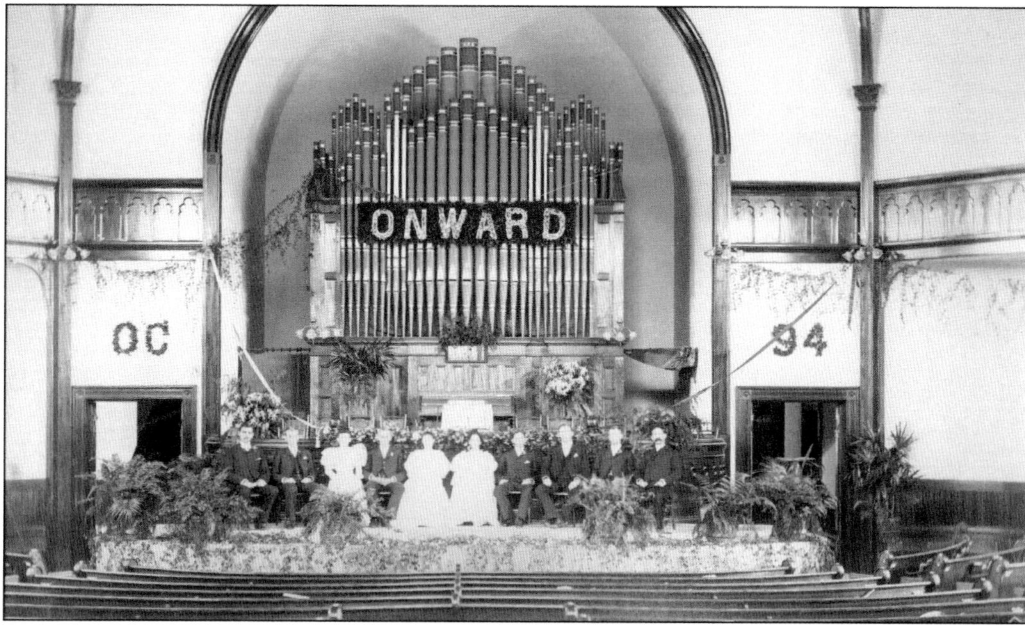

CENTRAL UNION CHURCH INTERIOR. This photograph of the interior shows the importance of the Christian mission "Onward." Considering the close connection between Central Union Church and Punahou School, one might speculate that the emblems above pertained to Oahu College (original name of the school) and the class of 1894. (Photograph by Hadley; Bishop Museum.)

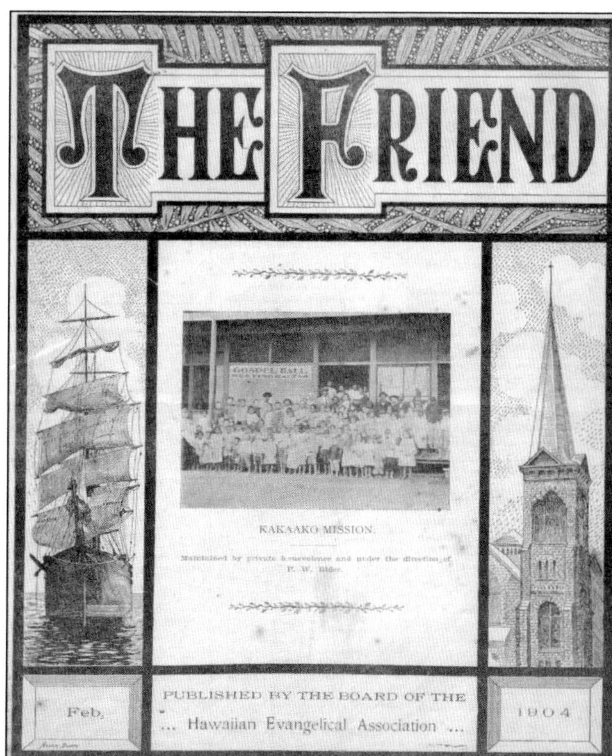
THE FRIEND

KAKAAKO MISSION.

Feb. 1904

PUBLISHED BY THE BOARD OF THE ... Hawaiian Evangelical Association ...

THE FRIEND, FEATURING THE KAKAAKO MISSION, 1904. Christian reverend Takie Okumura began this missionary project in 1902 in a room on the corner of South and Queen Streets. It was located in a "neglected part of the city, among some of the poorest and lowest of earth, divided among twenty-four nationalities." The neighbors were initially resistant to a gospel mission, but within a few years, it had expanded in ever-larger facilities with an assembly hall and play areas for children. (SRC.)

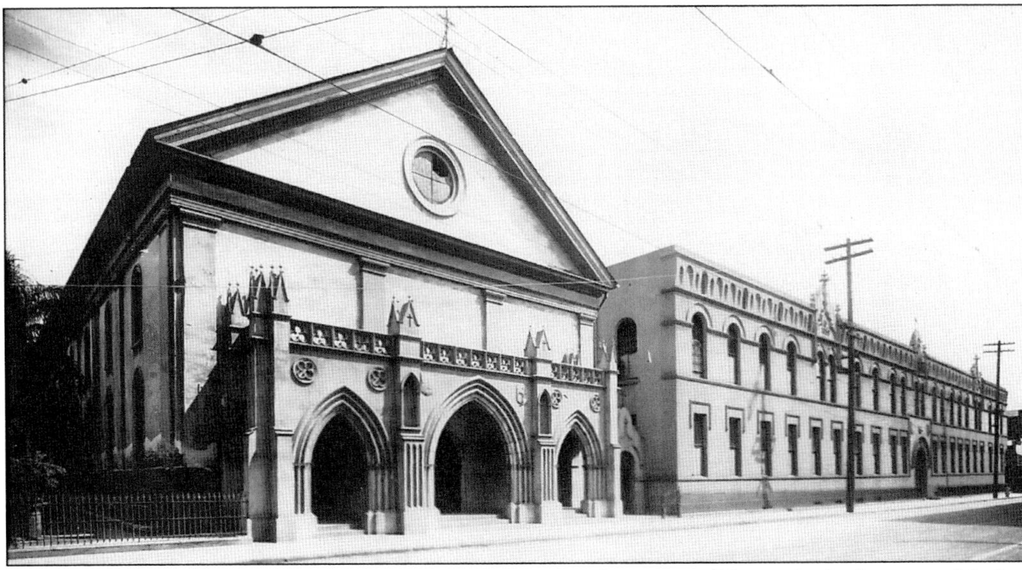

OUR LADY OF PEACE CATHEDRAL AND SACRED HEARTS CONVENT. The cathedral was established over Congregationalist objection and dedicated on August 15, 1843. It was constructed of coral blocks from the same reef as Kawaiahao Church and appeared similar until the exterior was plastered. Renovations undertaken by Bishop Louis Maigret in 1871 raised the building roof and installed decorative ceiling paneling, twin galleries, and windows from France. A Gothic-style portico was installed in 1910 by Bishop Libert Boeynames but was later removed. Heavy roof tiles were added in 1926 and the present front columns in 1929. The extra weight of the tiles required reinforcement of the building in 1940–1941, including adding tie-rods across the vaulted ceiling and concrete buttresses on the exterior. The building has had three different towers—an 1843 dome, an 1866 tall wooden spire, and the present square concrete structure from 1917. The Convent Building, inscribed with "1859" for the date that the sisters arrived, actually dates from 1901. In 1937, the sisters sold the Fort Street building to commercial interests and moved to Nuuanu. It was mostly demolished in 1991. (Above, HP; below, HSA.)

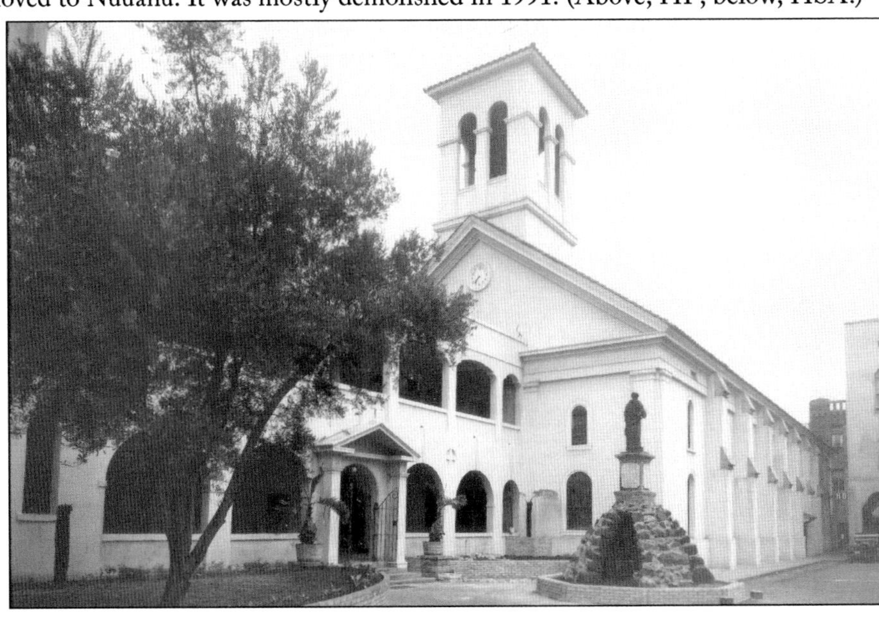

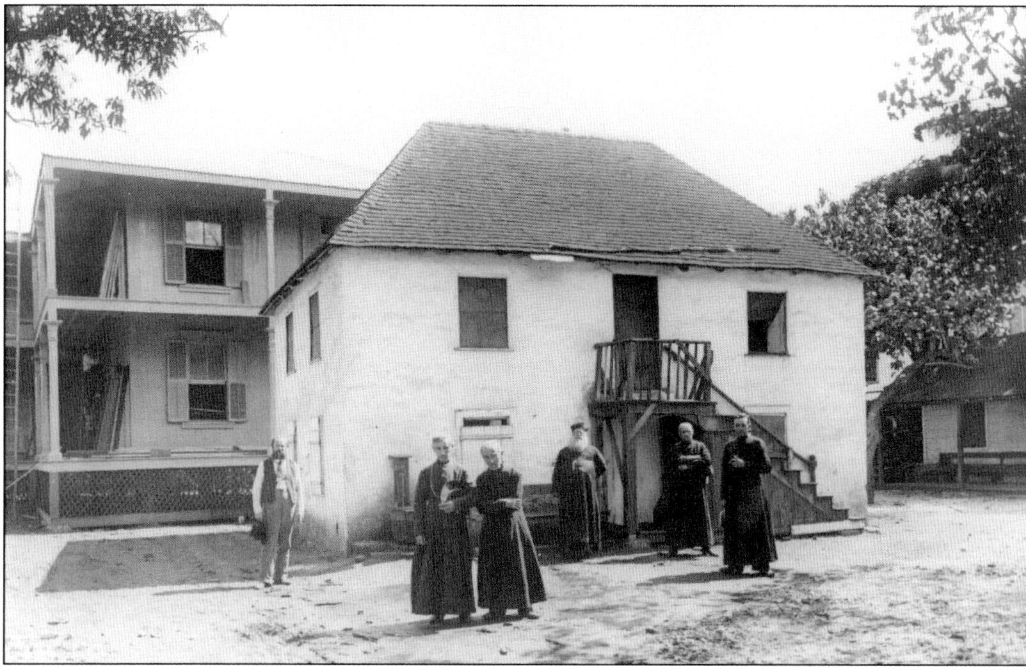

CHURCH GROUNDS. Clergy stand before one of the earliest Catholic church structures. Cathedral officials gradually acquired the Brewer and Jones properties mauka of the church. This view looks Diamond Head, and the building behind the adobe is a makai addition to the Jones residence. Such expansion led to the demolition of the adobe, whose site was marked by a statue of Our Lady of Peace placed on a basalt pedestal on the Diamond Head-mauka corner of the church (see page 52). (HP.)

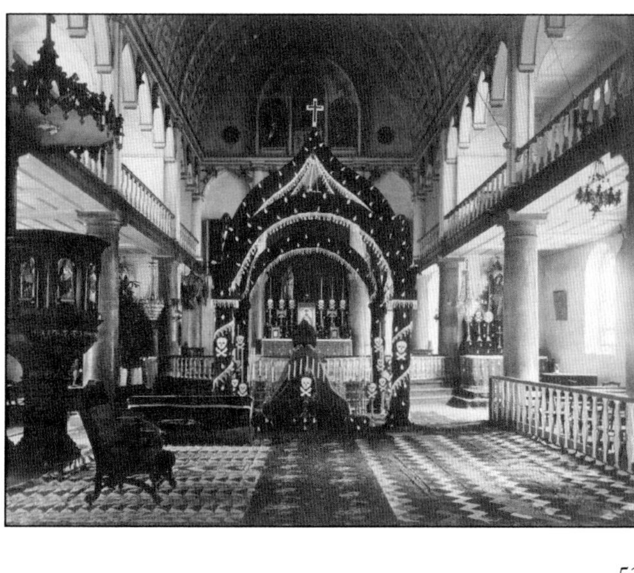

REGAL MASS FOR THE DEAD. This photograph shows the interior of Our Lady of Peace Cathedral, which was draped with funeral trappings for a mass on the death of King Alfonso XII of Spain in 1885. Note the prominent use of skull-and-crossbones symbols. Similar symbolism had been used over the dead for centuries in Europe and was placed upon graves at the first English settlement in America in Jamestown, Virginia. Such symbolism became unpopular in the United States by the 20th century. (HSA.)

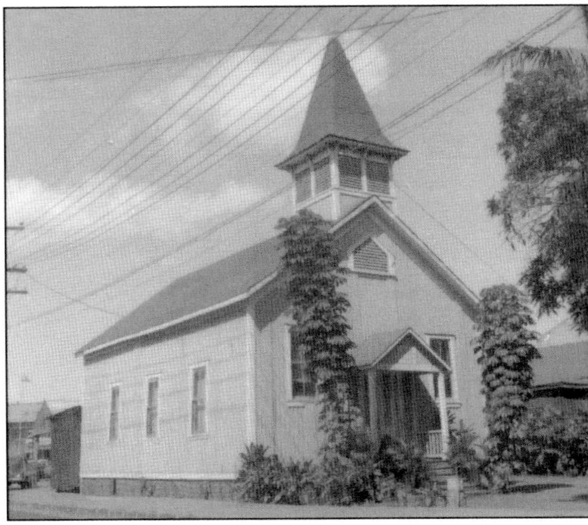 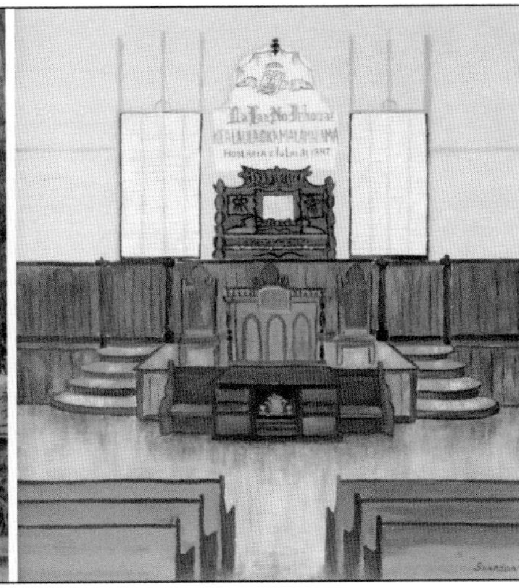

KE ALAULA OKA MALAMALAMA, HOOMANA NAAUAO O HAWAII, AND INTERIOR. This building was the mother church of the first independent Hawaiian Christian organization, founded on April 16, 1853, by Rev. John H. Poloailehua. This church was dedicated on July 31, 1897, by cofounder Rev. John Kekipi. In the back was the raised enclosed pew for the alii. Queen Kapiolani and Queen Liliuokalani both attended. Pictured on the right of the church is the house of the *kahu* (pastor). The photograph on the right is of the original church interior with pulpit. (Left photograph by Francis Haar; University of Hawaii Libraries–Jean Charlot Collection.)

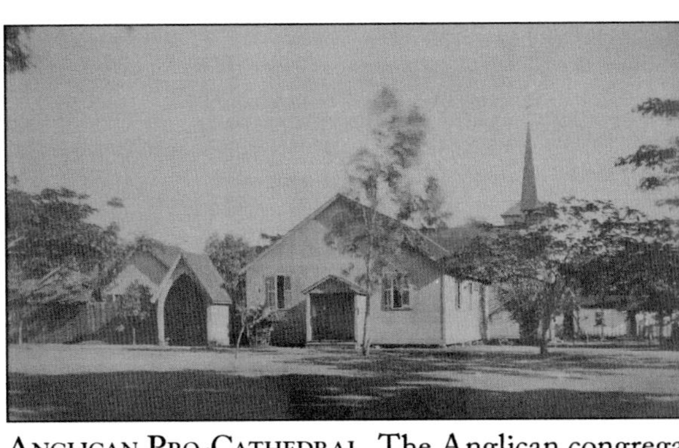 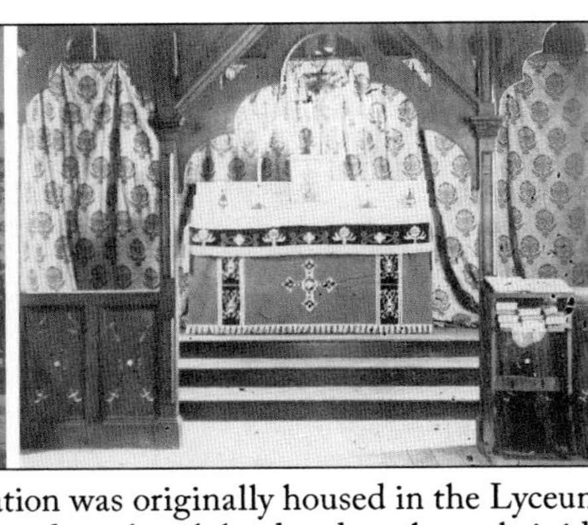

ANGLICAN PRO-CATHEDRAL. The Anglican congregation was originally housed in the Lyceum in 1862. In 1866, this wooden Pro-Cathedral was erected on church land and on the makai side of the bishop's house near Queen Emma Square. The simplicity of the structure can be seen in the sanctuary, including the wooden floor and cloth screens. The Pro-Cathedral was used for regular services for 20 years, after which it was used for Sunday school, Iolani School, and other purposes. It was demolished in 1909. (Left, HSA; right, EC.)

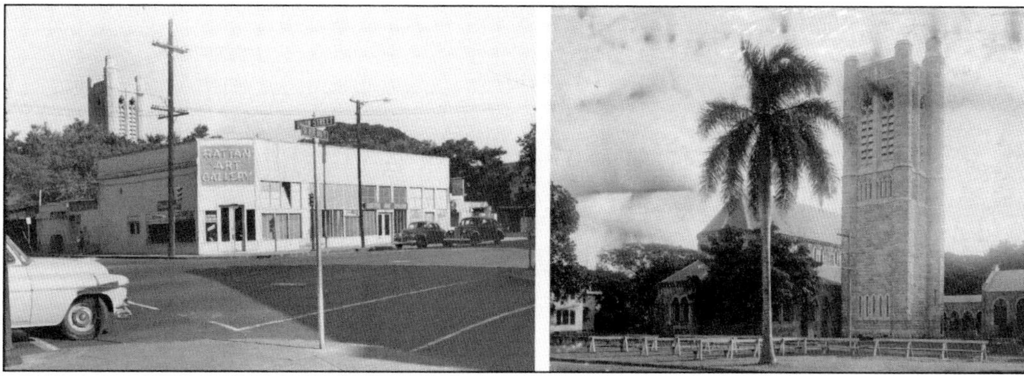

VIEWS OF ST. ANDREW'S CATHEDRAL. Kamehameha IV provided land near Queen Emma Square to the Hawaiian Reformed Catholic Church (Anglican Church). The makai grounds were acquired through the gifts of Davies Hall (1910), St. Peter's original property, and the 1951 purchase of Beretania Street lots. This resulted in the removal of businesses and the erection of the familiar rock wall, lawn, trees, plaza, and fountain. The tower (1912), built using local stone, memorializes Alice MacKintosh, a lifelong church member. (Left, EC; right, HSA.)

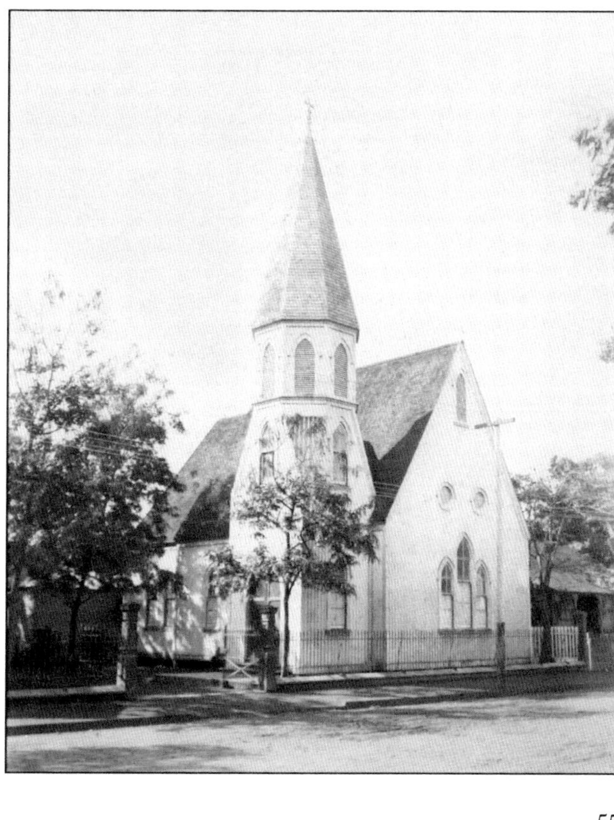

ORIGINAL ST. PETER'S CHURCH. In 1885, Queen Emma gave land makai of Emma Square to the Chinese Mission of the Anglican Church for St. Peter's, which opened in 1891. The initial site was too small, but the church was fortunate to receive a gift of $18,000 from Stephen Palmer of New York. This donation helped the church purchase a larger property up Queen Emma Street, which was still near the cathedral. The present building was consecrated in 1914. (Photograph by Frank Davey; Bishop Museum.)

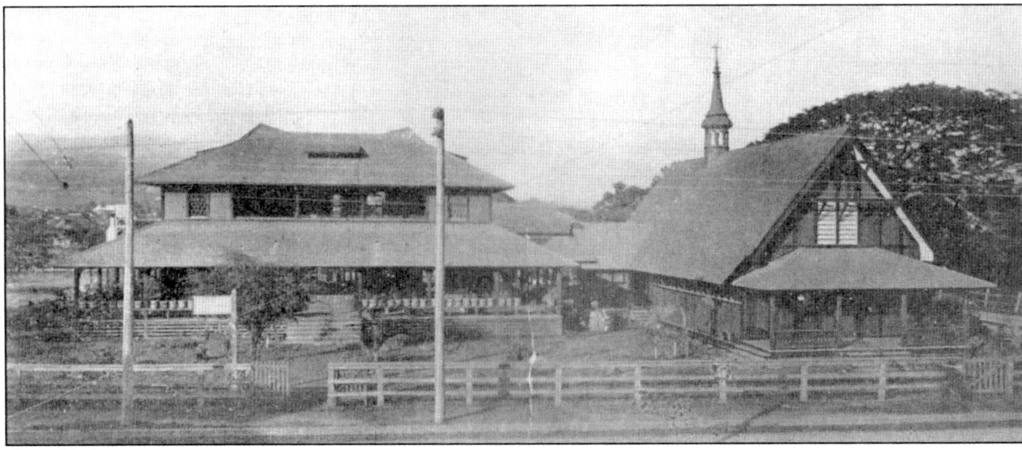

St. Elizabeth's Episcopal Church. Deaconess Emma Britt Drant came from Cincinnati to work with Chinese immigrants. Drant initially operated a night school on Robello Lane. By 1904, she acquired land on the mauka side of North King. On May 7, 1905, a church and mission house were consecrated. Later additions included a single men's lodging house and married couples' cottages, both intended to provide reasonable rents outside the tenements nearby. The 1905 building was razed in 1952, but its Tiffany window was retained.

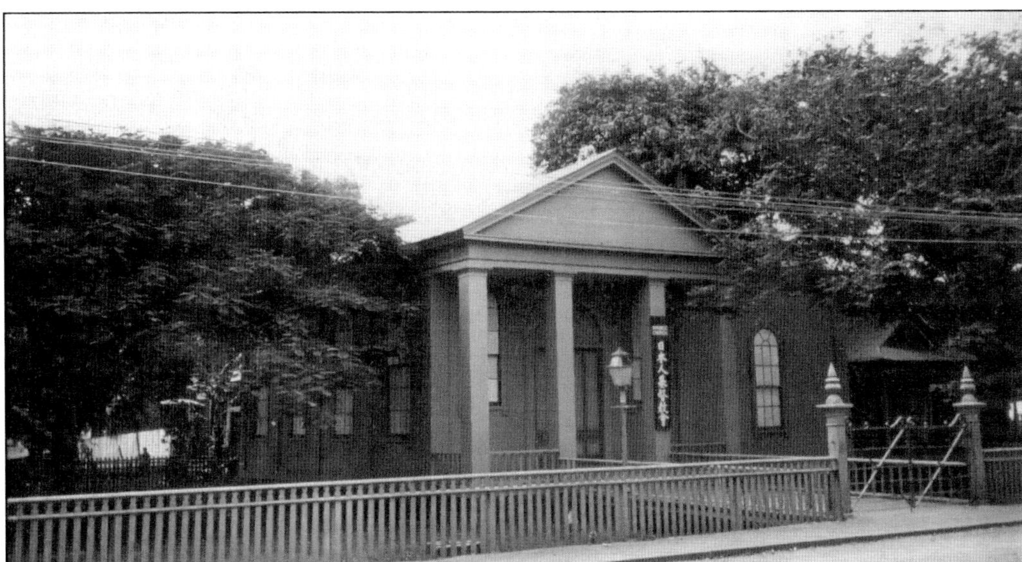

Lyceum. Located at the makai-Diamond Head corner of Kukui Street and Nuuanu, the Lyceum first served as a community meeting hall and then as the temporary home (1879–1881) of the Fort Street Chinese Church (later the First Chinese Church of Christ). The building became the permanent home (1896–1911) of the Japanese Independent Church (later Nuuanu Congregational Church). While the Lyceum was demolished in 1911, the congregation continued to meet at this site until 1950, when it moved to Nuuanu Street, mauka of School. (HSA.)

FORT STREET CHINESE CHURCH. In the late 1800s, the Hawaiian Evangelical Association (HEA) sought to reach Chinese immigrants by sponsoring Chinese immigrant preachers on plantations. By 1872, a Chinese Sabbath School opened at the Fort Street Church. The Chinese Christian Church of Honolulu, popularly known as the "Fort Street Chinese Church," was organized in 1879. Completed on January 2, 1881, on Fort mauka of Beretania, the church complex included a Chinese-language school. In 1929, the congregation relocated. It is today known as the First Chinese Church of Christ. (HSA.)

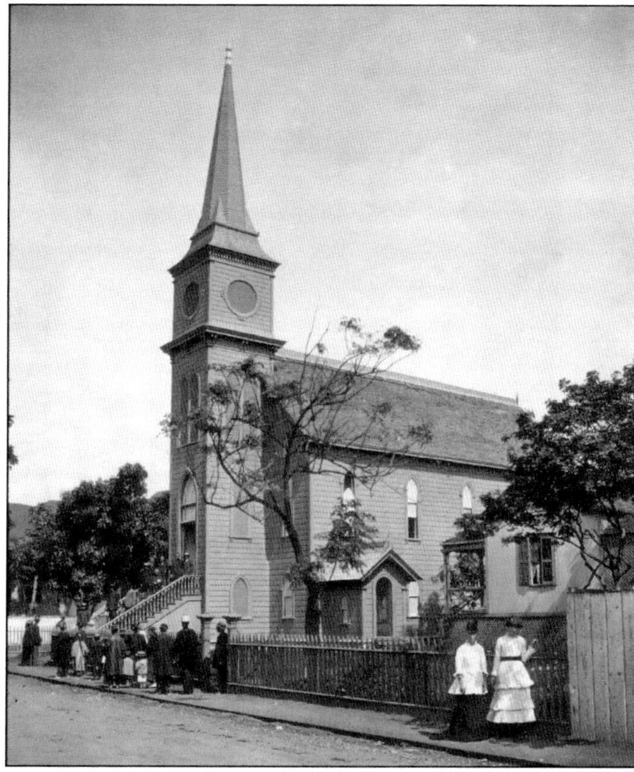

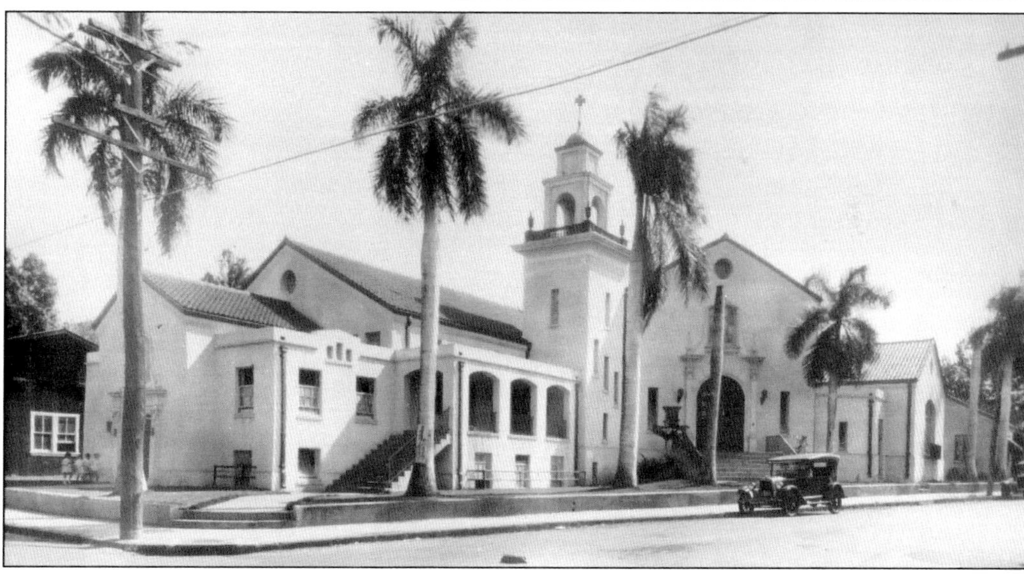

HARRIS MEMORIAL METHODIST CHURCH. In 1887, the Reverend Kanichi Miyama arrived to minister and comfort exploited Japanese plantation workers in Hawaii. A wooden sanctuary was first erected in 1894 on River Street, and a second one was constructed under the Reverend Gennosuke Motokawa in 1904. Over the next 20 years, the congregation became predominately English-speaking. The Harris Memorial Methodist Church (pictured), named for Bishop M.C. Harris, opened at the corner of Vineyard and Fort Streets in 1926; it was demolished in 1954. (HSA.)

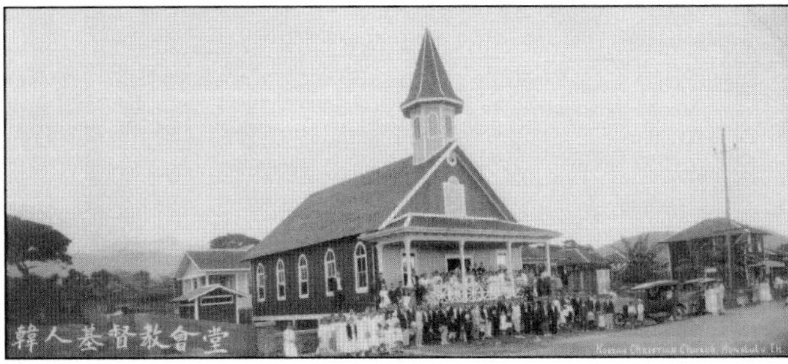

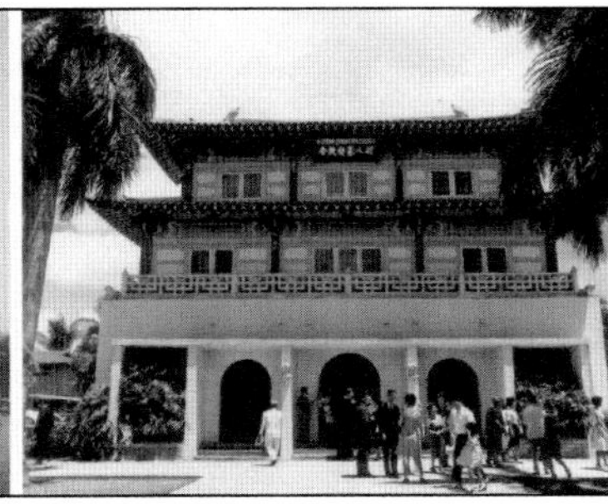

KOREAN CHRISTIAN CHURCH. Most Koreans arrived in Hawaii as Christians. The Korean Christian Church, supported by Hawaii educator and future Korean president Dr. Syngman Rhee, separated from the Korean Methodist Episcopal Church in 1918 and erected the building (left) in 1923. The coeducational Korean Christian Institute was located nearby. The wooden church was replaced with a three-story concrete building (right) that opened on April 24, 1938. (Left photograph by On Char/City Photo; Bishop Museum; right photograph by Nancy Bannick; HSA.)

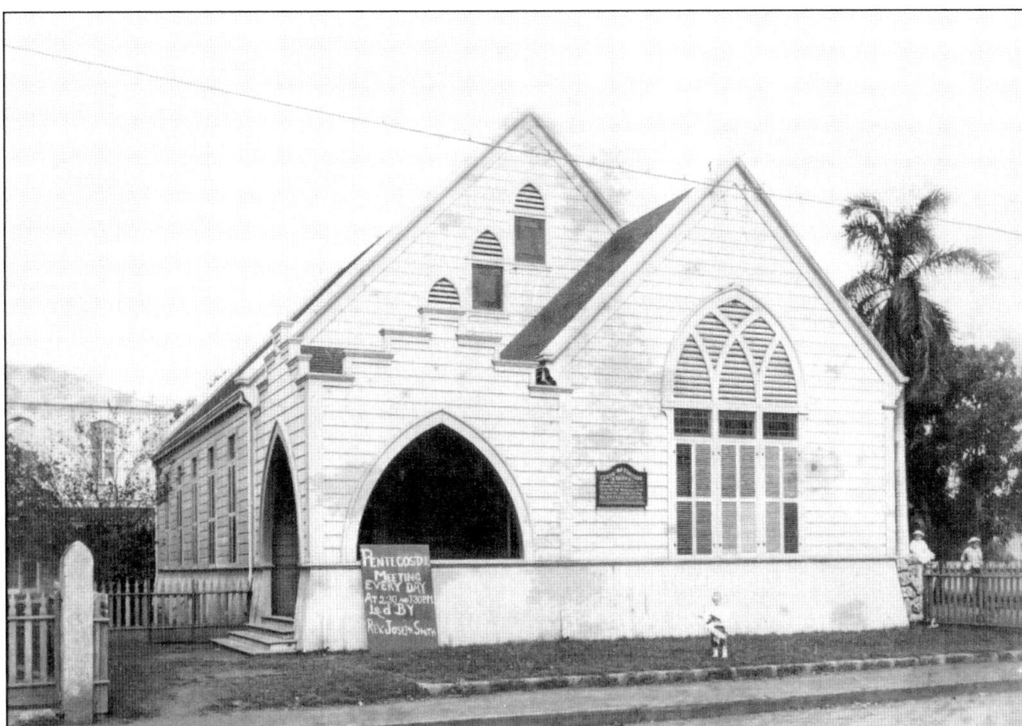

NEW USES FOR OLD CHURCHES. The First Methodist Church was founded in 1894, and a new building was erected on Beretania near Miller Street on April 19, 1896. The church was modest when compared to the other spire-clad churches on Beretania—so modest that its pastor moved his flock in 1910 to a more elaborate facility at Victoria and Beretania Streets. The sign in the photograph announces that the building will be housing a Pentecostal meeting every day. (Photograph by Frank Davey; HSA.)

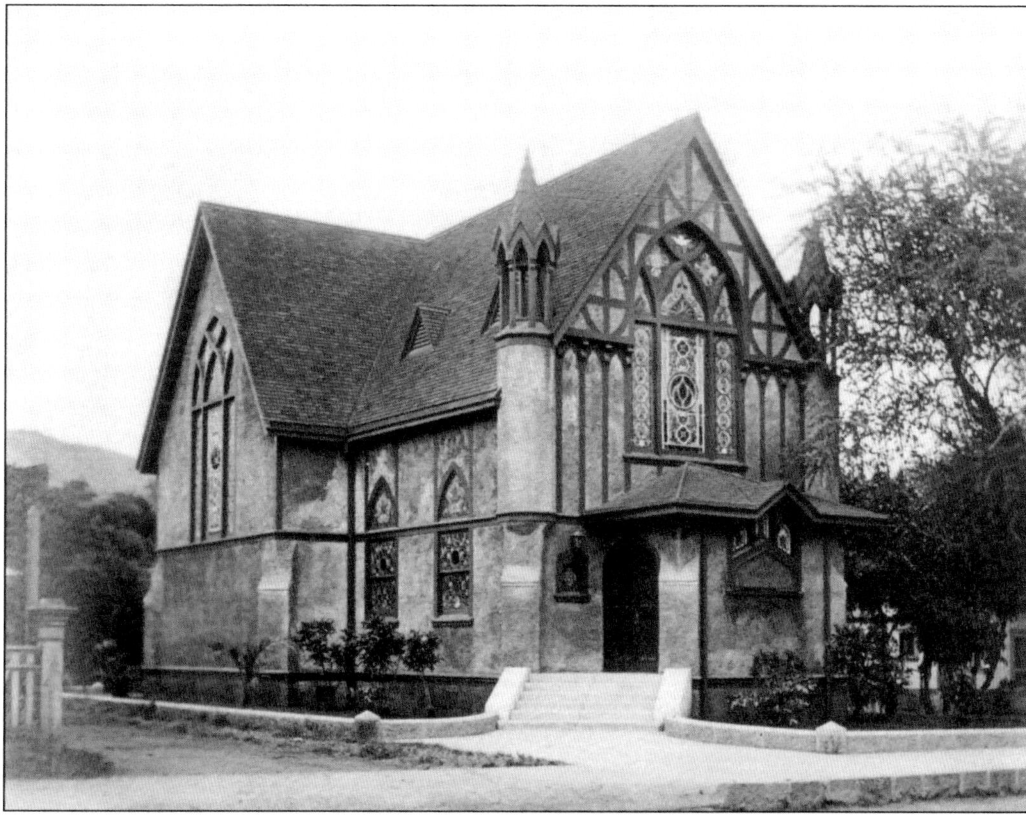

DEUTSCH EVANGELISCH LUTHERISCHE GEMEINDE ZU HONOLULU AND INTERIOR. In 1882, Lihue Plantation began a German-language school, and the following year, the Lihue Lutheran Church was established. In 1899, Johann Hackfield and employee Paul Isenberg each gave $25,000 towards a Lutheran church in Honolulu to celebrate H. Hackfeld and Company's 50th anniversary. Designed by the architectural firm of Ripley and Dickey, the new church was constructed at the corner of Punchbowl and Beretania Streets and opened in 1901. The company budgeted $9,769 for the project, and the building seated 150 people. The stained-glass windows over the front entrance, featuring fellow religious reformers Martin Luther and Philipp Melanchthon, were imported from Europe. The lectern, carved by local artist Frank N. Otremba, was said to be a copy of the lectern at Wartburg Castle in Eisenach, Germany, the same city where the New Testament was translated into German by Martin Luther in 1522. (Both, HSA.)

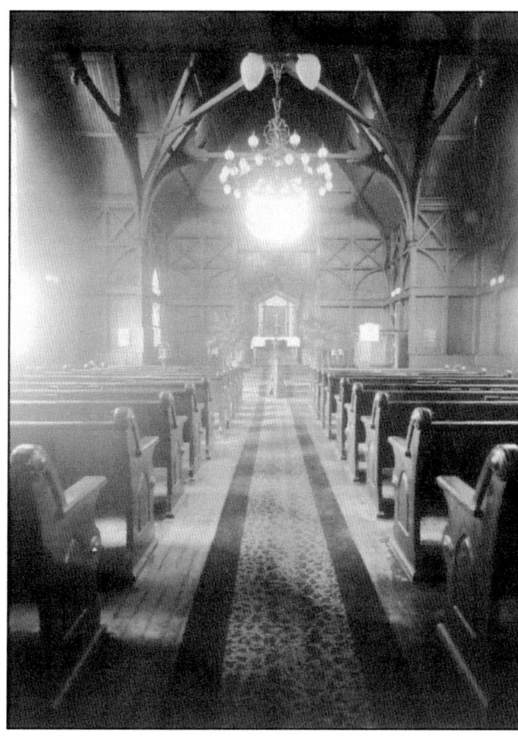

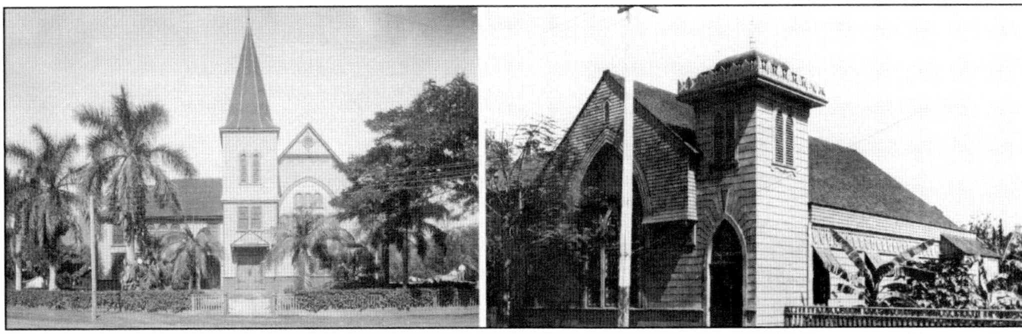

Portuguese Evangelical Church and Christian Church of Honolulu. Located at Miller and Punchbowl, the Portuguese Evangelical Church (left) was home to members who began the Easter Sunrise Service tradition at Punchbowl by trudging up the nearby hill. The church merged with Central Union Church in 1940, and the building was then converted into a hostel. Another church (right, denomination unknown) faced Alakea, near King, in 1895. A multipurpose church was there until 1914–1915, and then it moved to Kewalo Street, near Lunalilo Street. (Both, HSA.)

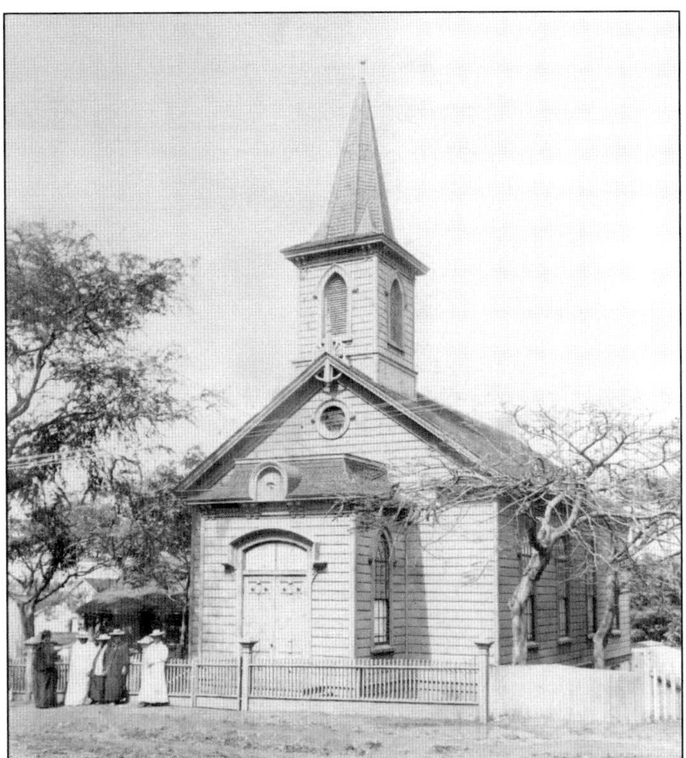

Church of the Latter-day Saints. This photograph, taken between 1897 and 1901, shows the Mormon Church, which stood on the Ewa side of Lusitana Street, at the present site of Kamamalu Market. After services, members would retreat from the heat inside by holding activities under trees Diamond Head of the church. This structure was torn down in 1920. The present church, financed in part through assistance from legendary local carnival entrepreneur E.K. Fernandez, was built mauka in 1959. (Photograph by Frank Davey; Bishop Museum.)

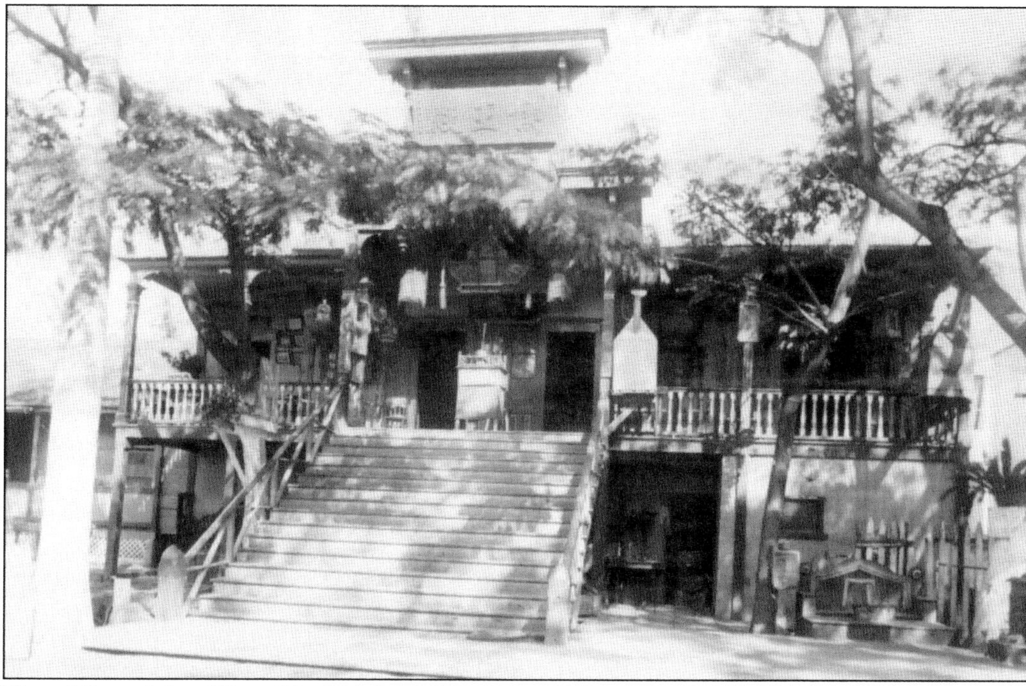

Huu Wong Miu (Hou Wang Miao). This joss house, or temple, was erected in honor of a count or marquis. This photograph was taken during the 1900 bubonic plague epidemic. The 1899 Dakin Fire Insurance map locates a large joss house just mauka of Beretania and Ewa of Kamakapili Church and another large house off Aala Lane. Incense was burned and wafted throughout the neighborhood. (HSA.)

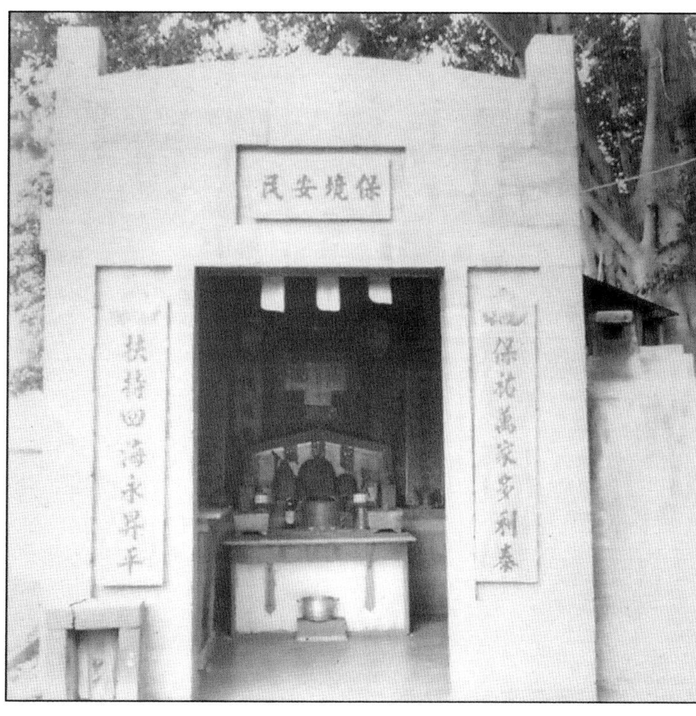

School Street Earth God Temple. These small shrines were found in every village in southeastern China. Villagers replicated their homeland's worshipful sites. The top horizontal plaque reads, "Protect the land and keep its people safe." The right plaque reads, "Bless ten thousand homes and much profit." The left plaque reads, "Upkeep the peace of the 'four seas' forever." Today, there is a seafaring temple located on River Street. Such temples could be found in all port towns in China. (Photograph by Nancy Bannick; HSA.)

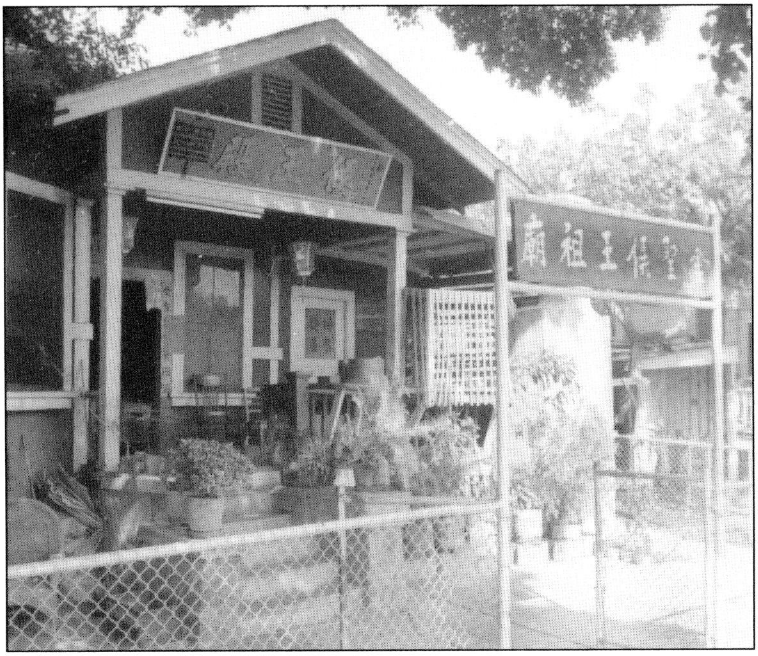

ADAPTIVE REUSE. This plantation-style building, with single walls, girt, and double-hung windows, was transformed for spiritual purposes. Such Chinese temples/shrines probably originated with people from rural villages where Daoist and Buddhist practices were intermingled. The informal translation from right to left says, "gold, saint, duke, king, ancestor, shrine." (Photograph by Francis Haar; UHL–JCC.)

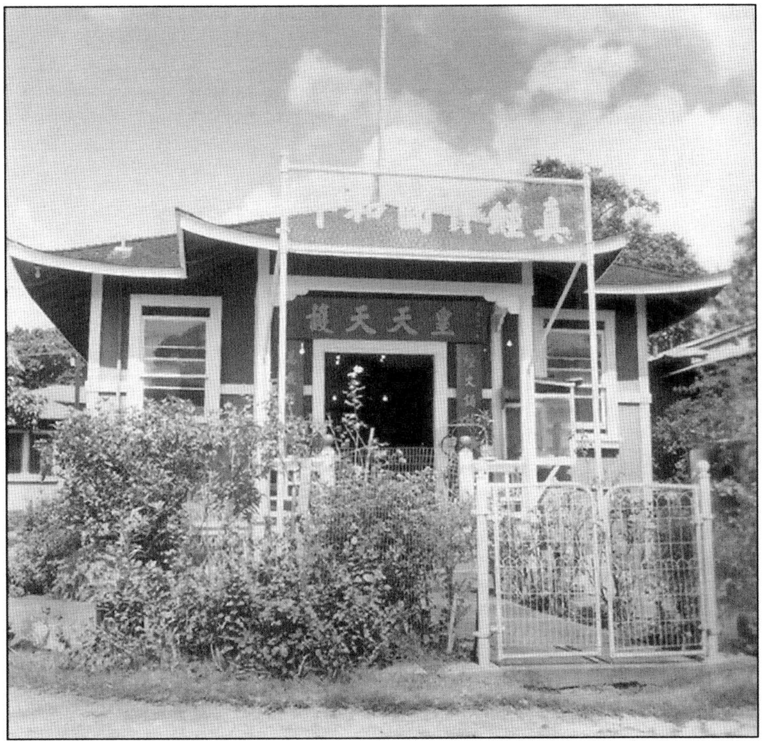

WONG-TIN TIN-HU DAOIST TEMPLE (HUANG TIAN TIAN FU). A rough translation of the sign reads, "real, sutra, treasure, country, peace (two characters)." Located at 298 North Kukui Street, this temple also lost out to the urban renewal bulldozer. (Photograph by Nancy Bannick; HSA.)

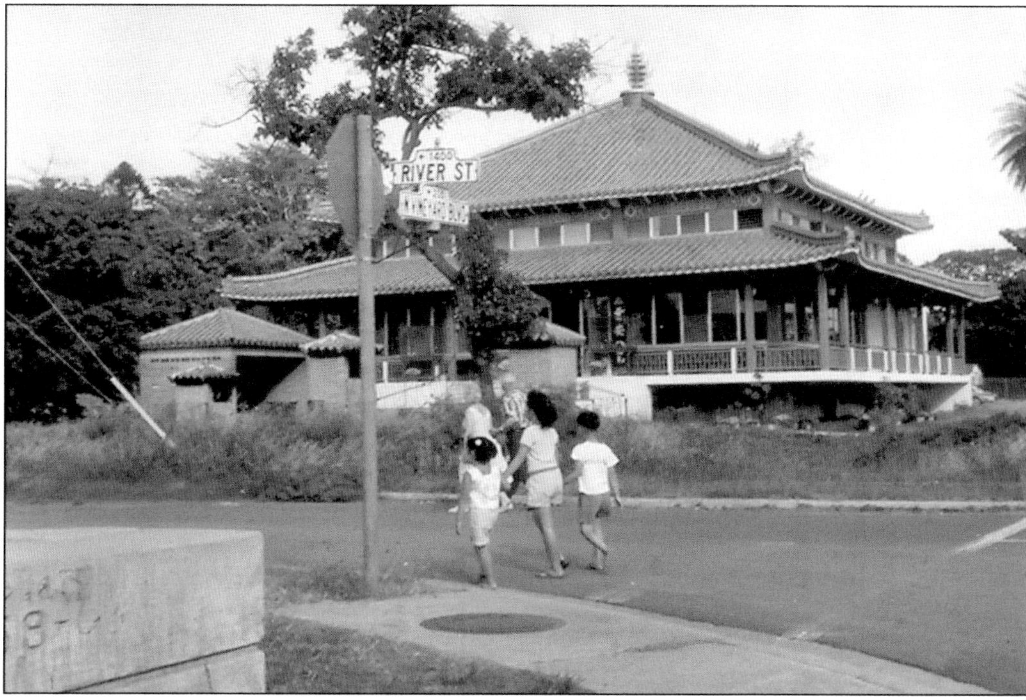

KWAN YIN MIAO (TEMPLE). Kwan Yin is the Buddhist goddess of mercy—one who sees and hears the cry from the human world. Folks in the early immigration period from southern China came together in informal worship. They likely met in an old wooden house before 1921. The current temple was reconstructed around 1960 at 170 North Vineyard Street. The funds for the building and the Kwan Yin statue were raised in a public-private partnership with the Chun Hoon family, a large donor. Worshippers bring offerings of fresh fruit and flowers and burn incense. (Both photographs by Nancy Bannick; HSA.)

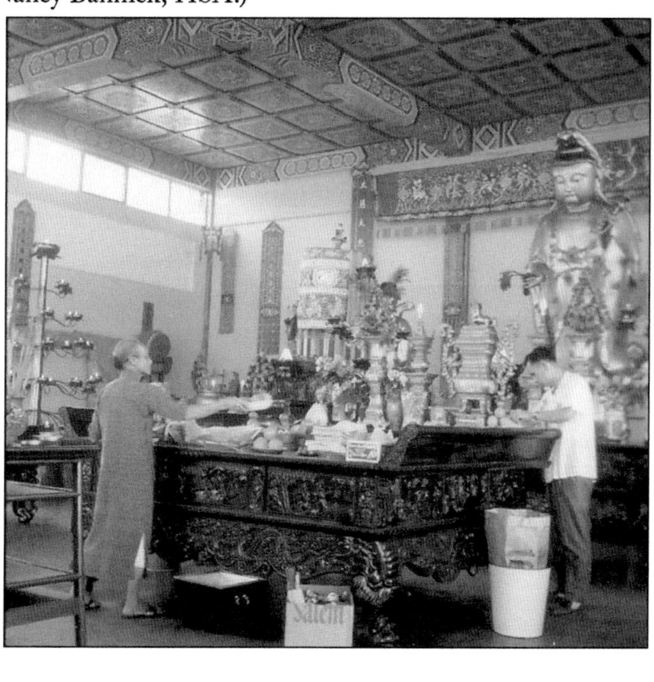

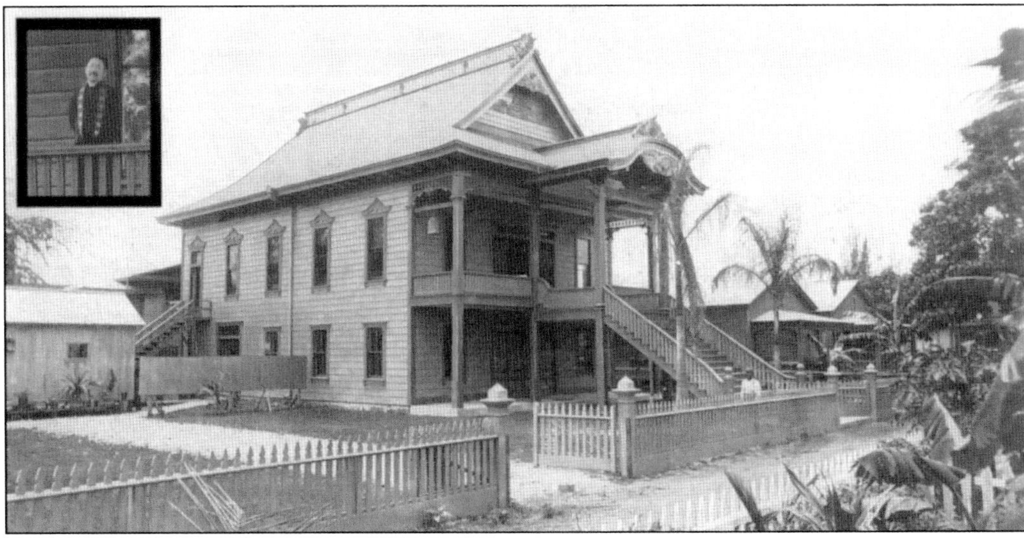

FORT STREET HONGWANJI–HONPA HONGWANJI MISSION OF HAWAII. The 1924 Japanese population in Hawaii, by prefectures of origin, were mostly from rural Hiroshima, Yamaguchi, Kumamoto Fukuoka, and Okinawa. The Buddhist Pure Land sect had the largest number of followers from this population in Hawaii and in Honolulu. Bishop Yemyo Imamura (inset) gave support to and adapted Japanese Buddhist teachings to Hawaii's climate. The first Honpa Hongwanji (above, pictured about 1899) was located at 1456 Fort Street near Kukui. Today, (below) the Betsuin (mission temple) and Gakuin (school) are located at 1727 Pali Highway. The architecture was inspired by Indian domes and towers, as Imamura and others promoted international Buddhism. Later, the towers were moved apart to expand the sanctuary. An automobile gate and curving entranceway reflected that the pedestrian parishioners now had cars. (Above, JCCH; below, HSA.)

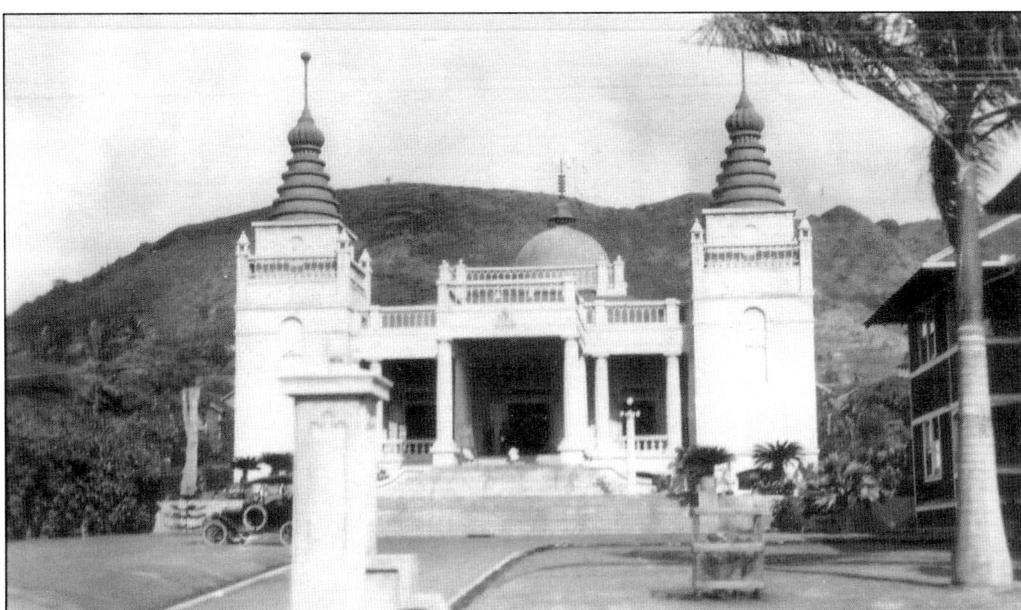

SOTO MISSION OF HAWAII–SOBOJI. The Soto Mission of Hawaii was founded in 1913 and originally located in Aala on Hall Street between Beretania and Kukui. It was housed in Yakushi Hall built by Rev. Ryogo Mitsunaga. In 1921, a Japanese-style temple opened here on Nuuanu Avenue. The present Indian-inspired building was dedicated in 1952. As with most Buddhist temples, the Soto Mission's activities include *O-bon* (event to honor the spirits of dead ancestors), New Year's, and Spring and Autumn services. (Photograph by Toshiharu Murai.)

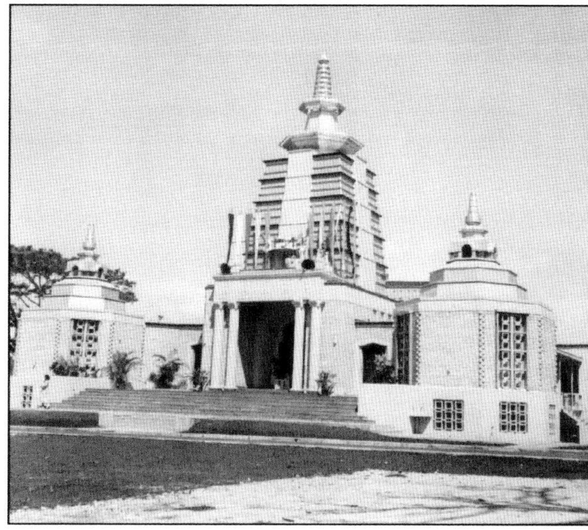

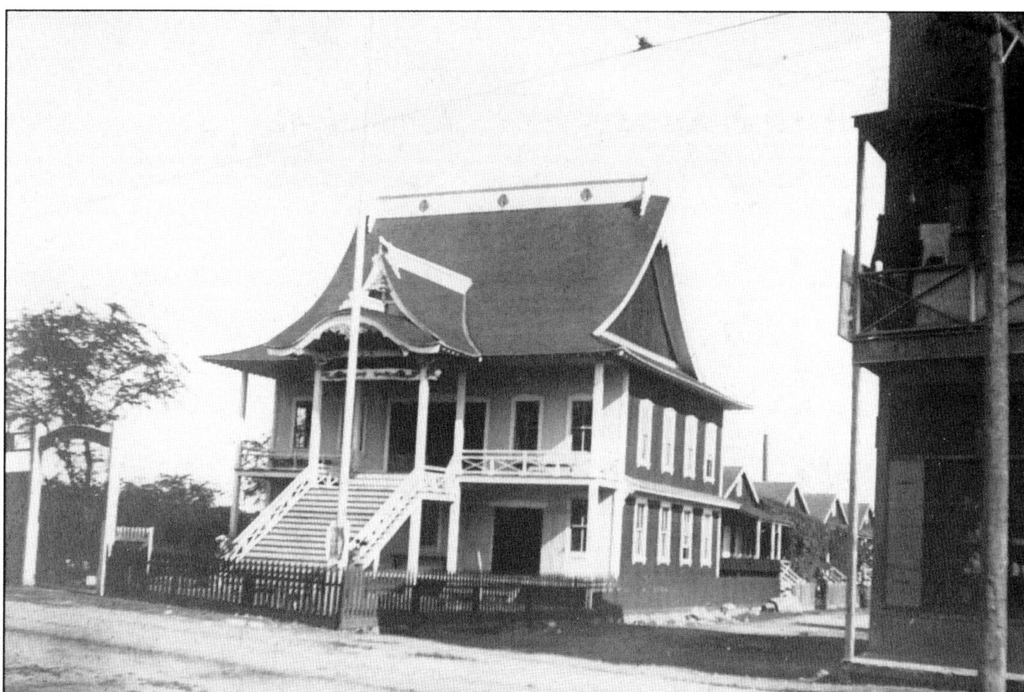

KAKAAKO JODO MISSION. The 1900 Chinatown fire displaced over 6,000 people, and among those were approximately 3,500 issei and nisei. They moved to other surrounding neighborhoods, such as Aala, Liliha, Kukui, Kauluwela, Iwilei, and Kakaako. At the same time, many of the plantation workers' contracts had concluded, and they swelled Honolulu Town. In 1907, Japanese Americans living in the Kakaako neighborhood founded the Kakaako Jodo Mission, built in a traditional Japanese-temple style. It was located at 738 South Street and moved to its present site in Makiki in 1932, becoming the Jodo Mission of Hawaii. (Bishop Museum.)

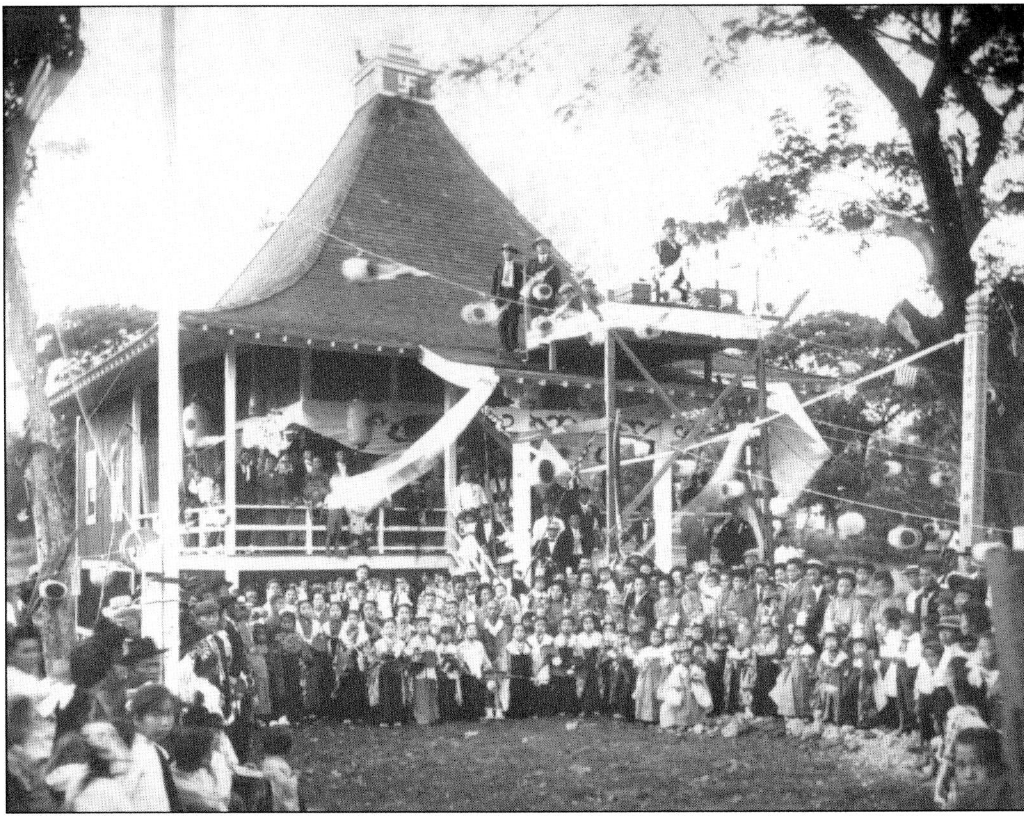

LILIHA SHINGONJI MISSION, 1911 AND 1931. The dedication of the new mission building (on the Ewa side of Liliha between School and Kuakini Streets) was celebrated by building a tower above the entrance. The men on top are engaged in *mochi maki* (throwing mochi [pounded rice treats] often stuffed with coins for good luck). A small girl or boy (*chigo*) was chosen to celebrate the occasion. The 1911 roof ridge had a swastika, a Sanskrit symbol that means the equivalent of "all is good." With the rise of Hitler in the 1930s, this symbol was quickly removed from all Buddhist temples. Note also the difference between the new roof in the 1931 roof celebration photograph and the earlier 1911 photograph. Prior to the outbreak of World War II, nisei Bishop Mitsumyo Tottori wrote a letter stating, "You are Americans and this is Hawaii." Some issei were resentful. For that, it is felt that he was looked on favorably by the military government and was not sent to a relocation camp. Ironically, he was later given an honor by the Japanese government. (Both, Liliha Shingonji Mission.)

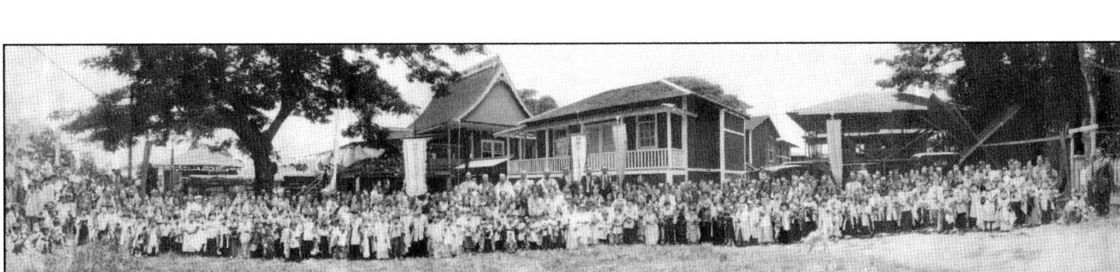

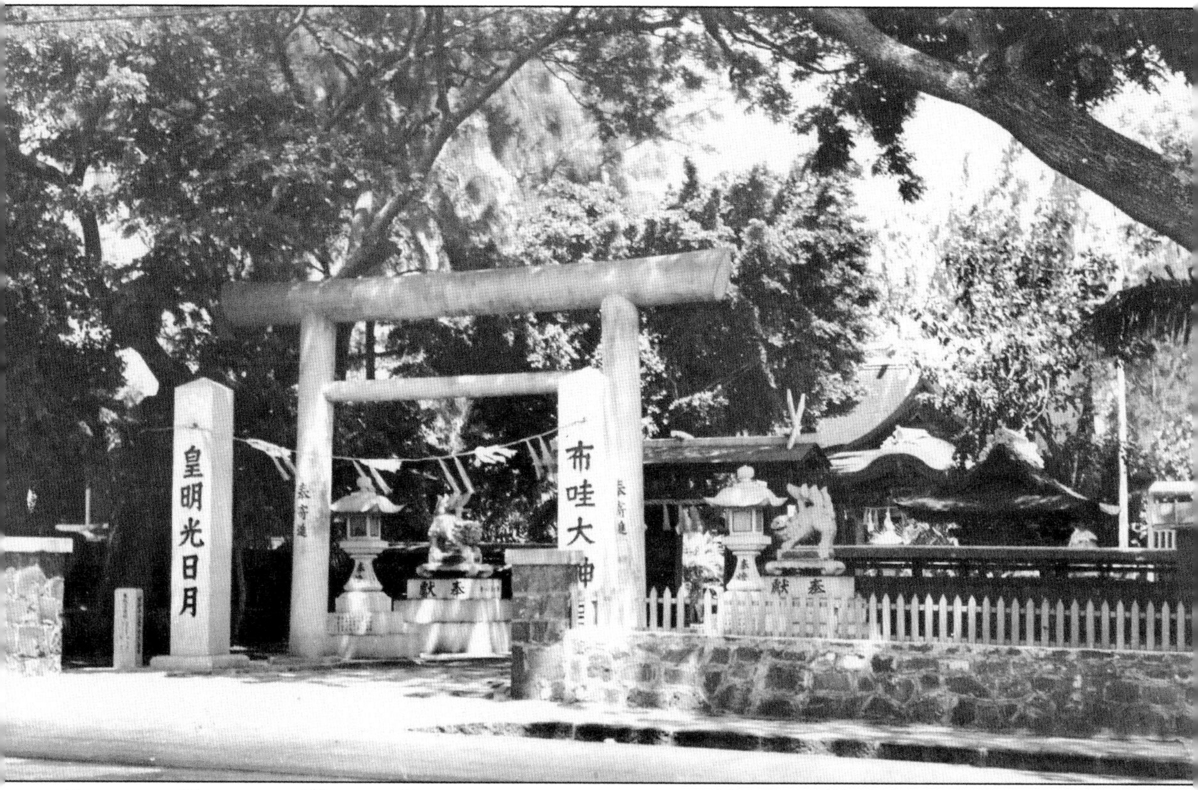

DIAJINGU TEMPLE OF HAWAII, ESTABLISHED AROUND 1903. Diajingu Temple was once located on the Diamond Head side of Liliha Street between Vineyard and School Streets. It embodied the complexity of the Japanese character and more particularly the special nature of the Hawaii–Japanese American character. Daijingu and other Shinto sects worship *kami* (spirits). However, Hawaii Daijingu differs from other shrines in honoring historical figures as kami, such as George Washington (as leader of America) and King Kamehameha I (as leader of Hawaii). In this transformative religious practice, Daijingu also honored Adm. Heihachiro Togo, victor in the 1905 Russo-Japanese War, as a living kami, embodying not just seafaring and naval militarism but also peaceful conciliation. The Japanese Americans held loyalties to both countries. In practice, the Hawaii Japanese-language schools honored flags, songs, and customs of both countries. And in Hawaii, as in Japan, there was no religious contradiction when attending a New Year's shrine ceremony (Shinto), *bon* dance (Buddhist), or sumo tournament (Shinto). When the Imperial Japanese Navy came into port prior to World War II, seamen obtained talismans and amulets at Daijingu for symbolic seafaring protection. (Photograph from the Tom Moriki Collection; JCCH.)

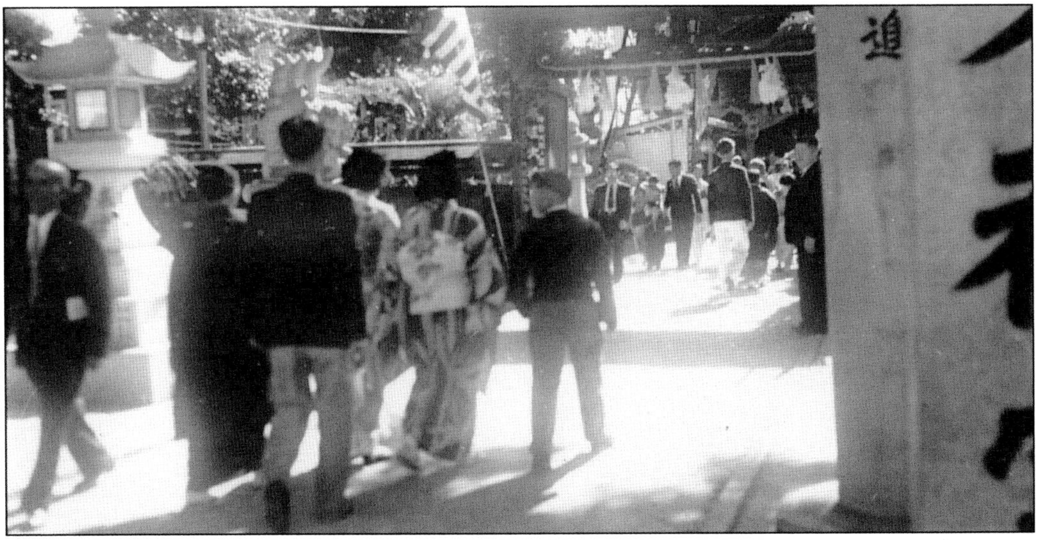

New Year's at Daijingu, 1939 and Blessings. At the entrance to the shrine are two pillars with *shiminawa* (a twisted straw rope), *gohei* (attached white paper streamers), the *torii* (gate), and the purification fountain. Note how very American this Japanese Shinto shrine was prior to World War II, as the American flag flies prominently. Children at ages seven, five, and three (below left) are taken to Shinto shrines for a *Shichi-Go-San* (seven-five-three) blessing. Below, in the 1938 photograph on the left, baby Harriet Natsuyama stands before the right of two guardian lion-dogs (*shishi* or *komainu*) with family friend Hanaoka-san, grandmother Yone Otsubo, mother, Yakue, and father, Kenjiro. The right guardian's mouth is open (*Ah*, to scare off demons), and the left guardian's mouth is closed (*Un*, to keep in the good spirits). It is a Daijingu tradition to paint green, yellow, and red details on the gray granite. In the photograph below on the right is a group of men celebrating *yakudoshi*, the benchmark for 41–42 years old. Bishop Kawasaki is front row center and Reverend Ikuma, his assistant, is to his left. (Photographs above and below left by Kenjiro Natsuyama; photograph below right from Florena Souza Collection; JCCH.)

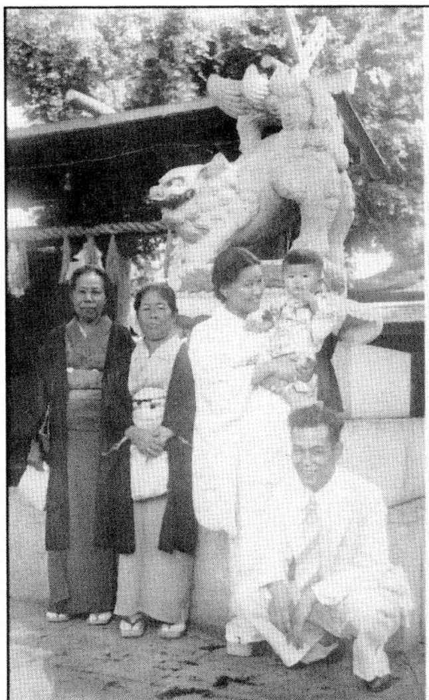

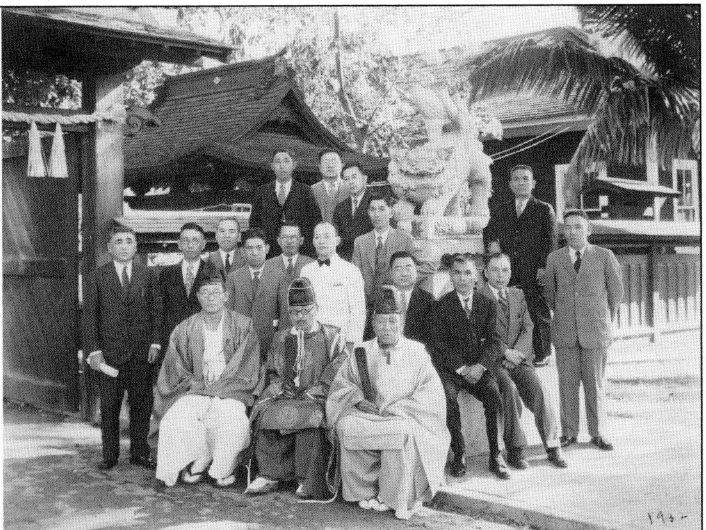

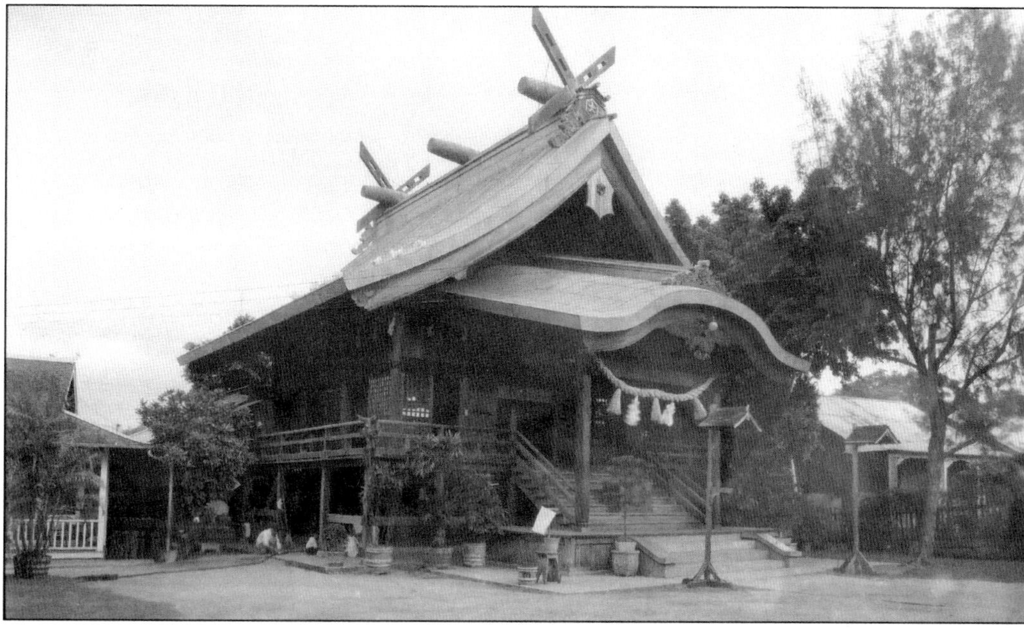

Izumo Taishakyo Mission, 1923. This wooden A-frame structure was inspired by Shimane Prefecture's classical Japanese shrine Taisha Machi. Founded in 1906 and built in 1923 mauka of Beretania and the Aala Triangle and on streets now no longer in existence, the shrine was designed by architect Hego Fuchino and built by master carpenter Ichisaburo Takata without the use of nails. The vertical cuts on the roof crosspieces indicate the primary kami, or male deity, Okuninushi, "Great Land Master." (The character *dai* (great) is shown in the inset below.) During World War II, the shrine was confiscated, and it became a City and County park. The shrine was plundered but belatedly returned to the membership in 1962. A major effort was undertaken to move and restore the shrine in its new location on College Walk. (Above, HHS; below, photograph by Francis Haar; UHL–JCC.)

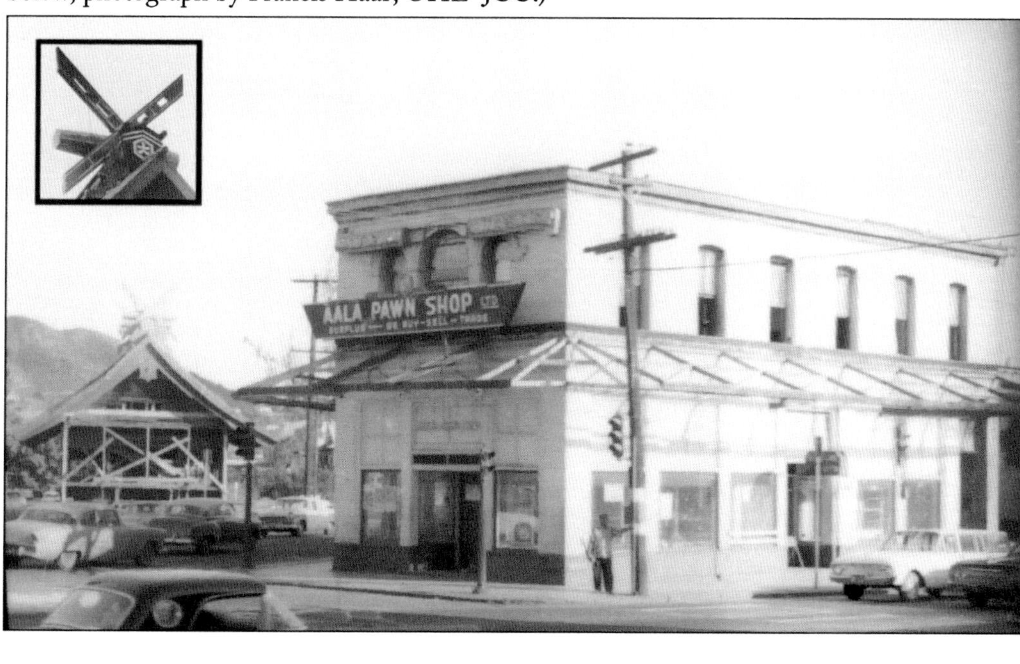

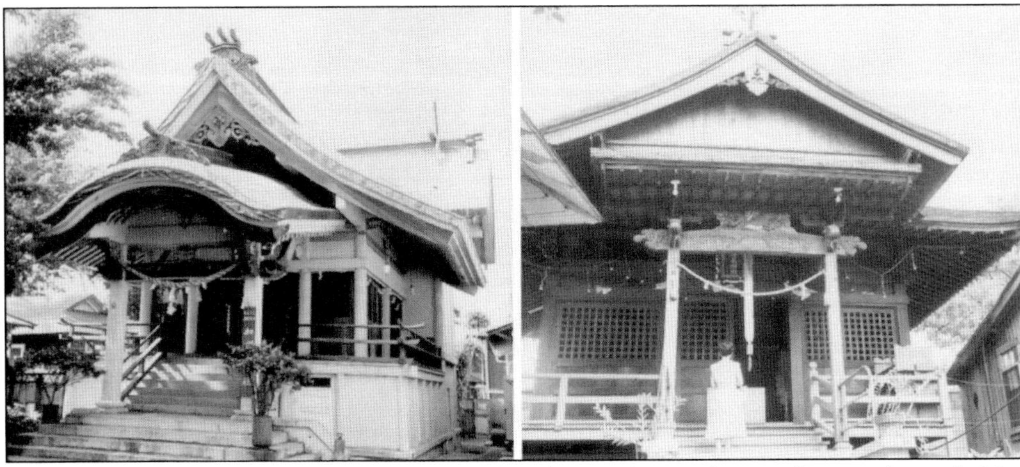

LOST KATO JINSHA ON BUCKLE LANE, 1911 (LEFT) AND COOKE STREET SHRINE (RIGHT). Note the characteristic Shinto shrine architectural features: raised main sanctuary, slightly curved gable roof, lanai extension over the entry way, carved animal imagery on the lanai lintel, and the shiminawa and gohei at the entryway. Urban renewal wiped out vulnerable downtown neighborhoods. Shrines such as Daijingu and Isumo Taisha survived, while less fortunate shrines' valuable artifacts and documents were given to remaining shrines in town for safekeeping. (Photographs by Nancy Bannick; HSA.)

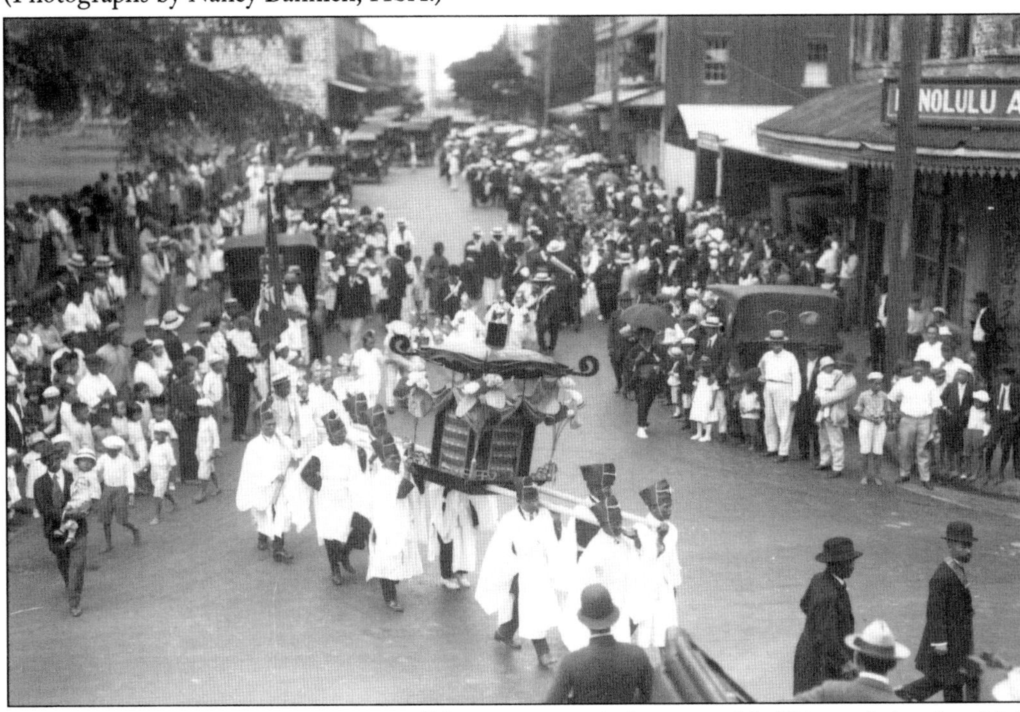

SHINTO PROCESSION, C. EARLY 1920S. Men carry a *mikoshi*, a portable Shinto shrine (a vehicle for kami) that was possibly made in Hawaii for nearby Izumo Taishakyo or Kato Jinsha. The procession is at the corner of Maunakea and Beretania. Behind are chigo, a long procession of children. The store on the right, Honolulu Auto Supply Co. Ltd., advertises automotive parts, repairs, and tires. On the left, people cling to the iron playground fence to view the festivities. (Photograph by Ray J. Baker; Bishop Museum.)

Four

The Wholesome Town and Free Time

In a pre-Internet society, face-to-face social interactions were very important both to those seeking goods, services, clients, and news while simultaneously integrating an ethnically diverse population. Although everyone in his or her free time eventually met at the waterfront, other town foci were many and varied.

Youngsters may have dropped by the playgrounds for pickup games of baseball, jumped in Nuuanu Stream or the harbor for a swim, or perhaps caught a parade. Youngsters may have walked to a nearby Y, where kids of many backgrounds could learn to interact. The Ys combined leisure activities with self-improvement programs, including games and athletics, crafts, and skill development for future jobs. The Y also provided night schools for working adults to better their lives.

For many folks, devoting their free time to helping others became a way of life. Medical institutions, such as Queen's Hospital founded by Queen Emma, provided health care for all, while the Chinese Hospital and the Japanese Charity Hospital improved the health of fellow countrymen. Fraternal and religious orders sought to ameliorate infirmities of the poor or ill.

For many folks, the importance of meeting at the Merchant Street post office, where letters were written and exchanged, cannot be overstated. Communications took months to travel across oceans—whether to China, Japan, or New England. Other regular meeting places were the locally owned retail shop, fountain drugstore, barbershop, pool hall, or perhaps even the special Elite Ice Cream Store on Hotel Street or the business rendezvous Hob Nob Café in the Young Hotel.

There were wondrous entertainment and shopping experiences, like chatting with fellow gawkers in the big stores of Kress, Woolworths, and then Longs, where there were so many bins and display shelves that just looking was a treat.

For very few coins, anyone could see a movie. There were no restrictions on class or ethnic background in the theaters. Originally just converted warehouses or enclosed lots, theaters evolved into richly adorned palaces, drawing thousands of citizens who wished to escape the rigors of everyday life. Facilities included the original live-performance theater near the Royal Hawaiian Hotel on Alakea, the Music Hall and Opera House on Mililani Street, and the Asahi, the first Japanese-drama theater, in two locations on Maunakea.

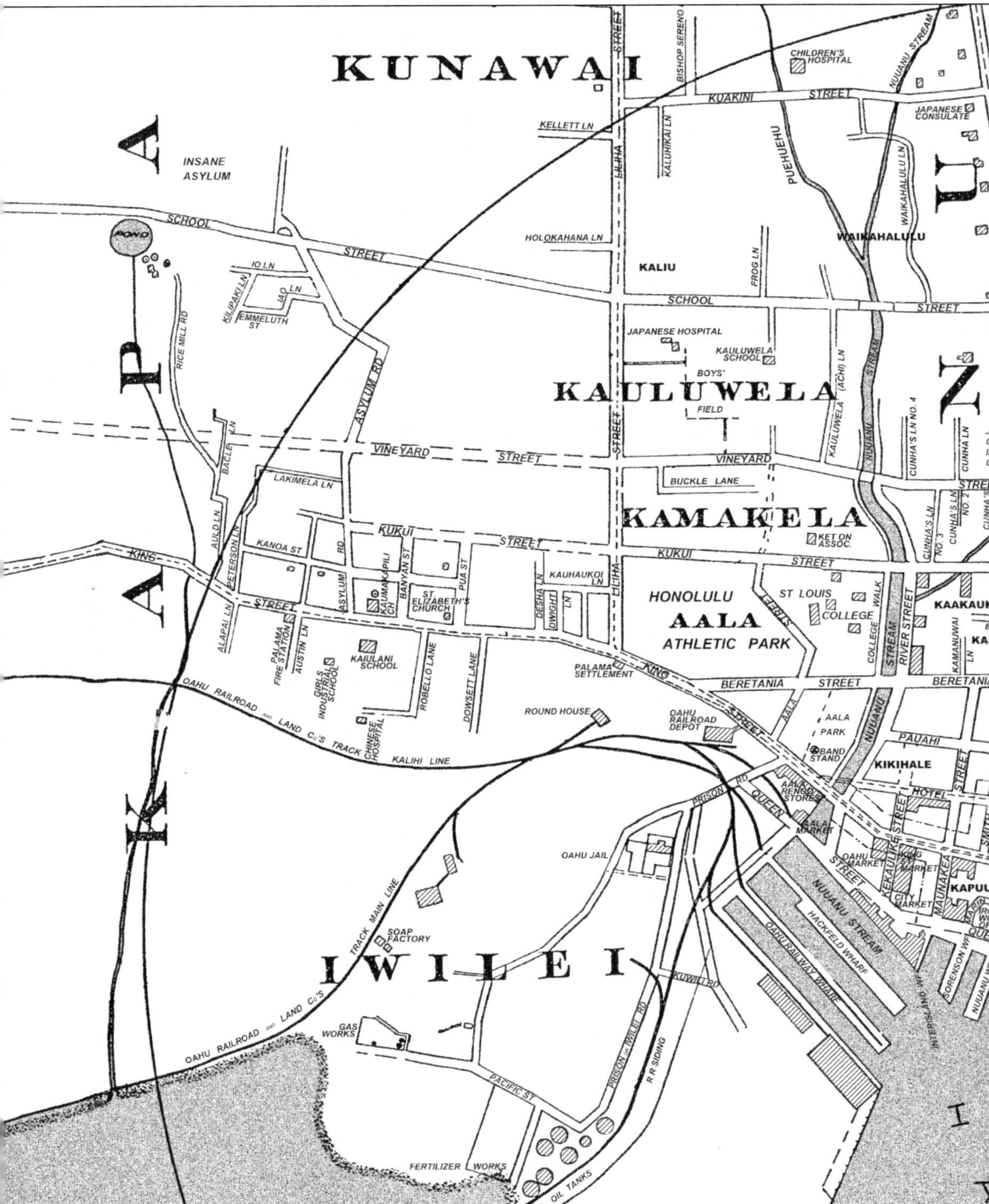

1912 MAP OF HONOLULU TOWN. This is a composite map comprised of overlays from the following: 1847 Metcalf/Lydgate original registered title map, 1899 Dakin Fire Insurance maps, 1912 fire department map, and 1914 and 1927 Sanborn Fire Insurance maps. Note that

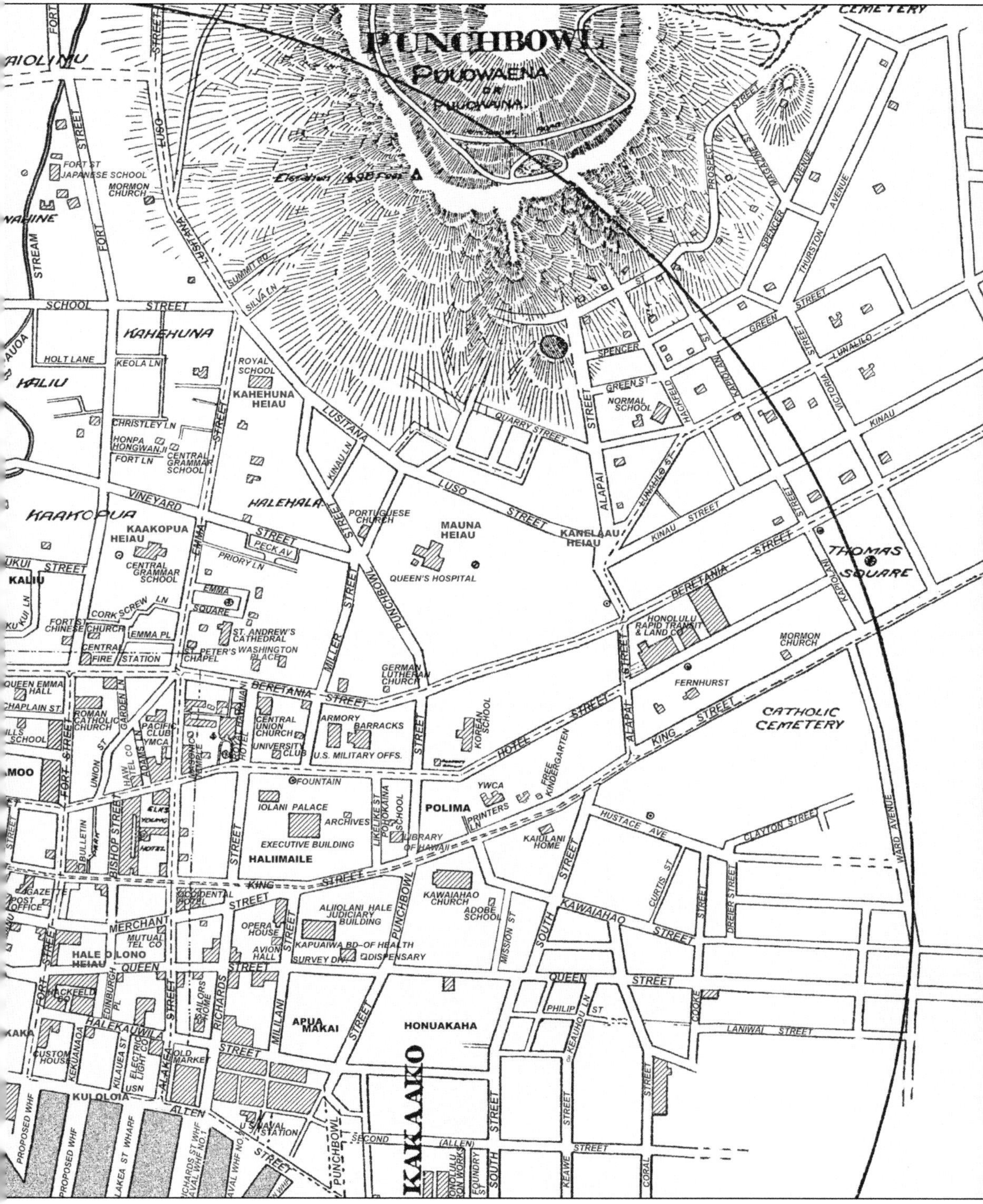

the center of the circle is the Central Fire Station, indicating the relative distance and time to respond to a fire alarm. The harbor and Punchbowl Crater acted as the makai and mauka edges of the town.

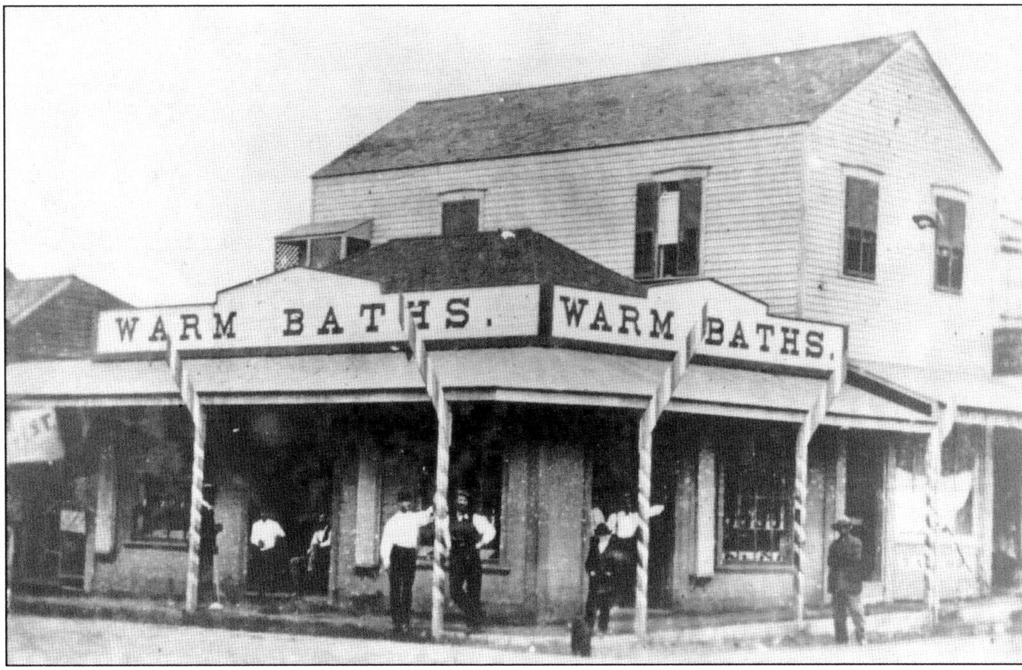

EVERYDAY SMALL-BUSINESS INTERACTIONS, 1869. The Wilkerson and Company Building on Fort Street has a dentist (partial sign, left), barbershop (striped poles throughout), and prominent sign for warm baths. The ground-floor wall of the next building lists a tailor. Men in shirtsleeves are shop clerks or business workers. The man on the far right, who is possibly Chinese, wears a homemade straw hat and long tunic shirt. (HSA.)

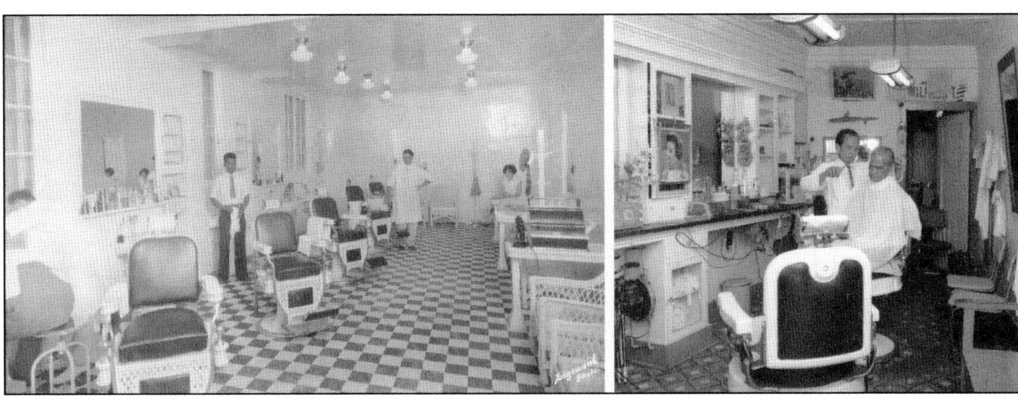

BARBERSHOPS AS GATHERING PLACES AND THE NEWS OF THE DAY. Young Hotel Barbershop (left) reflects developer Alexander Young's desire for a first-class hotel. The investment in tile decor and wicker-chair facilities in the barbershop was matched in the lobby and other meeting places in the hotel. Another barbershop (right) operated in close quarters and has the homeyness of cut flowers and a pinup, but it lacks the cleanliness and sterility of the Young Hotel. (Left, HSA; right, photograph by Francis Haar; UHL–JCC.)

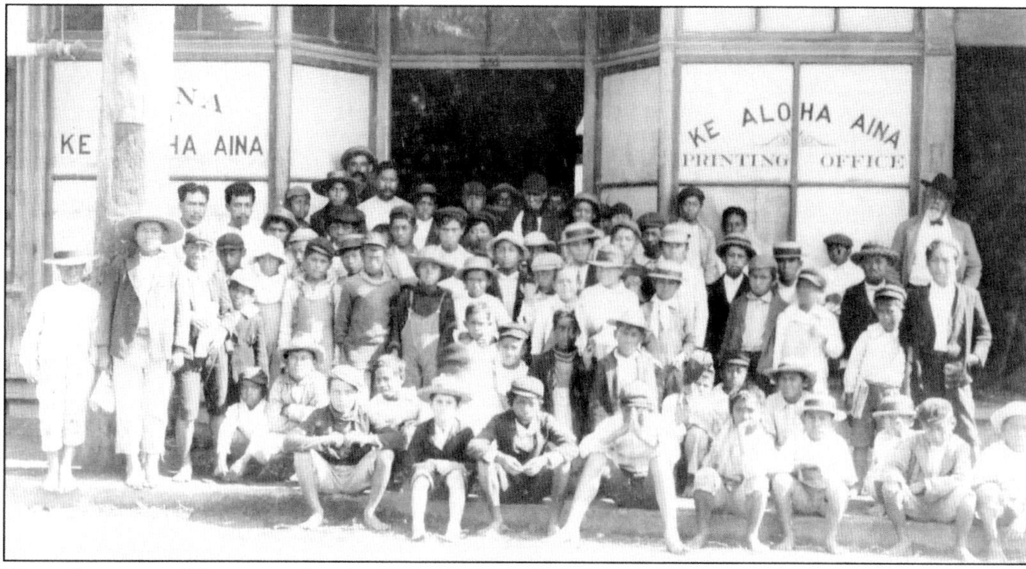

THE COCONUT WIRELESS. In the late 19th and early 20th centuries, there were dozens of newspapers printed in Honolulu. The newsboys seated here hawked their papers up and down the town streets. Joseph Nawahi, who opposed the 1893 overthrow of the Kingdom of Hawaii, published *Ke Aloha Aina*, one of the Hawaiian language newspapers printing editorials, news of the day, as well as ancient Hawaiian lore and sharp letters to the editor. (HSA.)

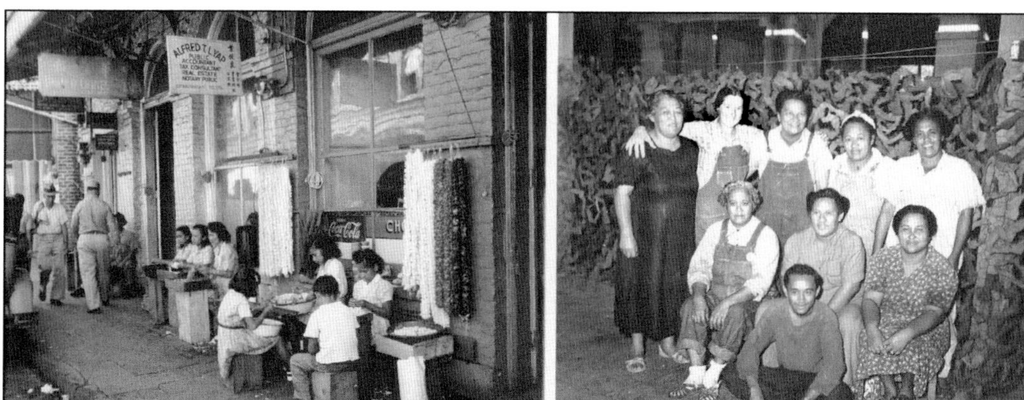

LEI SELLERS. Extended families (left) set up "shop" on Maunakea Street creating their lei on empty boxes that had contained goods shipped from China. Note that the sidewalk is the remnant of earlier trading with China—the granite blocks were used as shipboard ballast. Lei sellers and artist Juliette May Fraser (right) created camouflage during the war years. Lei sellers were hired because they had nimble fingers, and so they were thought to make the best camouflage weaving and patterning. (Left photograph by James Summerlin; Bishop Museum; right, University of Hawaii Library Archives.)

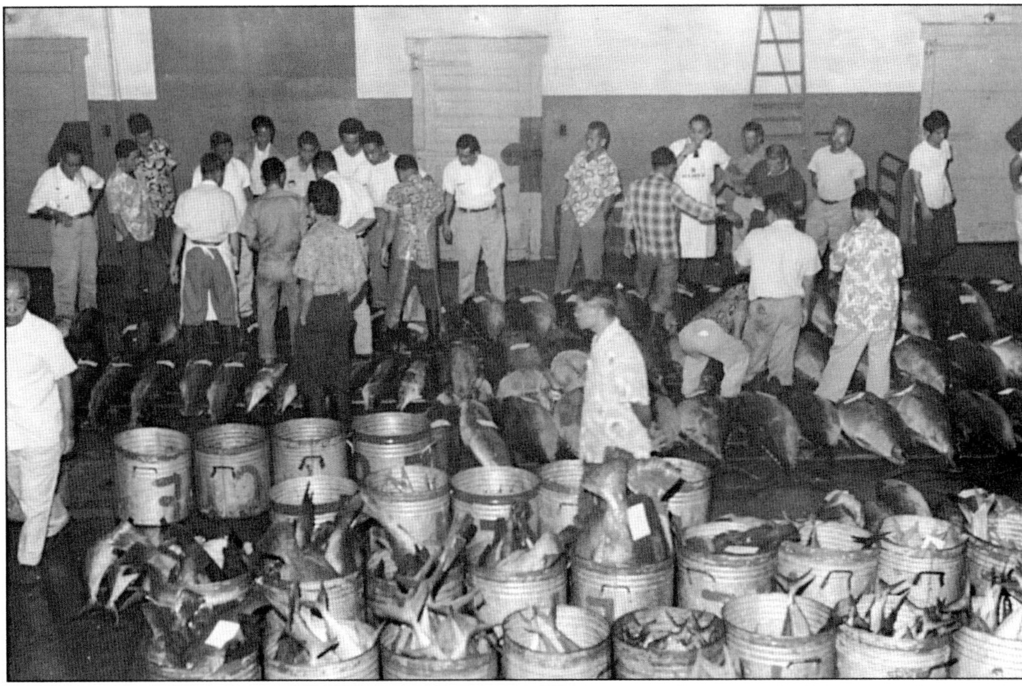

AUCTION AT THE OTANI FISH MARKET. This market had the misfortune of celebrating the opening of its new building on December 7, 1941. Matsujiro Otani was interned for the duration of the war, and his son continued the business. Nearby restaurants and fish markets bid on at least four types of fish that day at this gathering place, especially ahi (yellow fin tuna in the upper right of the photograph), used for delicious sashimi (sliced raw fish). (Matsujiro and Akira Otani Collection; JCCH.)

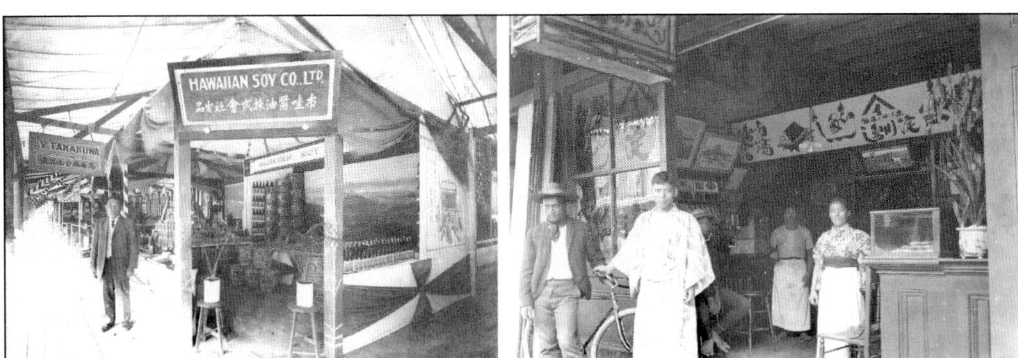

HAWAIIAN SOY COMPANY MARKET AND YODOGAWA SUSHI SHOP. Hoping for wider distribution, Hawaiian Soy Company (left) opened this small tentlike retail outlet located in one of the harborfront markets. Its *shoyu* distillery, with fermenting tanks and cooperage, was located on nearby Pua Lane. The Japanese store (right) announced catering and its *maki* (rolled) sushi specialty. Two Hawaiian men, probably customers, show early cultural mingling. (Dorothy C. Arakawa collection; JCCH and JCCH.)

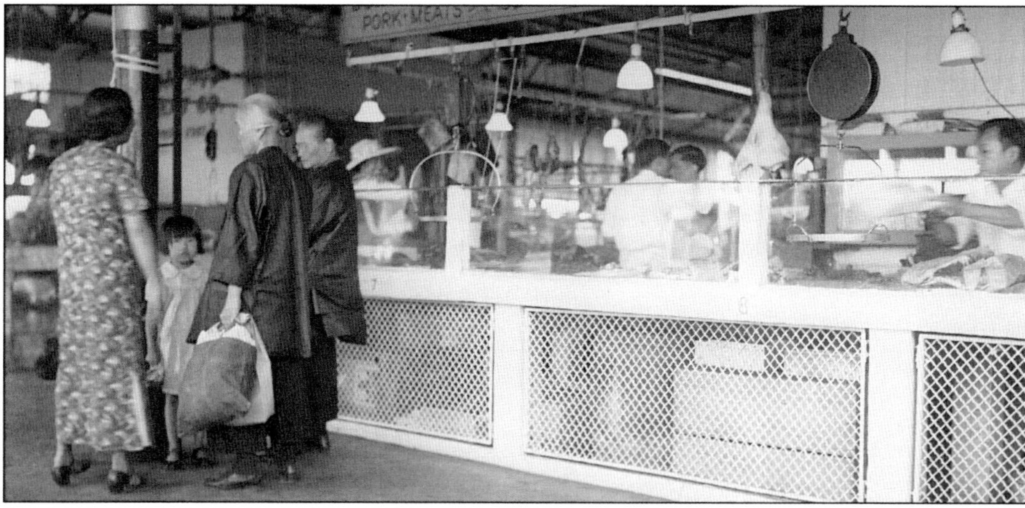

SHOPPING AT AALA MARKET, 1937. This meat market is selling pork, and the pig snout on the hook indicates that no part goes to waste. Three generations of Chinese American women have stopped to talk while shopping. The woman on the left wears a traditional *cheongsam* (long closely-fitted dress), the older women on the right has comfortably donned cool black-gummed (mud-treated) and silk *shan ku* (tunic and trousers), and the young girl wears a western-style short dress. (USAMH.)

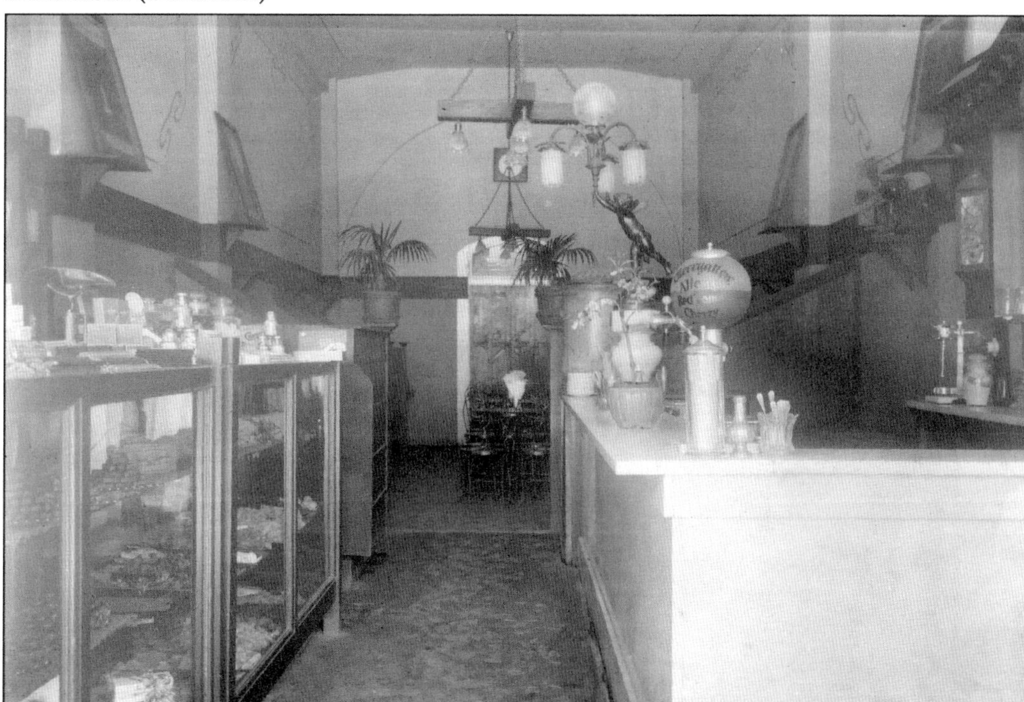

SODA AND SWEET SHOP. This narrow shop has lyrical hand decorations painted on the walls and scenic reproductions on wall shelves. The small parlor in the rear has room for a number of parties to gather while sipping their Cherryallen Red Tome Cherry sodas from the globe syrup dispenser in the central right. Candy could be purchased by the box or by the piece, weighed on the scale on top of the candy counter. (HSA.)

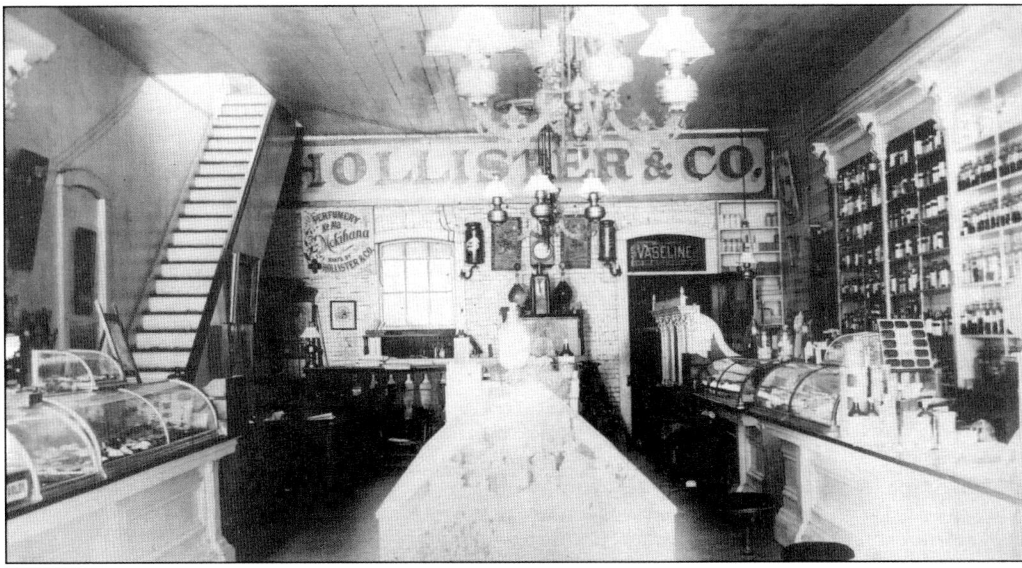

INSIDE HOLLISTER AND CO. DRUGSTORE. Candy display counters are on the left, while the back wall advertises "Perfumery Ke Ala Mokihana by Hollister Co." This indicates that perfumes are made on the premises. The advertisements also publicize that pills are "safe pleasant and reliable." The iconographic show-globes filled with colored water are the sign of an apothecary. On the right is the pharmacy where medicinal components are taken from the shelves and mixed in front of the patrons. (HSA.)

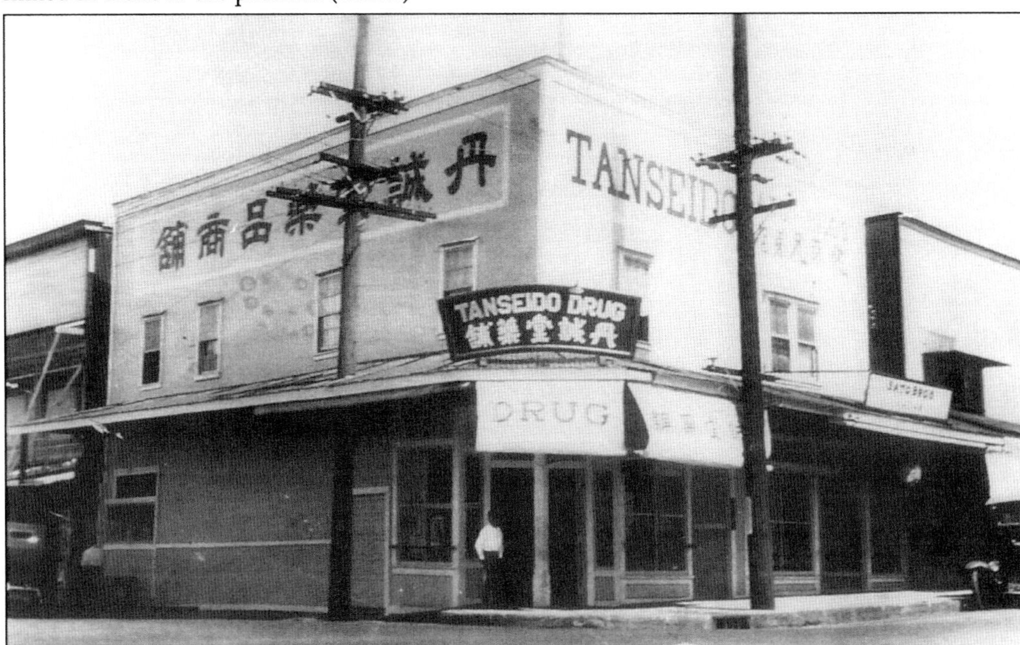

TANSEIDO YAKUHO-TANSEIDO DRUG STORE. Located at the corner of Beretania and River, this drugstore served the needs of the Japanese American community living in the Chinatown and Aala neighborhoods. This store sold drugs, cosmetics, and stationery. It was very well-positioned to receive lots of streetcar as well as pedestrian business. Sato Brothers Clothiers was next door. (Hoichi Ogawa collection; JCCH.)

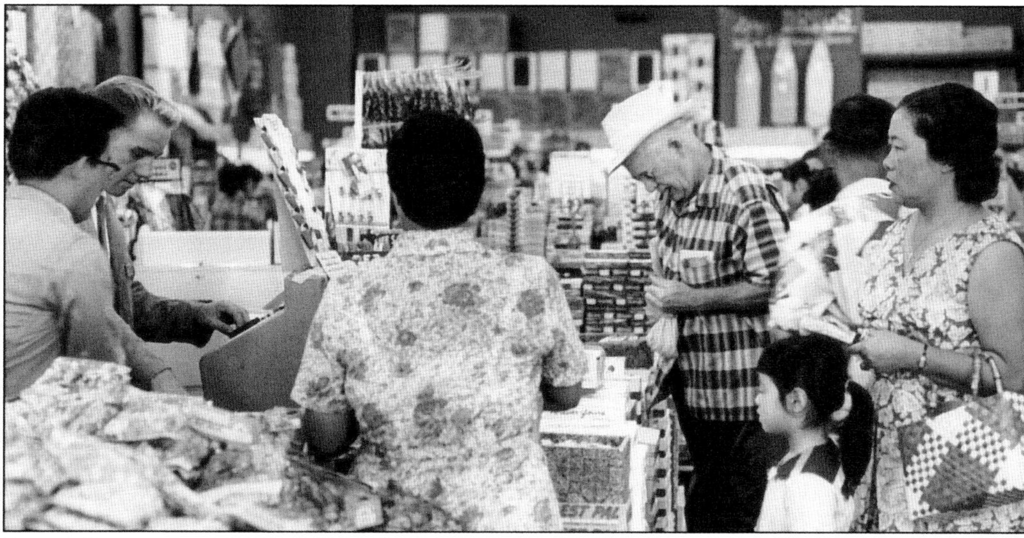

Longs Drugstore. Entrepreneur Joseph Long had created a chain of self-service combination drug, beverage, photographic supply, stationery, and household hardware stores in California. After vacationing in Hawaii on several occasions, he opened his 10th store at the makai-Ewa corner of Bishop and Hotel in March 1954. His stores, which kept prices low through volume sales, forced established retailers, such as Liberty House, to redefine their business models and move into more upscale wares. (HSA.)

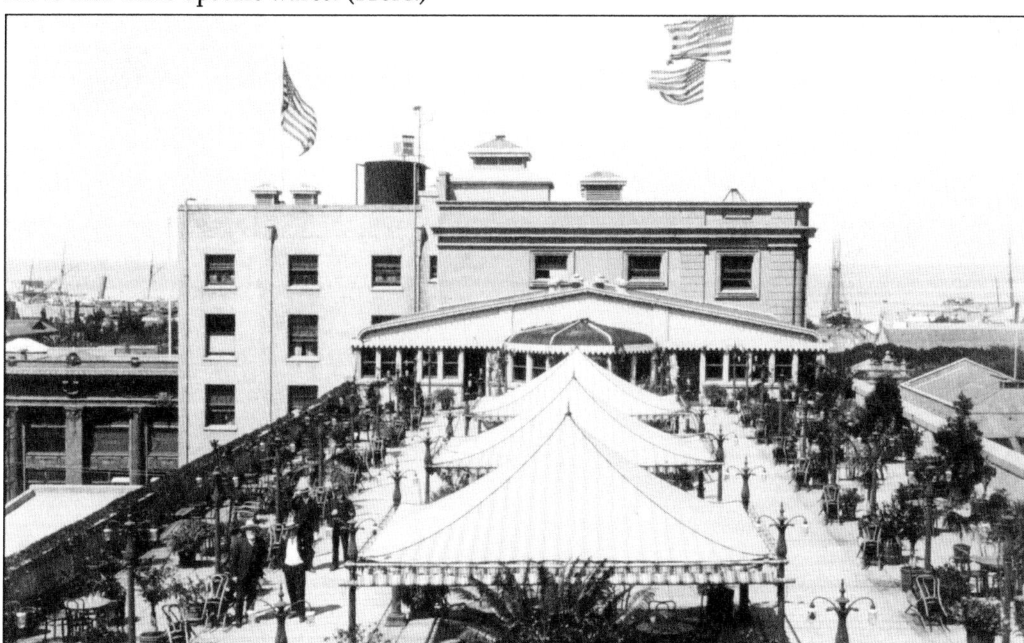

Alexander Young Hotel Rooftop Garden. Bishop Street owed its existence to Honolulu Iron Works manager and hotel pioneer Alexander Young. Young created the first Bishop Street block as street frontage for his building between Hotel and King in 1900 by dedicating the Diamond Head side (and getting Bishop Estate to donate the Ewa side) to the government. The July 31, 1903, gala opening of the Young Hotel drew 2,000 persons. The building had 192 rooms and suites and featured two sixth-floor dining rooms. (HSA.)

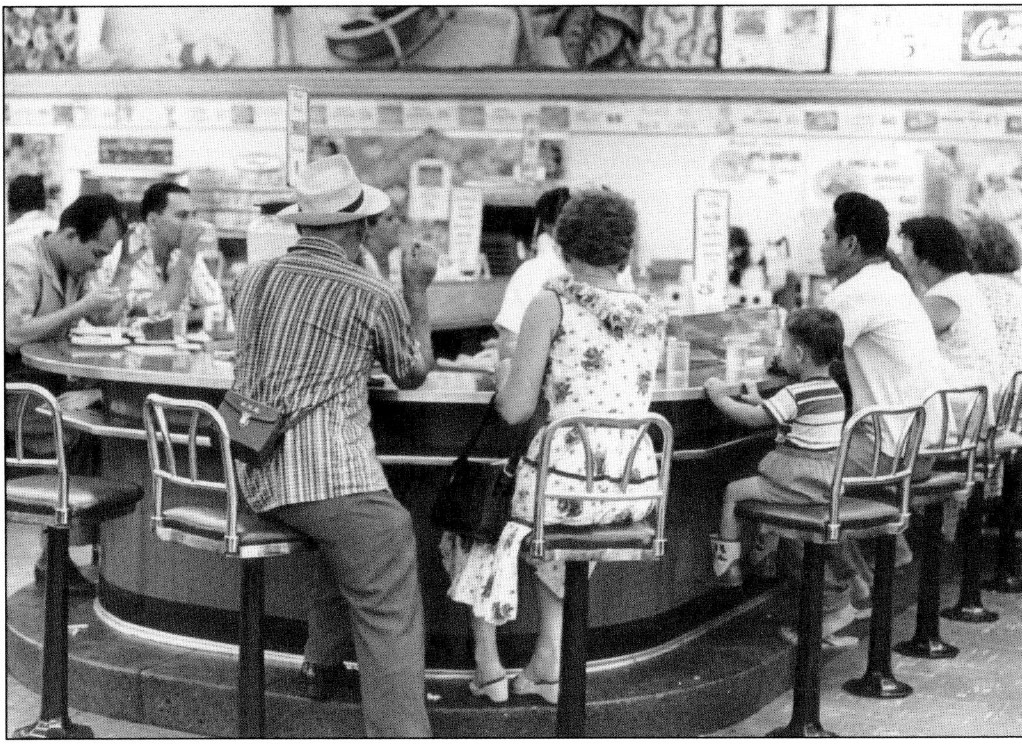

EVERYONE'S WELCOME AT WOOLWORTH'S. F.W. Woolworth was a retailing pioneer whose stores, known as five-and-dimes, contained popular restaurants. On opening day 1954, 3,000 people jam the new Woolworth's at Hotel and Fort—including its lunch counter. This was six years before civil rights lunch-counter sit-ins took place in the South. Honolulu's downtown lunch counter proved a popular, and certainly nondiscriminatory, place where everyone could gather and meet friends. (HSA.)

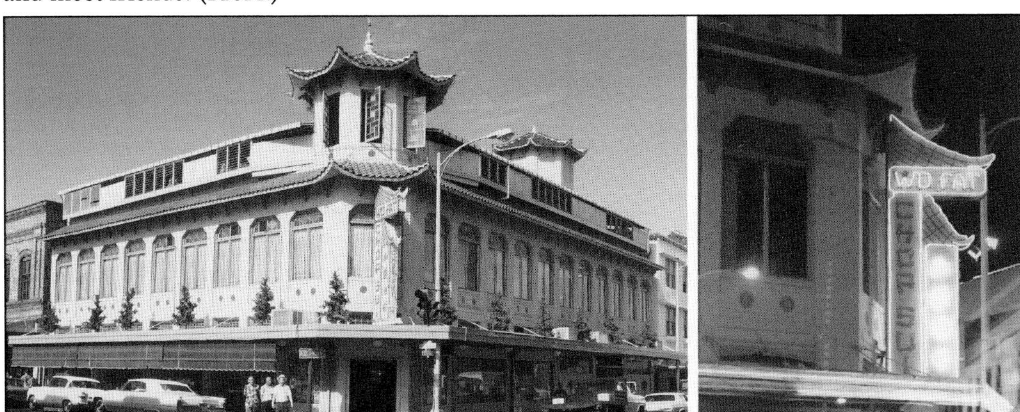

WO FAT. Located at Hotel and Maunakea, Wo Fat Chop Sui featured, as did most Chinese restaurants, Cantonese-style cooking. The Wo Fat vertical sign proclaimed this place for many family and business gatherings on the second floor. Robert "Bozo" Shigemura was a remarkable neon bender, who designed this and many of the signs in Honolulu, including the expansive original marquee for the Hawaii Theatre. (Photograph by Nancy Bannick; Historic Hawaii Foundation; photograph by William Lowe.)

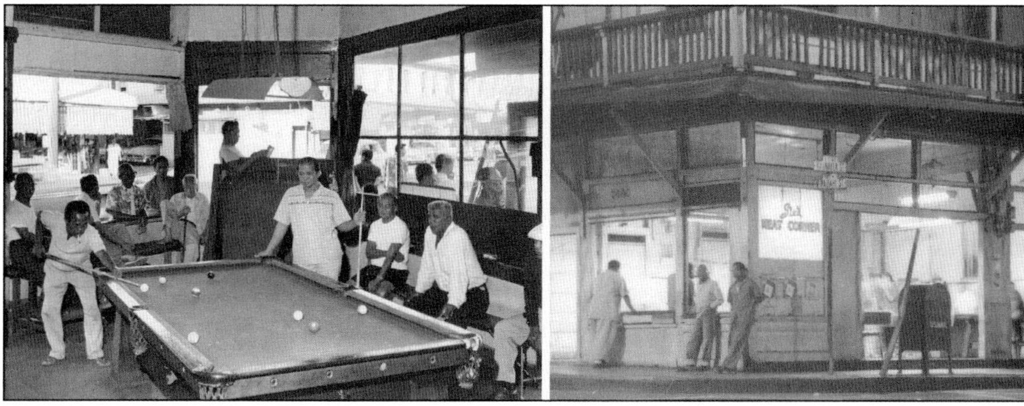

POOL SHARKS IN KUKUI, AND CHINATOWN POOL HALLS AT NIGHT. The pool halls were comfortable meeting places to speculate or to prove one's worth (different from the alii playing billiards). These pool halls in Kukui and on the corner of Maunakea and Pauahi Streets show the interest in pool and concentration involved. Siu's Meat Corner, a sign from an earlier establishment, does not faze the action of the pool sharks. (Photographs by Francis Haar; UHL–JCC.)

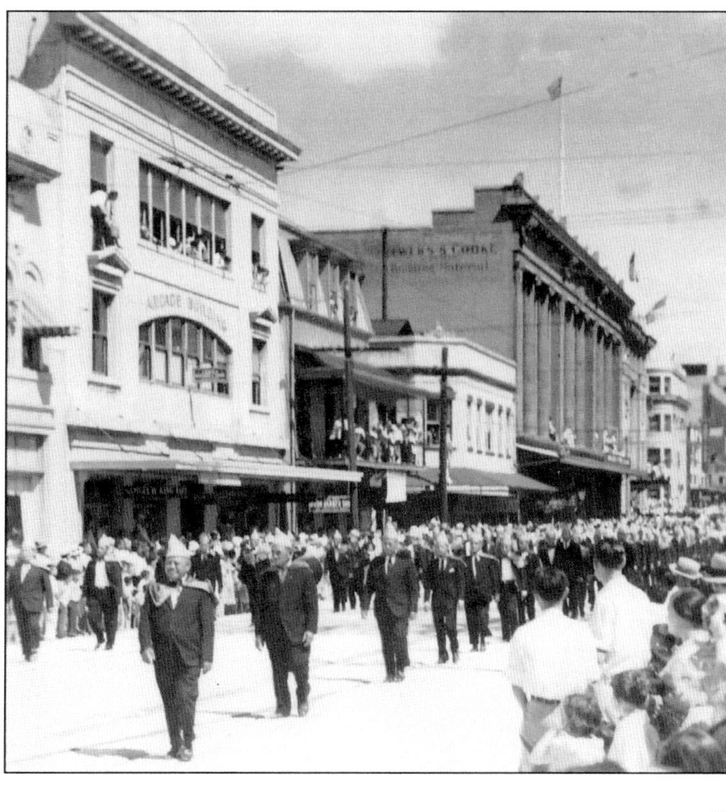

FESTIVITIES ON KING STREET. Before the relocation of retail to Ala Moana and the rise of tourism in Waikiki, parades proceeded from Aala Park to Iolani Palace. Here, members of the Royal Order of Kamehameha I march down South King. Judging by the spectators' clothing, this would be in the late 1950s. Behind the marchers are the original Hawaiian Electric Company and Arcade Buildings, the Occidental Hotel, and the dark-columned Lewers and Cooke Building. (USAMH.)

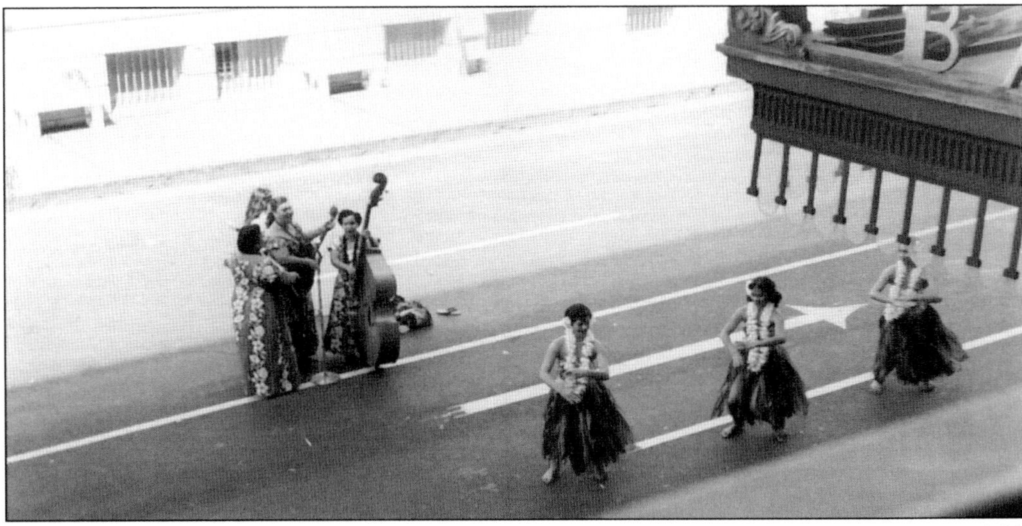

SPECIAL GATHERINGS AND INFORMAL ENTERTAINMENT. While the acoustic systems available were not very sophisticated, the idea of closing streets for local music and entertainment is not new. Above, four ladies serenade Bishop Street below South King while three others dance the hula. In front is the Damon Building, and behind the entertainers is the Bishop Trust Company Building. (Yamanaka/Angeles Collection.)

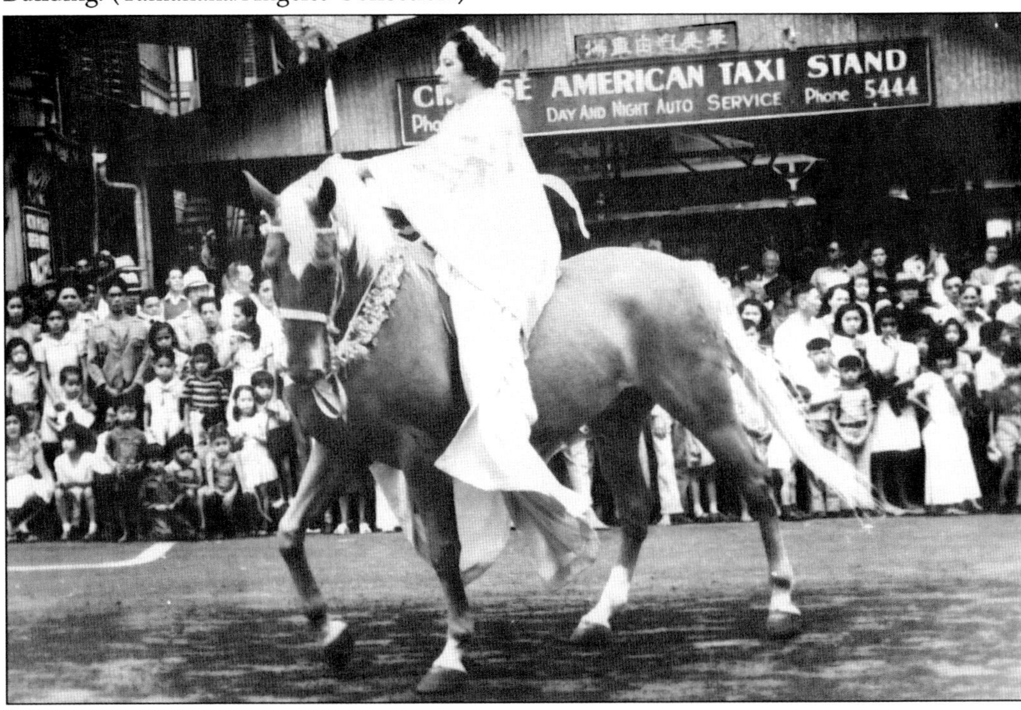

KAMEHAMEHA DAY *PAU* RIDER. King Kamehameha V established June 11 as a national holiday in 1871 to honor his ancestor Kamehameha the Great. In 1896, the legislature declared it the only holiday of royal origin to be recognized by the Republic of Hawaii. *Pau* riding in parades dates from the early 20th century. Here, eager children watch one rider in full regalia prance in front of the Chinese American Taxi Stand at 117 North Beretania Street. This photograph was taken sometime during the 1940s–1950s. (Photograph by Kenjiro Natsuyama.)

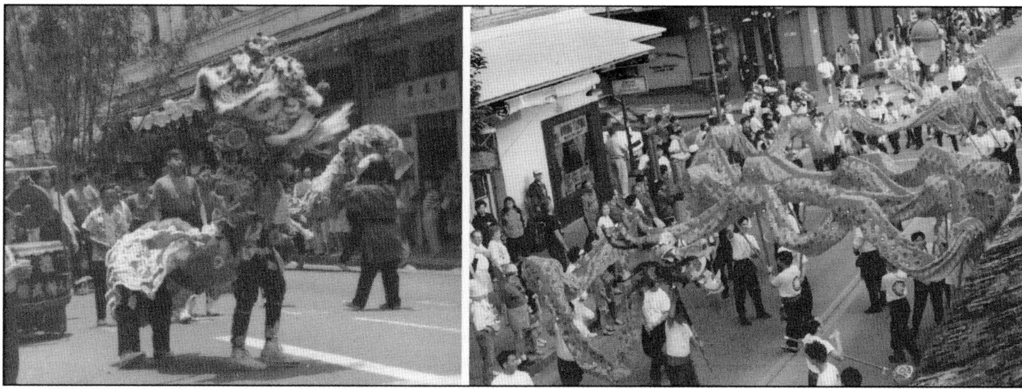

LION DANCE AND DRAGON PARADE IN CHINATOWN. A Chinese lion dance (left) celebrates the New Year's and many festive occasions, such as business openings. Spectators place money in the lion's mouth to offer good fortune for the coming year. The Chinese dragon (right) twists its way along Hotel Street. The moon (a ball on a stick in the lower right) guides the head of the dragon (lower middle of the photograph). (Left photograph by Francis Haar; UHL–JCC; right photograph by Kristina Larssen.)

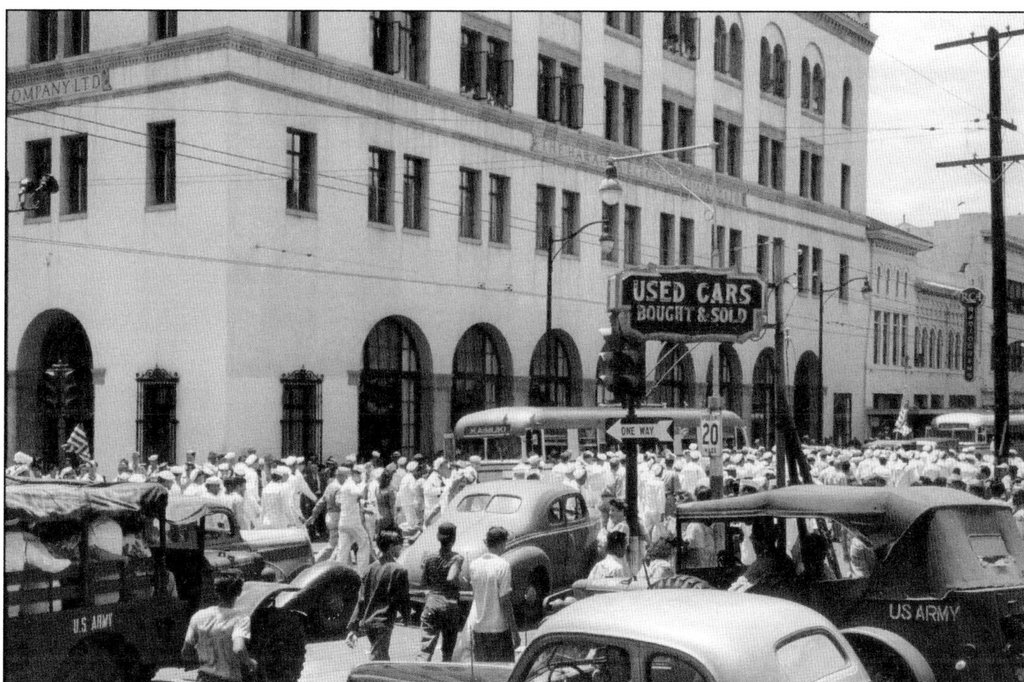

VJ DAY PARADE, AUGUST 14, 1945. People gather downtown as the news breaks. Sailors clog the intersection at King and Richards in a spontaneous parade. The *Star Bulletin* declared "Extra! It's Peace." World War II, and the involvement that had been thrust upon the United States with the bombing of Pearl Harbor on December 7, 1941, was over. The Hawaiian Electric Company is in the background. (HSA.)

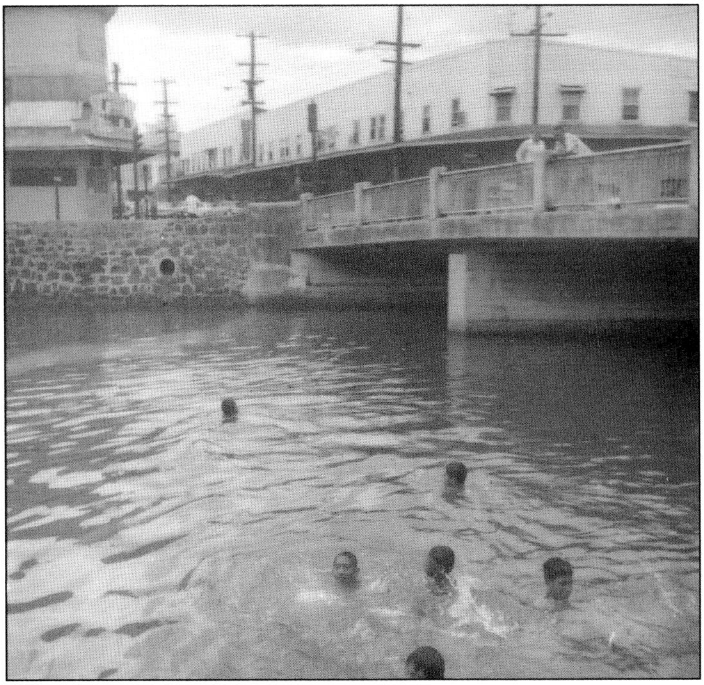

BOYS SWIMMING IN NUUANU STREAM. Jumping from the Hotel Street bridge, the boys are having great fun swimming in the mix of salt and brackish water of the Nuuanu Stream, presumably at high tide. Wooden buildings at the corner of River and Hotel are shown in the background. (Photograph by Francis Haar; UHL–JCC.)

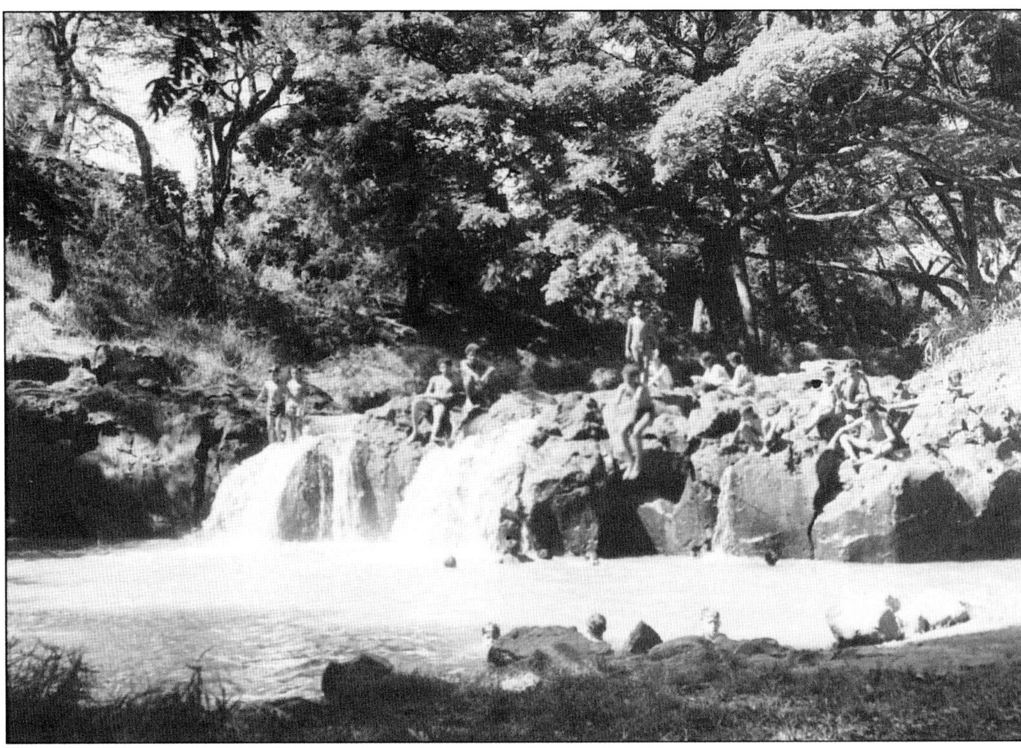

WAIKAHALULU FALLS. Like the nearby Kapena Falls, Waikahalulu provided recreational opportunities for generations within a short walking distance from town. Former Queen Liliuokalani gifted the falls and the surrounding area to the public as a park, which now bears her name. (Photograph by Toshiharu Murai.)

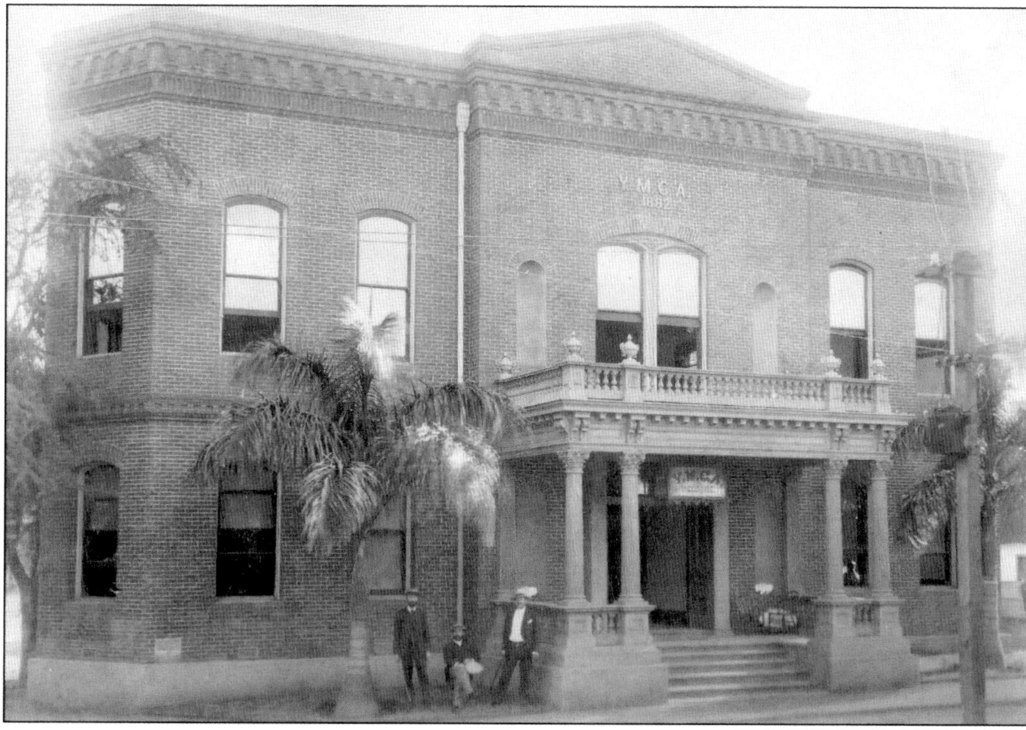

THE WELCOMING Y. This YMCA was founded on April 30, 1869, and Sanford Dole was the first president. King Kalakaua dedicated the Y building on the mauka-Ewa corner of Alakea and Hotel on April 21, 1883. It contained an office, parlor, committee room, reading room, and assembly room. The rear yard accommodated outbuildings. The structure was extended in 1895 on the Ewa side for a gymnasium addition, which allowed the organization to offer a fourfold program of social, educational, physical, and religious activities. (HHS.)

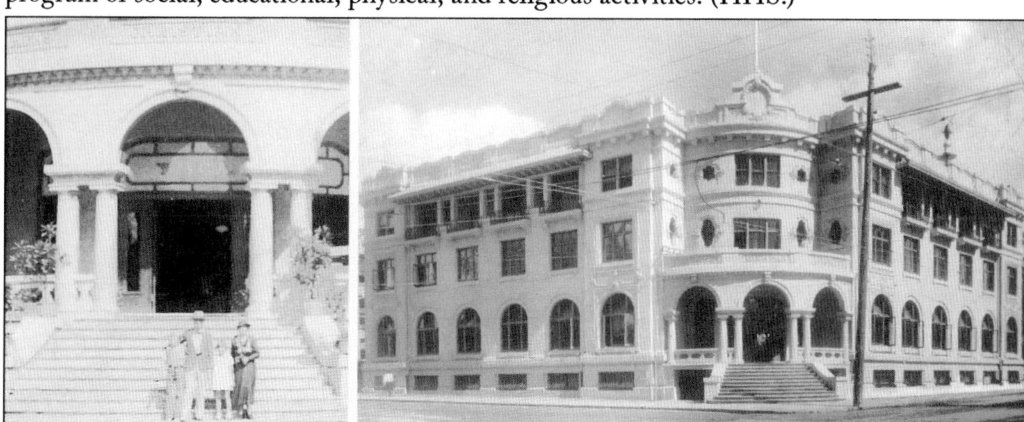

YMCA, 1911. Prior to World War II, YMCA board members wanted to exclude Japanese Americans. General secretary Ralph G. Cole (pictured in this 1935 detail photograph with his family) stood fast and said all were welcome. Located across Hotel Street from the older Y, the 1911 building boasted two cornerstones—the 1882 structure's inscribed motto of Kamehameha III and a new one listing the year of installation. The Y featured rooms for music, billiards, and other games, as well as a cafeteria, gymnasium, dormitory, and (in 1915) a pool. (Left, Cole/ Nordyke Family; right, HSA.)

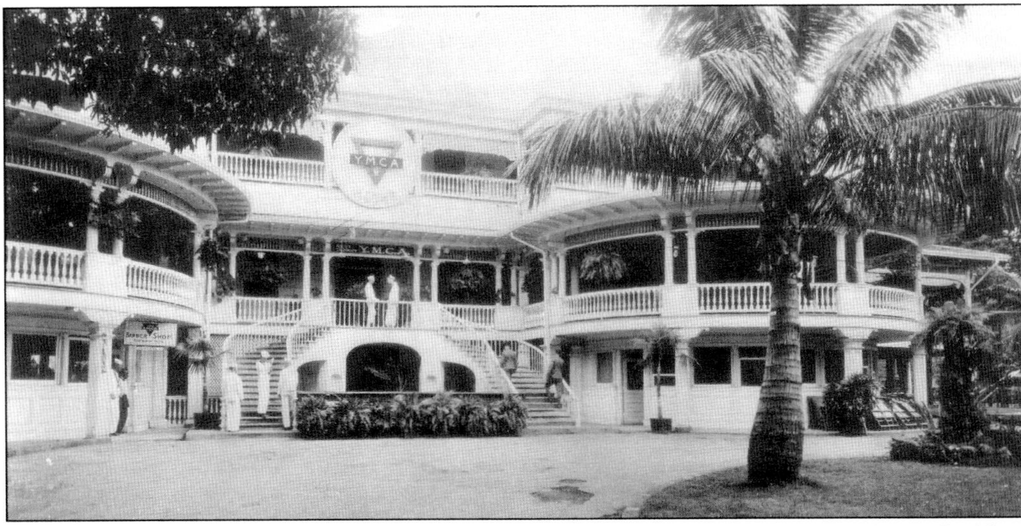

ARMY-NAVY YMCA. When the United States entered World War I, large numbers of soldiers were expected in Honolulu. There existed no place for enlisted men to obtain reasonably priced sleeping quarters. The old Royal Hawaiian Hotel was purchased and converted into an Army-Navy YMCA. The first floor was remodeled and two cottages rebuilt, providing sleeping quarters for 500 men with rates per night at 25¢ in the dorm, 50¢ or 75¢ for rooms without bath, and $1 for room with bath. (HSA.)

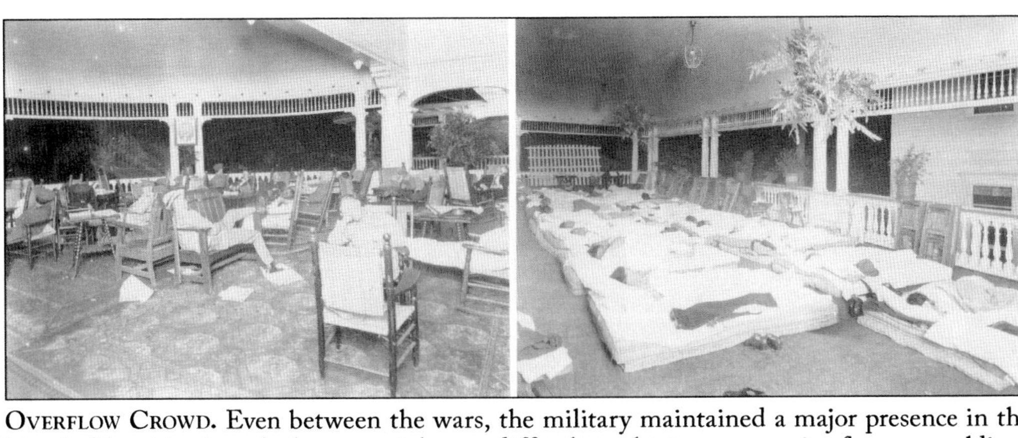

OVERFLOW CROWD. Even between the wars, the military maintained a major presence in the islands. Travel back to the bases at night was difficult to obtain or expensive for many soldiers. In these photographs from 1926, the number of soldiers seeking accommodations at the Army-Navy YMCA had filled all 500 beds, and those unlucky enough to arrive last are forced to sleep on mattresses on the lanai floor or on the furniture. (HSA.)

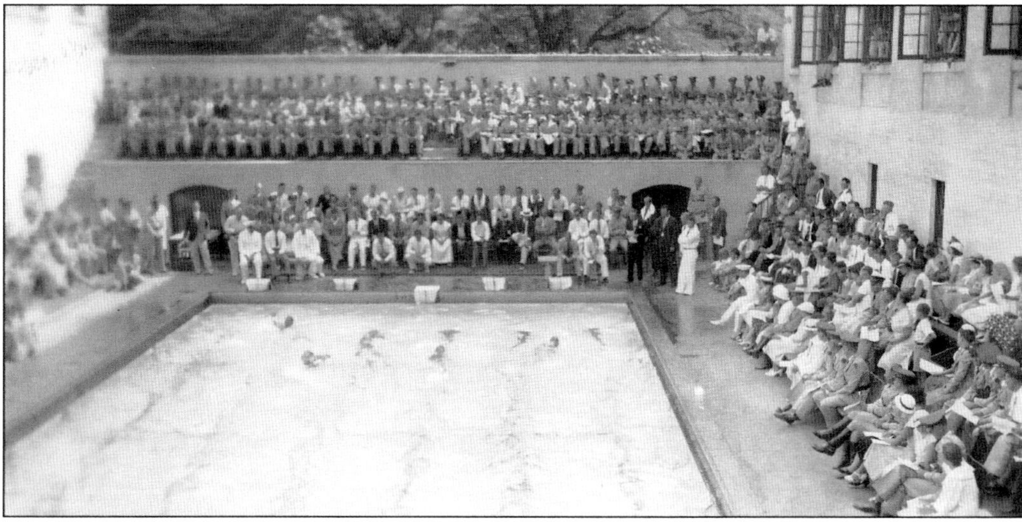

SECOND ARMY-NAVY YMCA, 1931. The old Royal Hawaiian Hotel Y eventually succumbed to termites and age. The Alakea side of the property was sold to raise funds. Designed by Lincoln Rogers, Walter Emory, and Marshall Webb, the new building complemented the architecture of the new Hawaiian Electric Company, federal buildings, and Honolulu City Hall. Shaped in a "U" pattern, it featured a gracious front lobby, cafeteria, gymnasium, auditorium, offices, meeting rooms, and living quarters. In the center was the pool, complete with second-story viewing stands. (USAMH.)

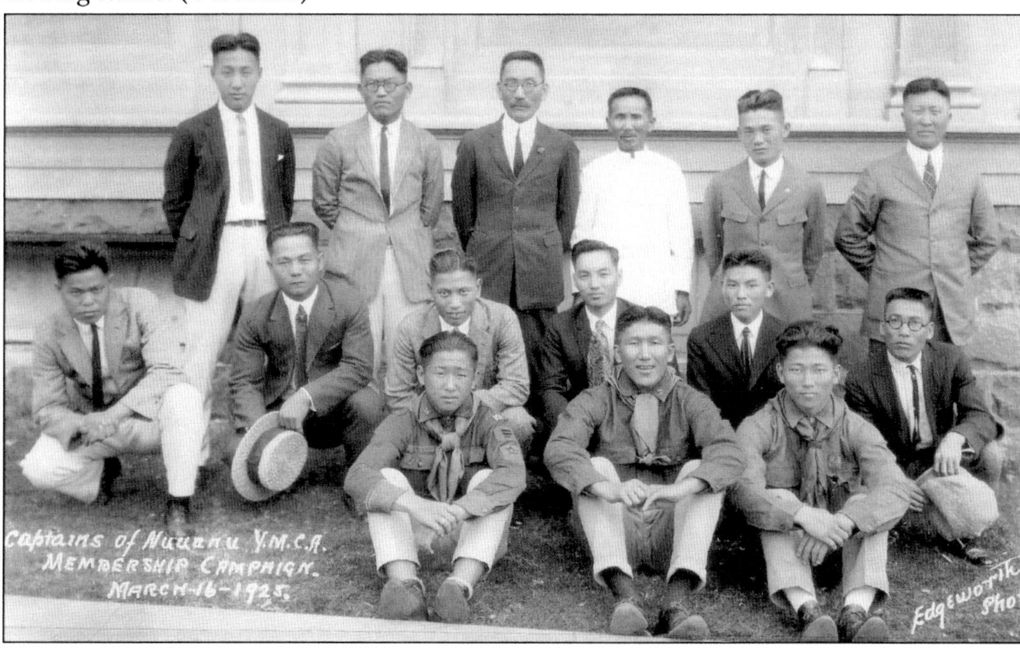

NUUANU YMCA. Race had been a contentious issue within the YMCA, but evangelism fostered reaching out to other nationalities. Significantly, between 1887 and 1891, Chinese, Japanese, Hawaiian, and Portuguese groups were all meeting in Queen Emma Hall for educational and social activities. In 1917, leaders Dr. Iga Mori, Chung K. Ai and Dr. Syngman Rhee agreed to support a multiethnic Y, which opened the next year. These are the multiethnic Y membership campaign captains of the Nuuanu YMCA in 1925. (HSA.)

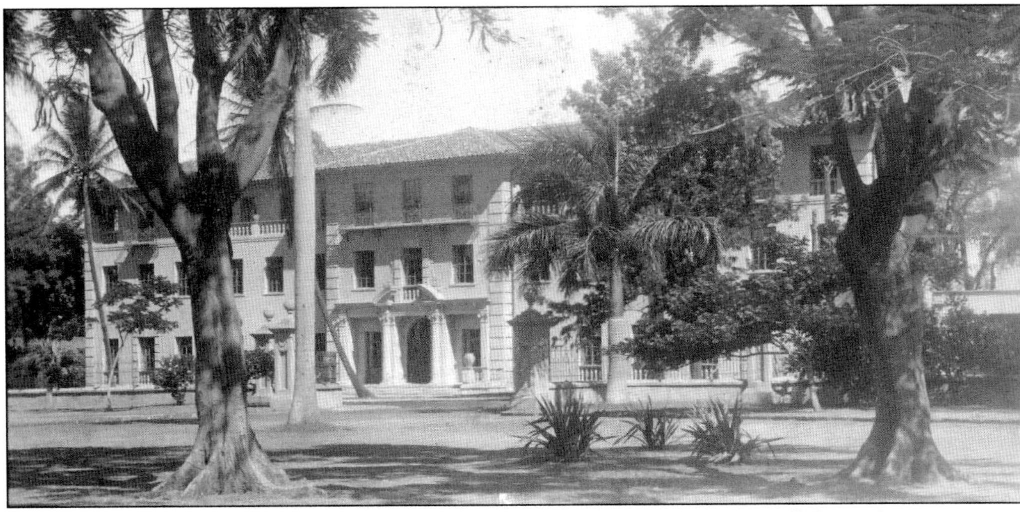

LANIAKEA (RICHARDS STREET) YWCA. Meaning "broadening horizons," Laniakea was an apt name for this facility designed by Julia Morgan. Morgan was the first woman to gain entry to the prestigious architecture program at the École des Beaux-Arts in Paris, France. Morgan produced this building "long-distance" while working at William Randolph Hearst's castle in San Simeon, California. She had associates send detailed written and photographic reports weekly by sea to her mainland office. The building opened in 1927. (HSA.)

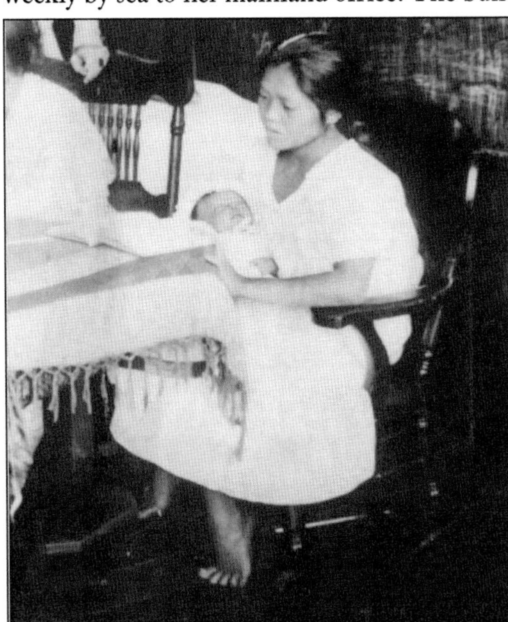

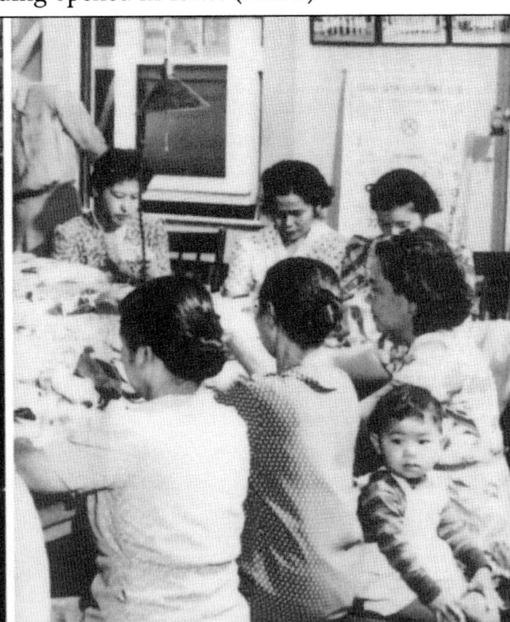

RICHARDS STREET'S YWCA ACTIVITIES. The YW was about the uplifting of community. It reached out to young women of all backgrounds. Activities included athletics, camping, night schools, night adult schools, healthy mother and baby classes (left), cooking classes, and dances. During World War II, Laniakea was one of the most active locations of the Hawaiian war effort (right), as women made bandages and sewed hospital slippers. For many nights, these hardworking volunteers found themselves working after curfew and spending the night at the Y. (Richards Street YWCA.)

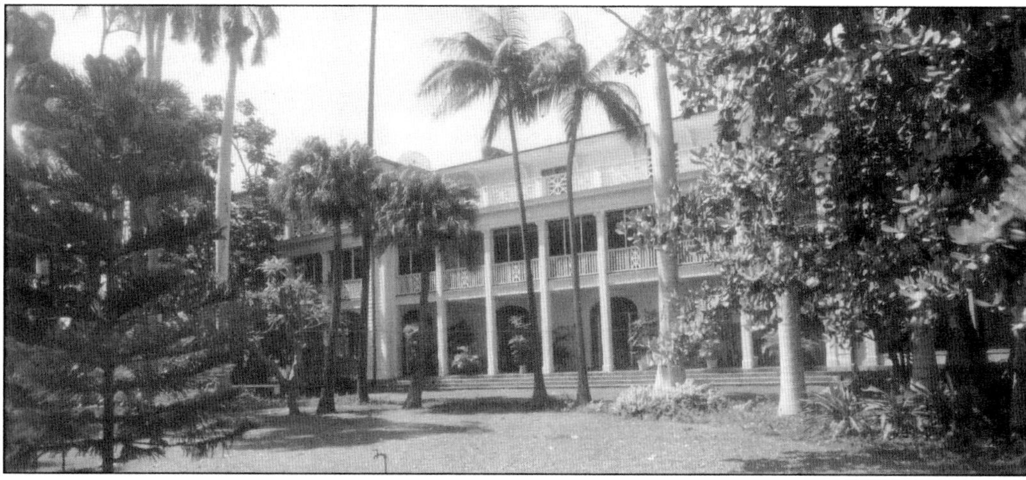

FIRST FERNHURST YWCA. In 1871, Joseph B. and Juliette Atherton moved to a home they named Fernhurst at the corner of Alapai and King. Three of their children in 1919 gave the property to the YWCA in memory of their sister Kate. This Fernhurst YWCA, also designed by Julia Morgan, provided affordable housing for 60 girls. During World War II, the YWCA held USO functions. In 1952, the land was sold to Honolulu Rapid Transit Co. Ltd., and the Y facility relocated to the corner of Wilder and Punahou Streets. (HSA.)

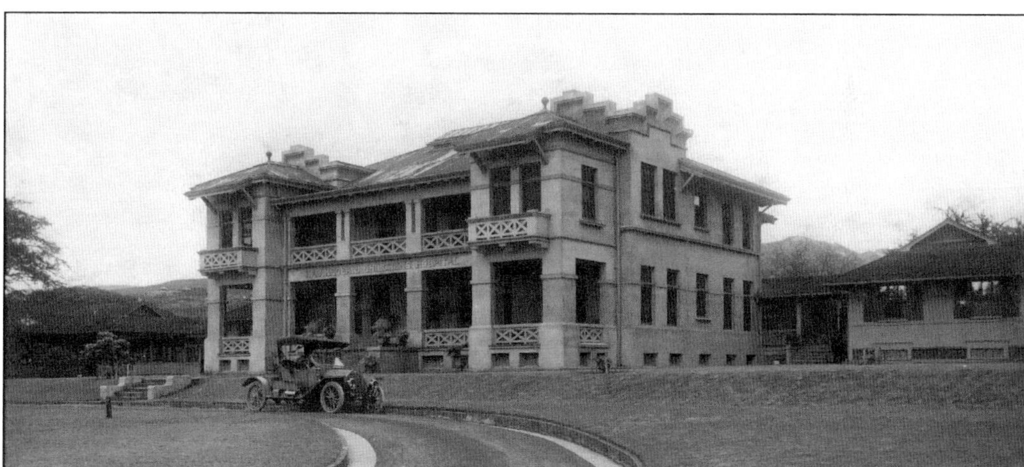

KAUIKEOLANI CHILDREN'S HOSPITAL. Located on the mauka side of Kuakini Street, the facility was erected in 1908 to combat a high infant mortality rate. Albert Wilcox gave $55,000 for the cause, and the general community donated $50,000. It was named after Wilcox's wife, Emma Kauikeolani Napoleon Mahelona Wilcox. In 1953, the hospital founded the Rehabilitation Center of Hawaii, which took over the property when, in 1978, Kauikeolani Children's Hospital merged with the Kapiolani Maternity and Gynecological Hospital. (HSA.)

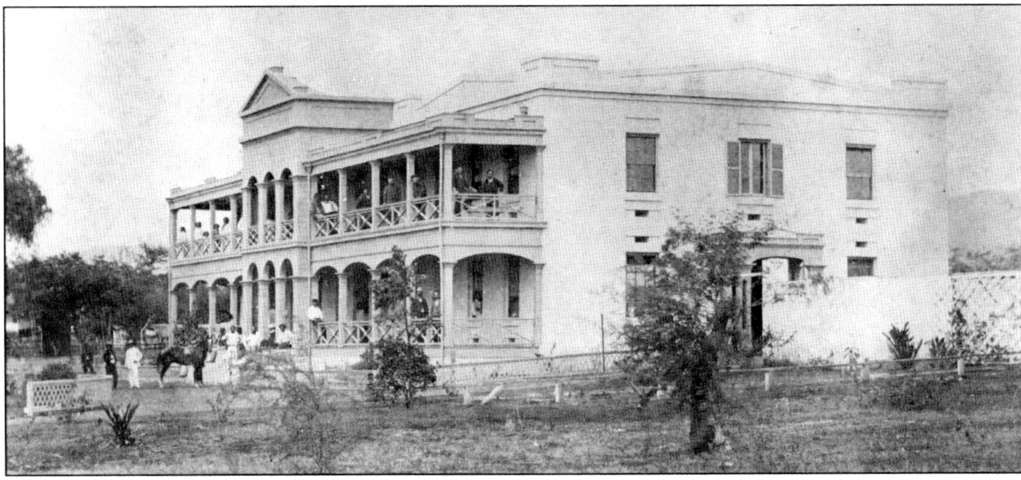

WHOLESOME CARE FOR THE SICK—QUEEN'S HOSPITAL. Queen's Hospital, founded in 1859, began as a temporary clinic at King and Fort. In 1860, the trustees of the hospital purchased nine acres of land on Punchbowl Street from Kaisara Kapaakea and his wife, Analea Keohokalole (parents of Kalakaua and Liliuokalani). The first hospital building was made of coral blocks and designed by architect Theodore Heuck. It opened in 1860 after a Masonic ceremony. The cornerstone contained photographs of benefactors King Kamehameha IV and Queen Emma. Charles Reed Bishop financed an 1893 Bishop Wing and 1905 Pauahi Wing Ewa of the original building. The first Pauahi makai facade closely resembled the open lanai of the original building, so much so that when the original building was demolished in 1922, the facade of the Pauahi Wing was altered to follow that of the C.W. Dickey's new main Queen Emma Building. (Both, HSA.)

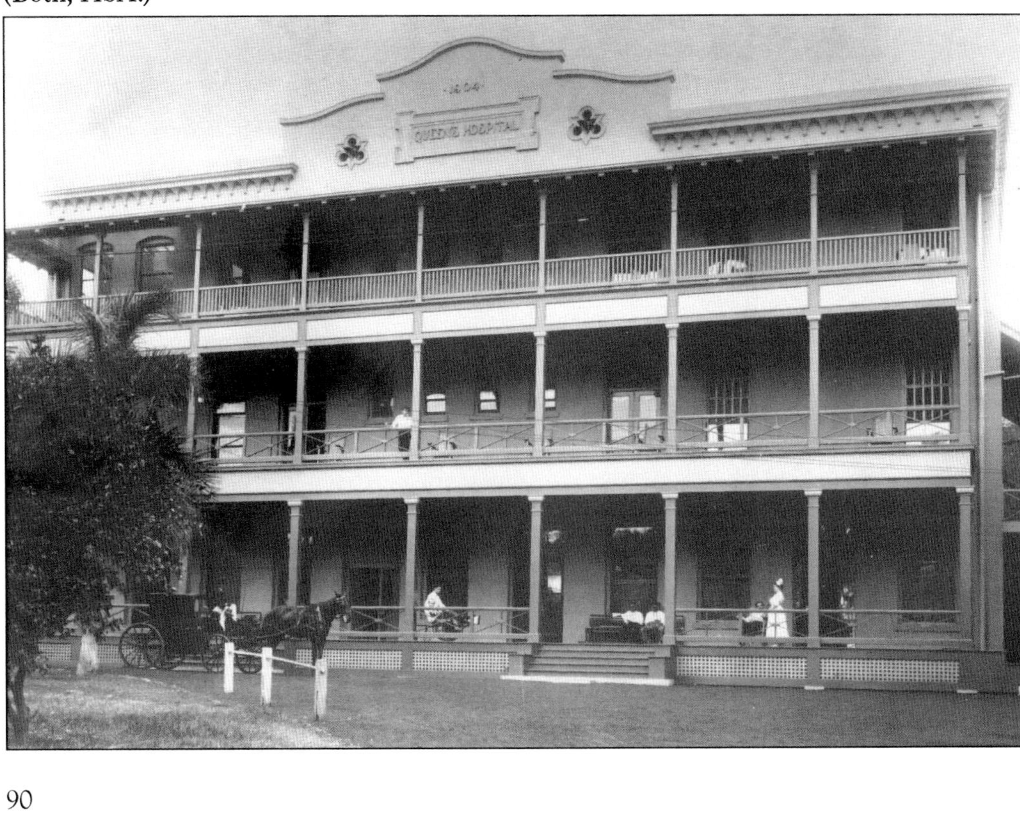

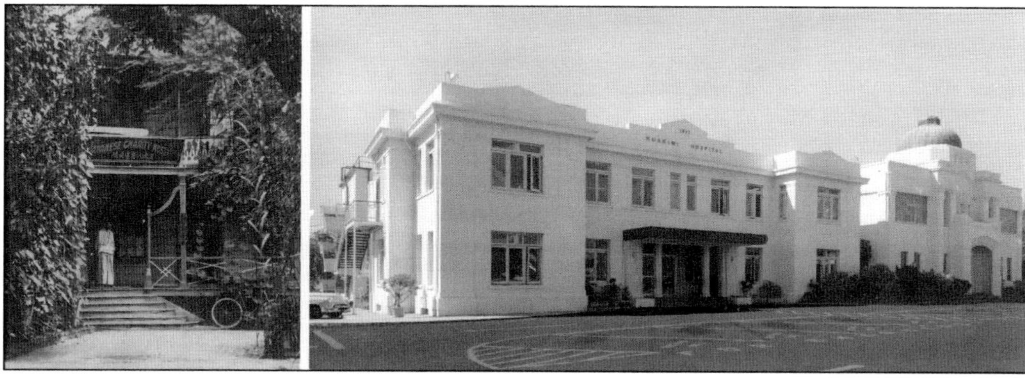

Japanese Charity Hospital. In 1892, the Japanese Benevolent Society began assisting Japanese suffering from disease, poverty, and other afflictions. The Chinatown fire of 1900 spurred the society to develop a hospital. The hospital began on North King in 1900, moved to Liliha in 1902, and has remained at Kuakini since 1917. A gift from Emperor Hirohito of Japan in 1934 helped finance the copper-domed building. The facility name was changed in 1942 to Kuakini Hospital and Home. (HSA and Kuakini Hospital.)

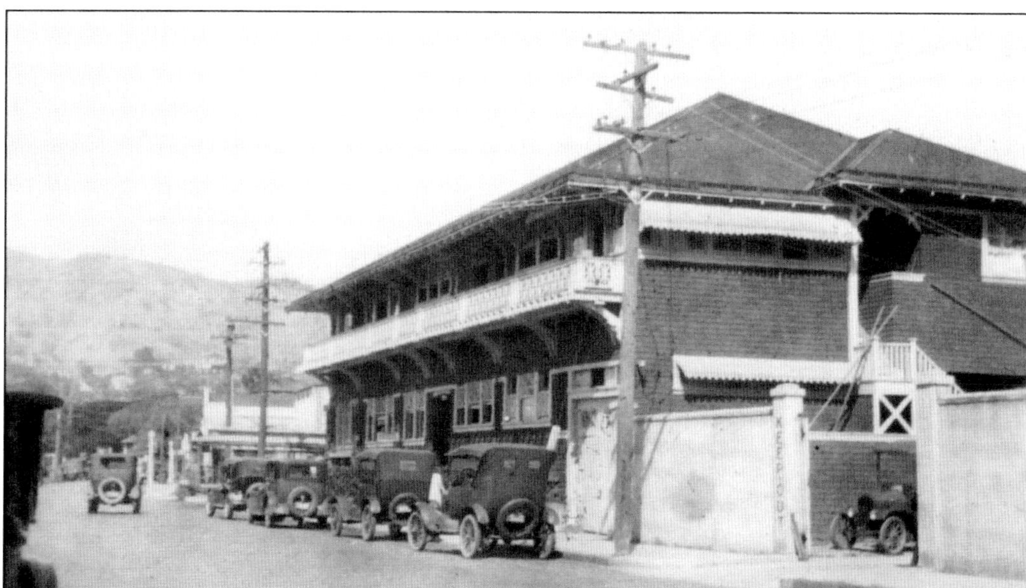

The Clinic. Dr. George Straub left Germany to avoid a court martial. He arrived in 1908, first working at Queen's Hospital. In 1912, Straub constructed this building at Miller and Beretania Streets as a combination home and office. The elderly Queen Liliuokalani, who lived across Beretania, was one of his patients. In 1921, he partnered with former Army doctors at The Clinic. In 1933, The Clinic moved to the present Strode Building on Young Street. The organization became known as Straub Clinic in 1952. (Bishop Museum.)

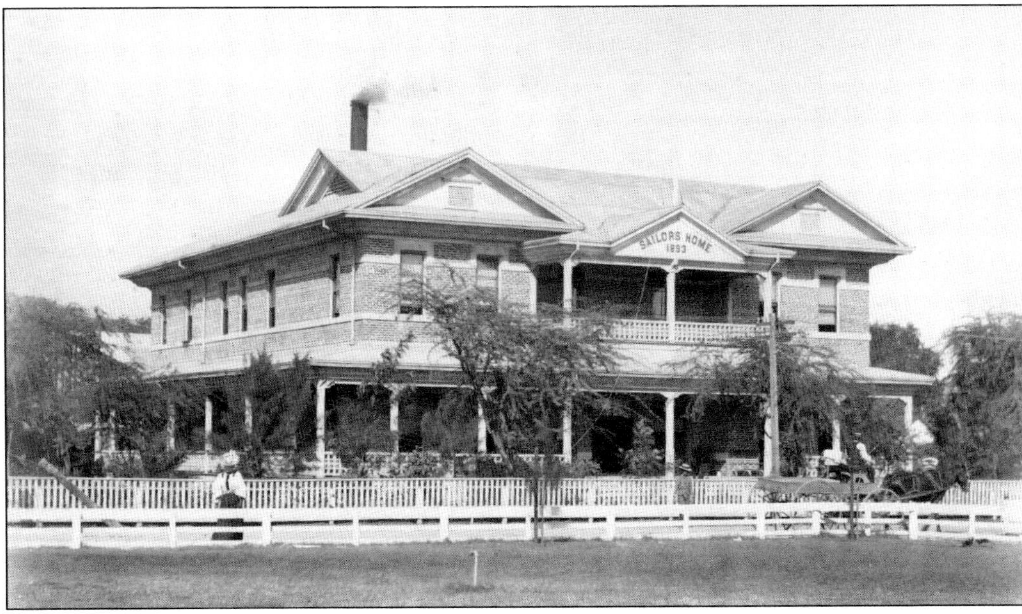

SAILORS' HOME AND SEAMEN'S INSTITUTE, 1893. The Honolulu Sailors' Home provided mariners with room and board at a reasonable price. The first three-story home was opened in September 1856 at Bethel and Merchant. The fire of 1886 forced the razing of the building. The facility reappeared in 1895 on Alakea (pictured) and joined with the Episcopal Seamen's Institute in 1907. The C.B. Ripley–designed building served as a club during the war. (Photograph by Frank Davey; Bishop Museum.)

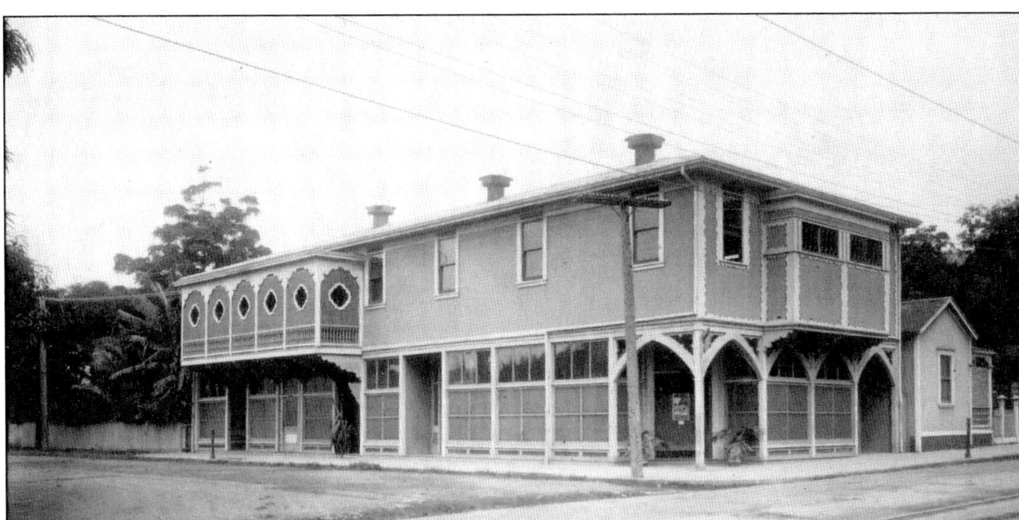

KILOHANA ART LEAGUE, CORNER OF MILLER AND BERETANIA STREETS. In 1894, this galvanizing group of artists, including founding member *kamaaina* D. Howard Hitchcock, began sponsoring exhibitions of local artists' work, including those of the Volcano School. One rare, yet notable, urban Hitchcock painting, *Honolulu Harbor from the Commercial Club,* depicts the 1920 dusky, calm harbor, Sand Island, Waianae Coast, and beyond from atop the McCandless Building. King Brothers Art Store also exhibited artworks and sold art supplies. (HSA.)

Young Hin in Front of His Son's Beaux Arts Store on Bethel Street, c. 1940s. This was an all-purpose art store selling a variety of art supplies, framing, and John Young's artwork. John's father was concerned that his son's store would not be successful, but John became an internationally recognized artist. Notice the wartime poster shows a big US boot kicking a bent-over Hitler, with the caption "A Good Buy / Bonds / is Good Bye to / Bunds." This poster was printed by an art supply company. (John Young Foundation.)

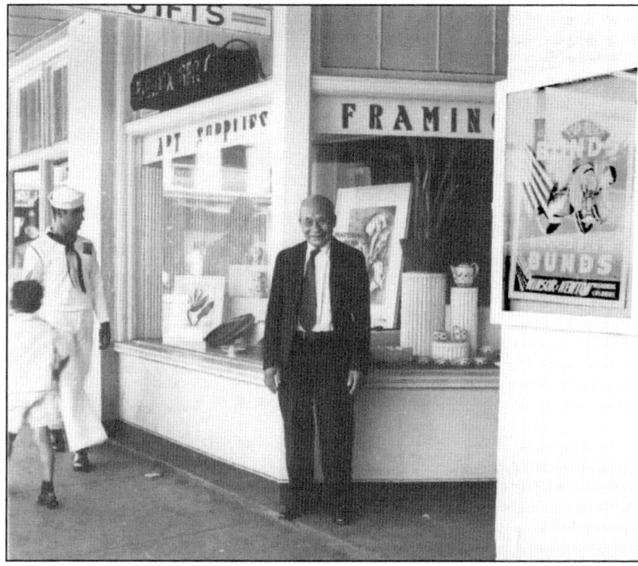

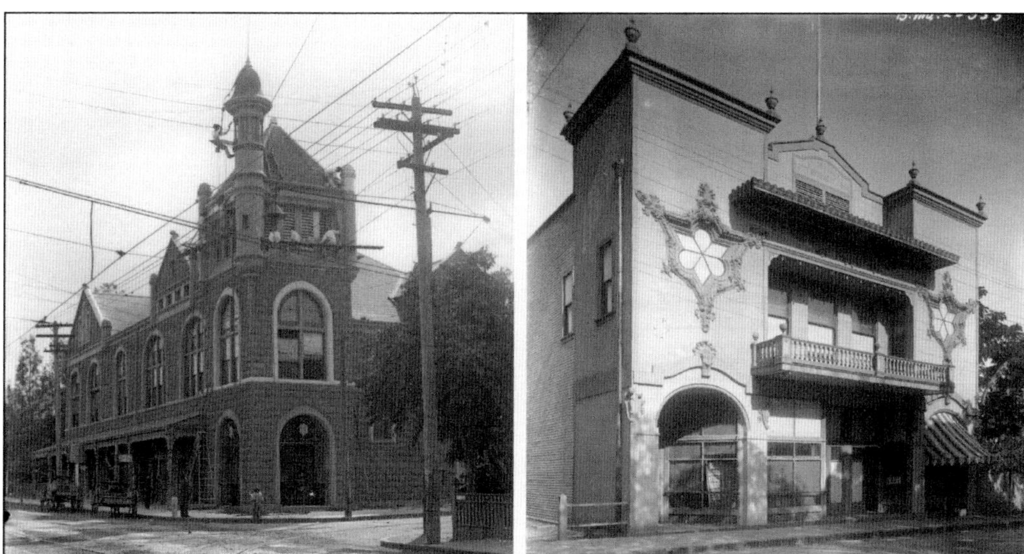

The Fraternal Orders, Masonic Temple, and San Antonio Society Hall. These organizations emphasized community and charity work. The Masons, active since 1843, are known for funding Shriners' hospitals and medical research. The Masonic lodge (left) was dedicated in 1893. The San Antonio Society (photograph taken in 1913) began offering assistance to the Portuguese community in 1877 and ultimately focused on providing funds against sickness and for the support of widows with children. (Photographs by L.E. Edgeworth; Bishop Museum.)

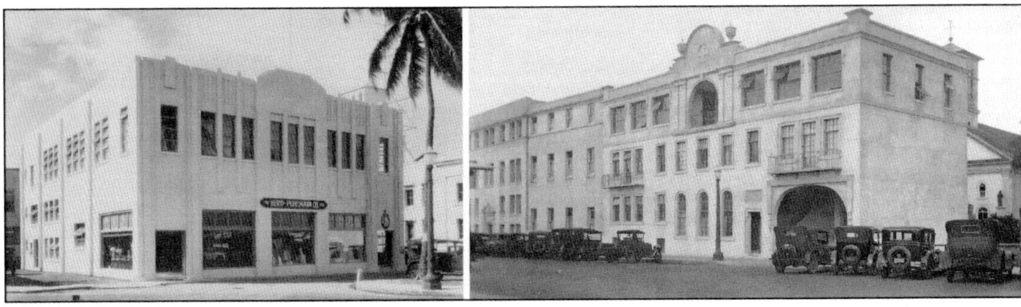

THE KNIGHTS OF PYTHIAS AND KNIGHTS OF COLUMBUS. The Knights of Pythias (left), in Hawaii since 1884, is nonsectarian and promotes cooperation, friendship, and goodwill. It funds playground facilities, hearing equipment for deaf children, and guide dogs for the blind. Its building was erected in 1930 between Union Street and Garden Lane. The Knights of Columbus (right), located on the Ewa side of Bishop Street, seeks to promote Catholic morality, education, and charity. Our Lady of Peace Cathedral was behind. (HSA and HP.)

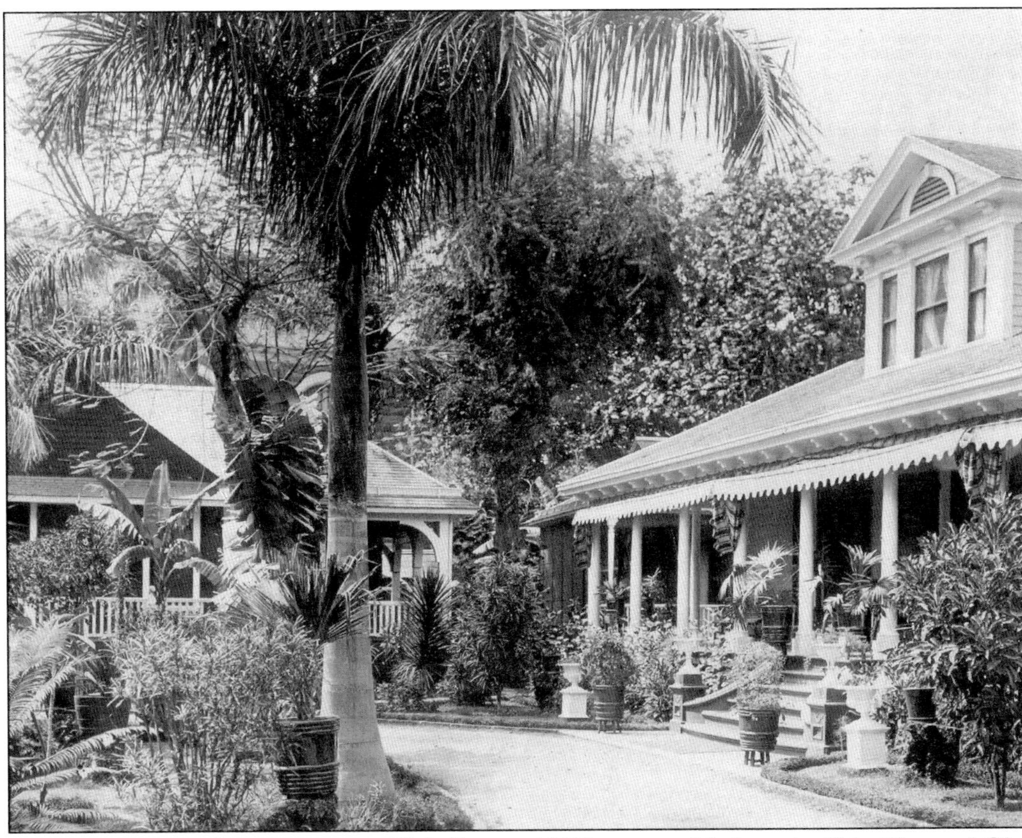

UNIVERSITY CLUB. The University Club (begun 1903) was modeled on the Yale-Harvard Club where many missionary children were members. The organization rented part of the Royal Hawaiian Hotel grounds and supported establishing a College of Hawaii. Once the college was created, the club established scholarship programs. The club also supported a college club for college women and the Footlights Club, a forerunner of the Honolulu Community Theatre. The University Club merged with the Pacific Club in 1930. (HSA.)

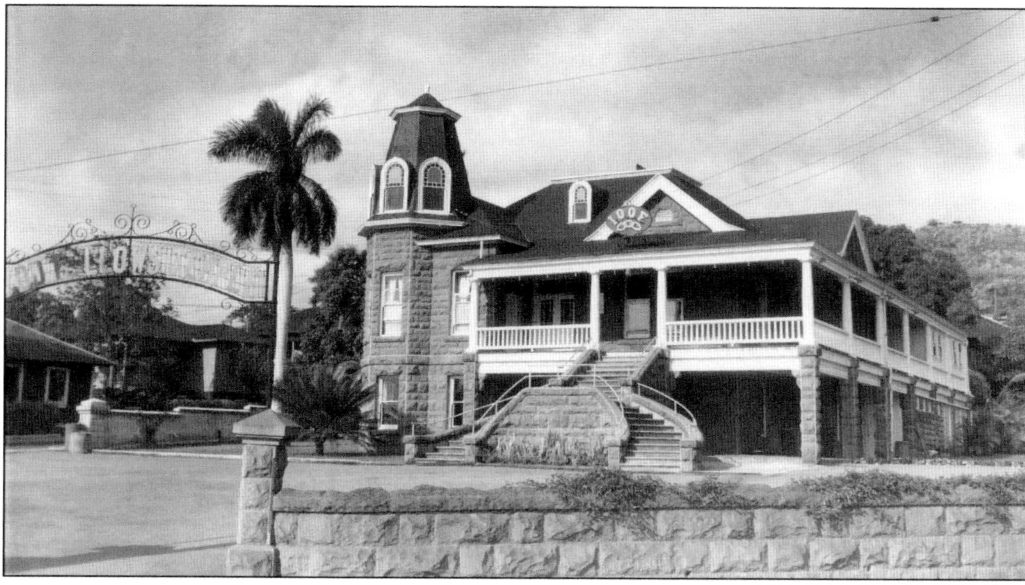

INDEPENDENT ORDER OF ODD FELLOWS (IOOF). Members of this benevolent society begun in 18th-century England were considered "odd" because they were organized to give aid to the needy without recognition. The first IOOF building in Honolulu was erected near the mauka-Ewa corner of Fort and King in 1859. This structure, at Alapai and Lunalilo Streets, served as the Lusitana Society headquarters before becoming the IOOF hall in 1924. The IOOF moved to Atkinson Boulevard in 1947. (Bishop Museum.)

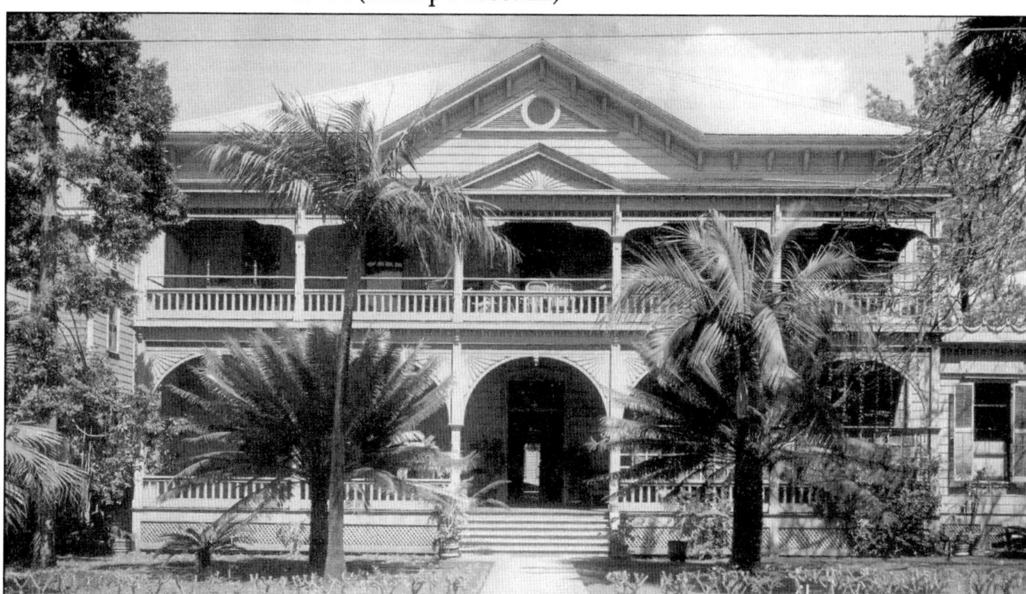

THE PACIFIC CLUB. Often thought of locally as an organization for the well-to-do, the club began life in 1851 known as, of all things, "The Mess" on Maunakea Street. It then became the British Club based upon the citizenship of the majority of its members before branching out more widely as the Pacific Club. It was located from 1861 to 1926 on a lot between Union and Alakea Streets (pictured), and then it relocated to the former Archibald Cleghorn/James Campbell residence on Queen Emma Street. (HSA.)

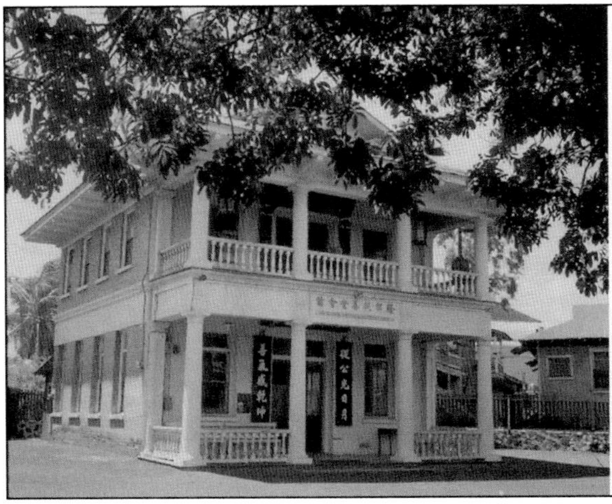

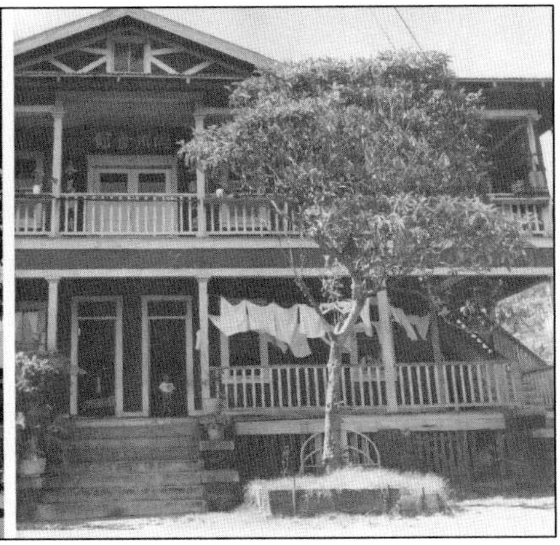

LUNG DO CHUNG SIN TONG BENEVOLENT SOCIETY AND KWONG CHAU SOCIETY (GUO ZHOU HUI GUAN). This tong (left) aided Chinese immigrants from Lung Doo/Longdu Province. This Aala Lane building, constructed in 1895, served as a meeting hall and residence for indigent members. The vertical placards on either side of the door were poetic couplets for good fortune for the tong. The Kwong Chau Society (right), the oldest Chinese society in the country, was built in 1922 on Webb Lane. (Photographs by Nancy Bannick; HSA.)

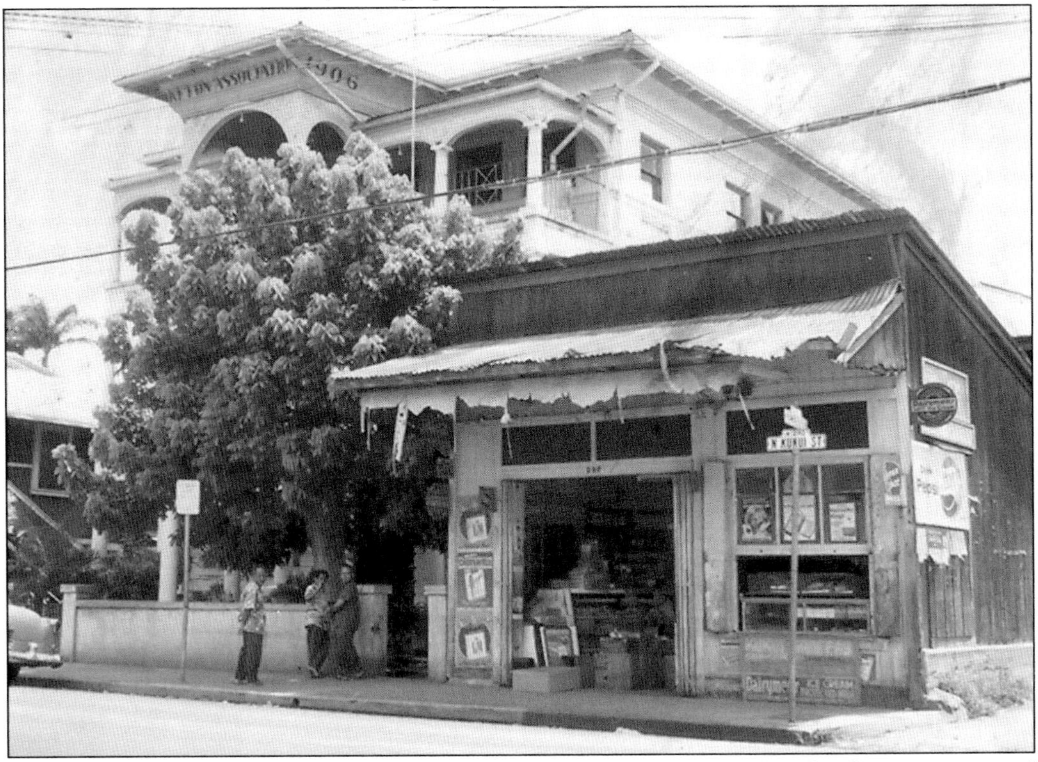

KET ON ASSOCIATION. Founded in the Kaneohe area in 1869, the Ket On Society is a triad fraternal organization. In 1899, the society moved to North Kukui Street, and on January 8, 1904, Dr. Sun Yat Sen became a member before returning home to establish the Republic of China. Ket On, like many similar organizations, rented out part of its premises for income to support itself. Note the small grocery on the right. (Photograph by Nancy Bannick; HSA.)

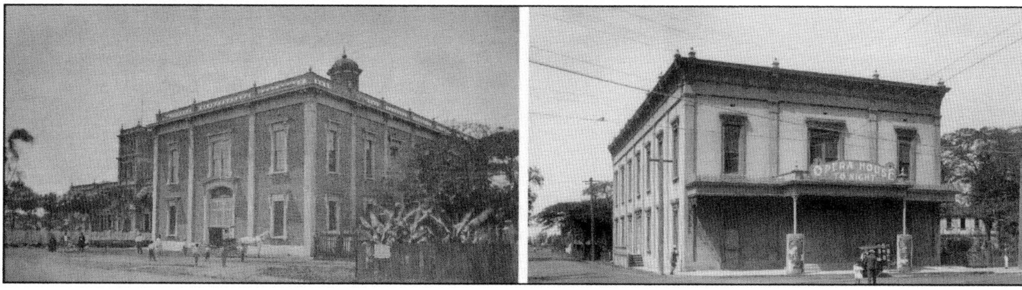

THEATERS, MUSIC HALL, AND OPERA HOUSE. The Music Hall, opened in 1881 at Mililani and South King Streets, witnessed the January 17, 1893, overthrow of the monarchy. It burned in 1895, but a new Opera House opened the next year. Both facilities benefited from the talents of both local and international production companies. The first public film showing in Honolulu occurred here in 1897. The Opera House was demolished in 1917, and the US Post Office Custom House and Court House took its place in 1922. (HSA.)

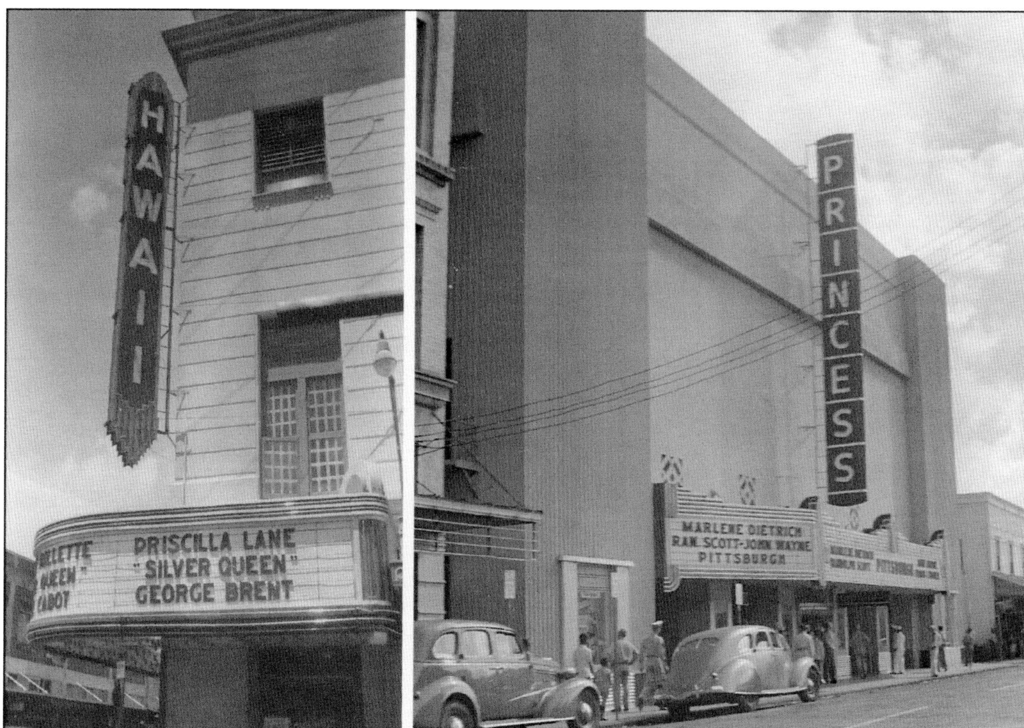

HAWAII AND PRINCESS THEATRES. The Hawaii and Princess Theatres were second-generation showplaces both built on the sites of previous entertainment venues. The theaters bridged the gap from vaudeville to films in 1922 by being equipped for both live performances and moving pictures. Their interiors were elaborate, featuring art, spacious lobbies, and plush seating. Later, remodeling of the Hawaii featured the neon of Robert "Bozo" Shigemura, while the original arched entrances of the Princess Theatre were eliminated by architect Vladimir Ossipoff. (USAMH.)

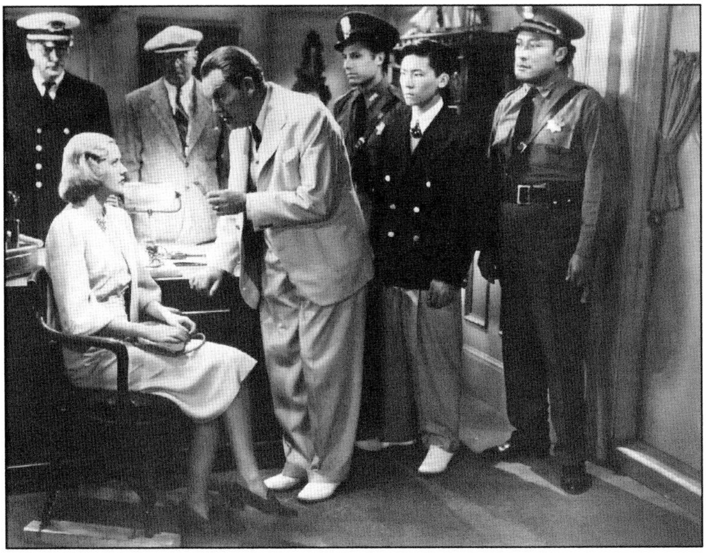

Charlie Chan in Honolulu. On shipboard in Honolulu Harbor, Charlie Chan questions a witness in this film still. It was filmed in 1938 and mostly on sound stages with a few stock and rear-screen projection shots of palm trees and harbor. Note two pieces of wood were placed under the actress's chair to establish the filmmaking sight lines. The actors are Sidney Toler as Charlie and Victor Sen Yung as Number Two Son. (Anonymous.)

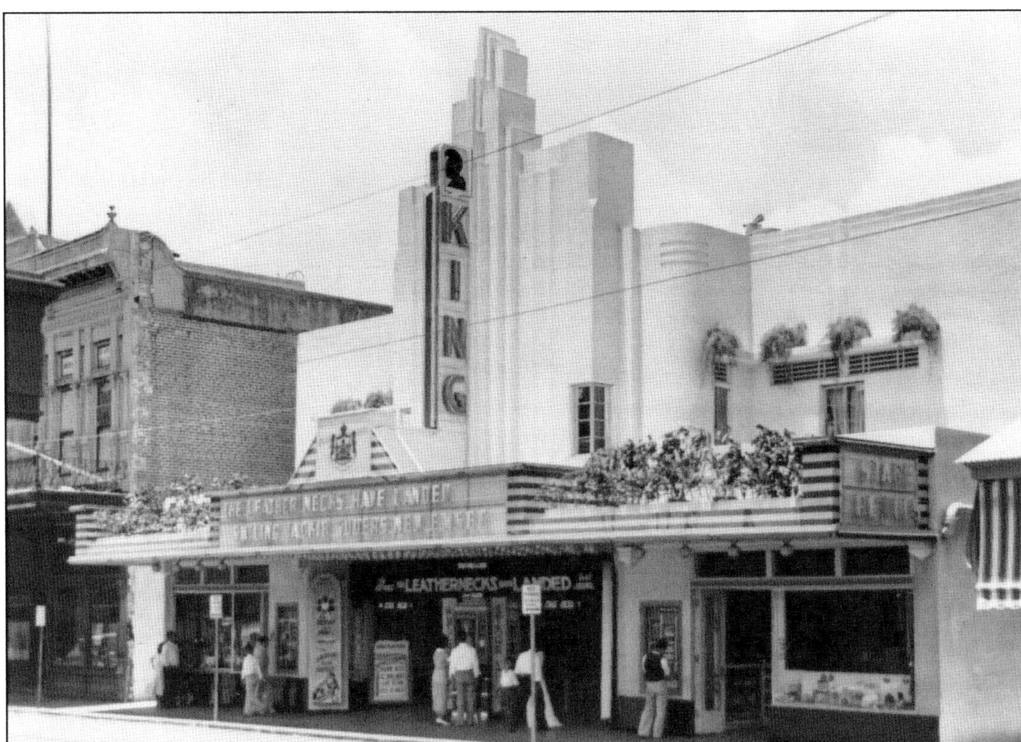

King Theatre. Located on the makai side of King Street between Bethel and Fort, the King Theatre opened in 1935 as a combination motion picture and live-entertainment facility. It originally had 1,000 seats and was the city's last vaudeville theater. The King was the site of the world premieres of Elvis Presley's *Blue Hawaii*, *Hawaiian Paradise,* and *Girls, Girls, Girls.* The theater was later subdivided before closing in 1986. It was the last of downtown's movie showcases. (USAMH.)

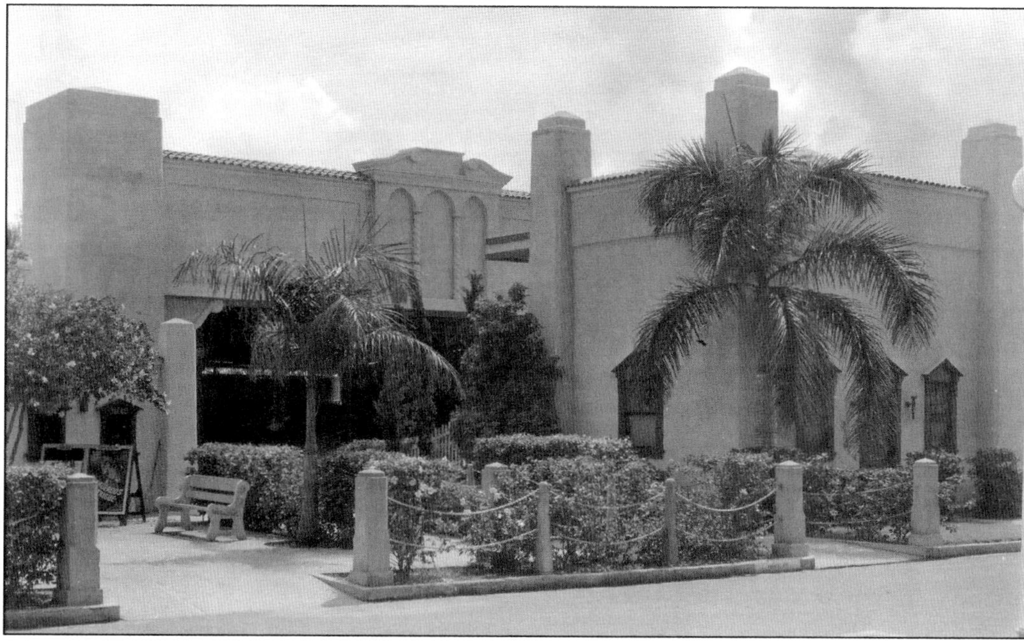

FORT ARMSTRONG THEATRE. Named for Maui-born and US Civil War Union hero Gen. Samuel C. Armstrong, Fort Armstrong was developed by filling in 76 acres of Kaakaukukui Reef. The Fort Armstrong Theatre used inexpensive trusses that allowed open-air ventilation. Its Moorish Revival architecture was popular for theaters of the 1930s and reminds one of Laurel and Hardy Foreign Legion movie sets. Forrest Avenue and an elaborate wall along Ala Moana Boulevard are all that is left of the base. (Both, USAMH.)

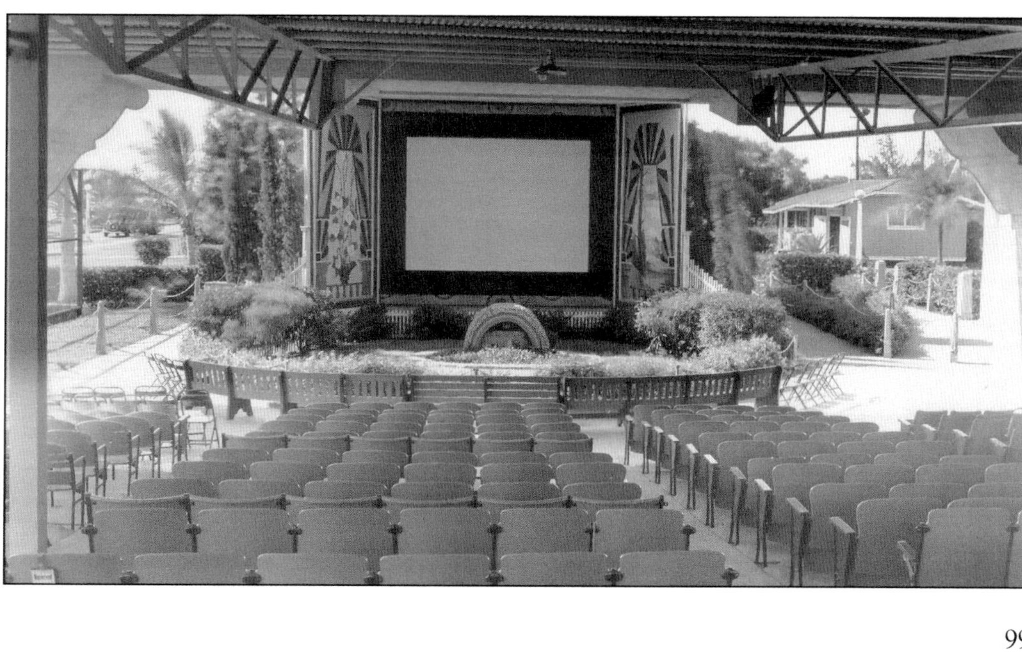

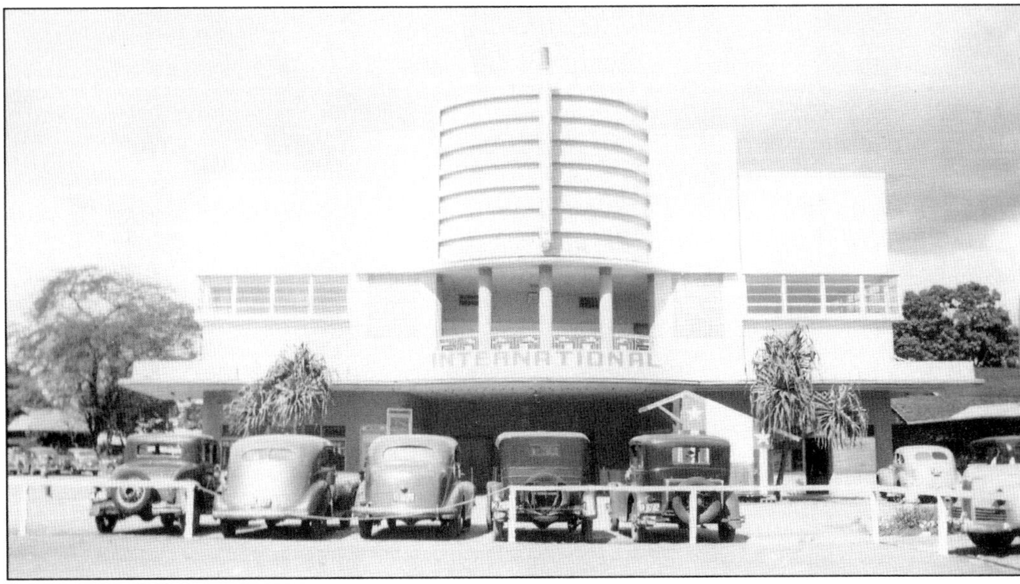

THE INTERNATIONAL THEATRE. The International Theatre (Kokusai) had the misfortune of opening on May 7, 1941, at 1246 Aala Street Extension (Ewa of the Toyo Theatre) and closed when the war broke out on December 7. Later reopening, it showed Hollywood films until closing in 1963. Its rounded Streamline Moderne architecture, designed by local architect Hego Fuchino, was a departure from the Asian-themed theaters or the palaces in downtown and Aala. (USAMH.)

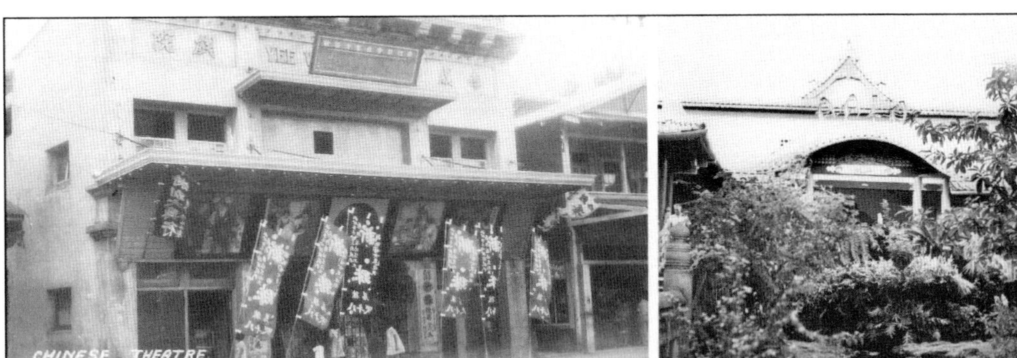

AALA THEATRES. There were two Aala Theatres. The earliest Aala Theatre (1079 Aala Street) was built around 1903 to stage Chinese drama and later displayed Japanese programs. It was known under many names, including Tong Lock, Honolulu, Aala, and Asia before closing in the 1960s. During the war, Toyo Theatre at 1230 College Walk (right) was renamed Aala (1942), and later restored to Toyo (1953). Simultaneously, the movies changed from Japanese releases, to second-run Hollywood movies, and back to Japanese films. (Left, Lowell Angell Collection; right photograph by Toshiharu Murai.)

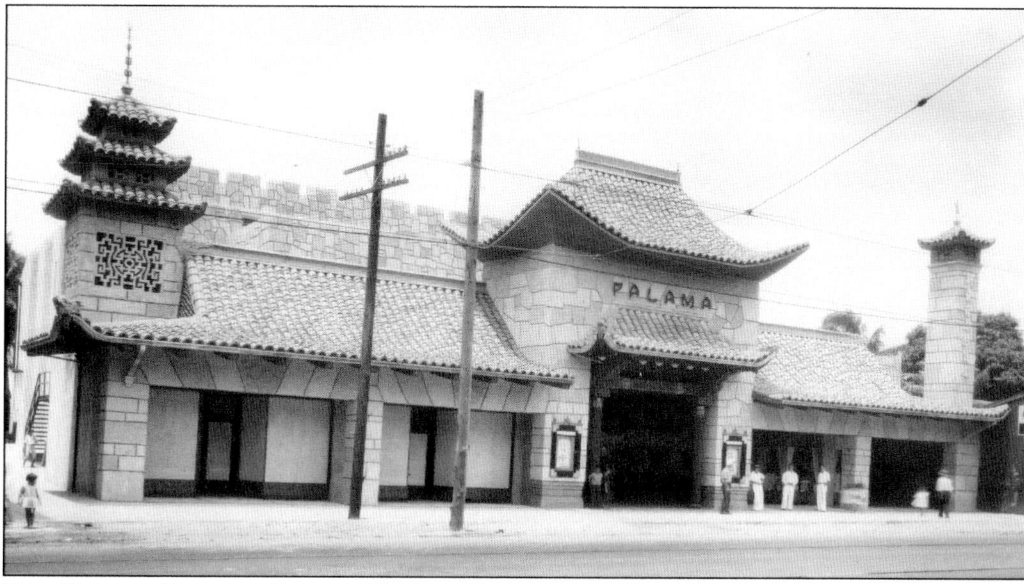

NEW PALAMA THEATRE. Designed by Lou E. Davis, the New Palama Theatre was constructed in 1930. The building seated 1,400 and evoked the flavor of nearby China and Japantowns through illuminated pagoda towers, green glazed terra-cotta tiles, and art copied from Peking's Forbidden City. The theater boasted an extra-large lobby and four-store arcade. It closed in the 1960s, was reopened in 1970 by Filipino movie star Fernando Poe Jr. (who renamed it Zamboanga), but closed again within the decade. (HSA.)

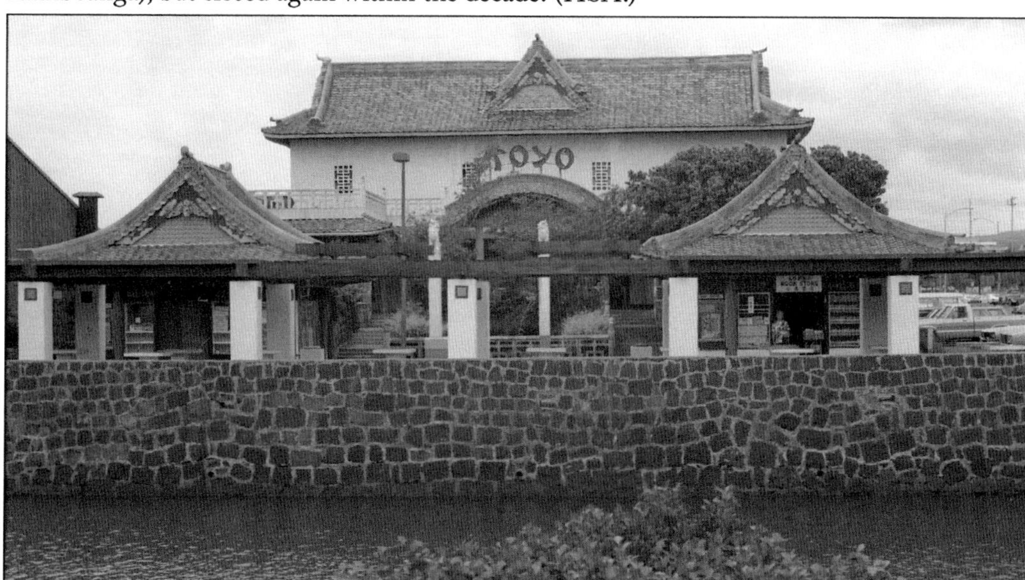

TOYO THEATRE. This 1,000-seat theater was intended to show primarily Japanese films, many of which were *chambara* (samurai sword-fighting films), to the large Japanese American population in Chinatown, Aala, Liliha, Iwilei, and Palama. This movie house was designed by premier architect Charles Dickey, who paid exquisite attention to Japanese architectural details. At the time of its construction in 1938, the Japanese-speaking Honolulu Town was 30–40 percent of the population. (Photograph by Nancy Bannick; HHF.)

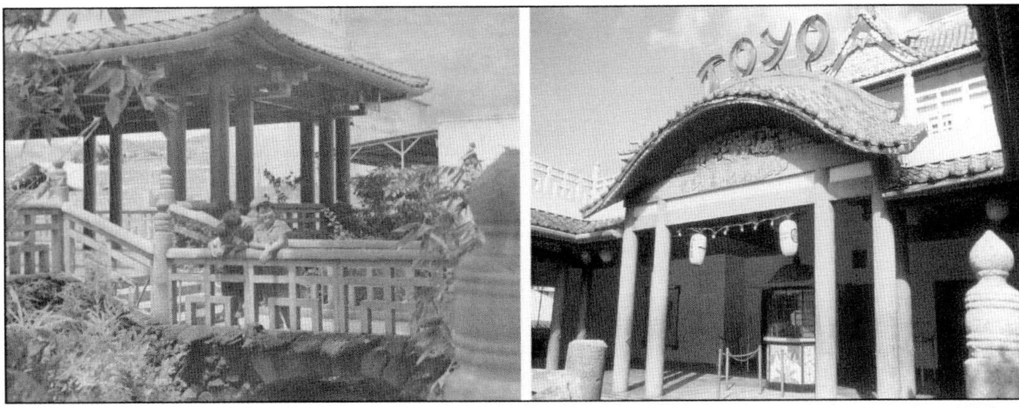

TOYO THEATRE ARCHED BRIDGE AND LANAI. In 1938, Harriet Natsuyama, her mother, Yakue, and her brother, Ernest, stand on the arched bridge over the pond within the front gardens of the Toyo Theatre. The koi (carp) gracefully swam below. Beyond the bridge, a *karahafu* (undulating Japanese gabled lanai roof) focused moviegoers toward the ornate box office and actual entrance to the theater. (Left photograph by Kenjiro Natsuyama; right photograph by Brian Suzuki.)

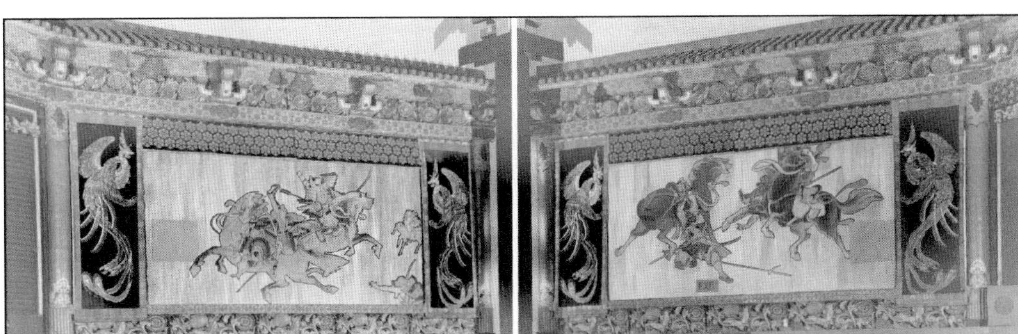

PHOENIX AND SAMURAI SWORD FIGHTING ACTION SCENES INSIDE THE TOYO. Samurai were often closely associated with fighting skills while on horseback. The highly ornate gold ornamentation more closely resembled Buddhist temple sanctuaries rather than the austere settings in samurai film classics of the 1930s. Note the horizontal motif, above the samurai horse scenes, has ornamental Buddhist temple brackets used to support the cantilevers of heavy tiled roofs. (SHPD.)

Five

The Raucous Nighttown

It has been suggested that, during the whaling era, the islands' economy was significantly supported by prostitution. The government's policy on this vice varied over time. In 1900, nondescript and supervised "bull pens" constructed of wood in Iwilei were patrolled by policemen day and night. When Honolulu's social elite succeeded in closing these facilities in 1917, staff and clientele were dispersed underground into areas such as Aala. By 1940, prostitution was still technically illegal, but new facilities had appeared throughout downtown due to an unofficial policy of efficiently meeting market demand for "servicing" ever-larger numbers of military personnel. The "ladies of the evening" reacted to the increased war workload in 1942 by striking against police rules that limited their mobility and rights of domicile, determining rightly that the military would force local police chief William Gabrielson to rescind such policies. By September 1944, the coming Allied victory had moved theater of war operations away from Hawaii and thus changed the local political equation. The brothels were then closed.

But Honolulu's downtown has been, and continues to be, notorious for its nightly entertainment excesses. The Reverend Samuel C. Damon, whose Seaman's Bethel (Church) stood on King Street in the mid-1800s, had as his immediate neighbors grog shops, dance halls, and other facilities of questionable character. When Queen's Hospital opened in 1859, the discussion was whether prostitutes should receive medical aid. The hospital compromised and placed prostitute patients in a substandard building on the grounds.

For much of the 20th century, Hotel Street was the epicenter of entertainment and drinking. In the 1930s, shortwave radios brought jazz to Hawaii musicians, and the Casino Ballroom at Beretania and Nuuanu successfully broadcast the Brown Cats and its dance hall jazz locally. African Americans lived in the area but surprisingly found Hawaii's openness for all peoples did not extend to the clubs—African American musicians could perform but not be patrons. The musicians changed the climate and also secured mainland union-scale pay. There was a great burst of jazz clubs during the war years and into the 1950s as the influx of military swelled the jazz audiences and number of musicians playing. With the postwar decrease of the military and the new entertainment center of Waikiki, Hotel Street's energy waned.

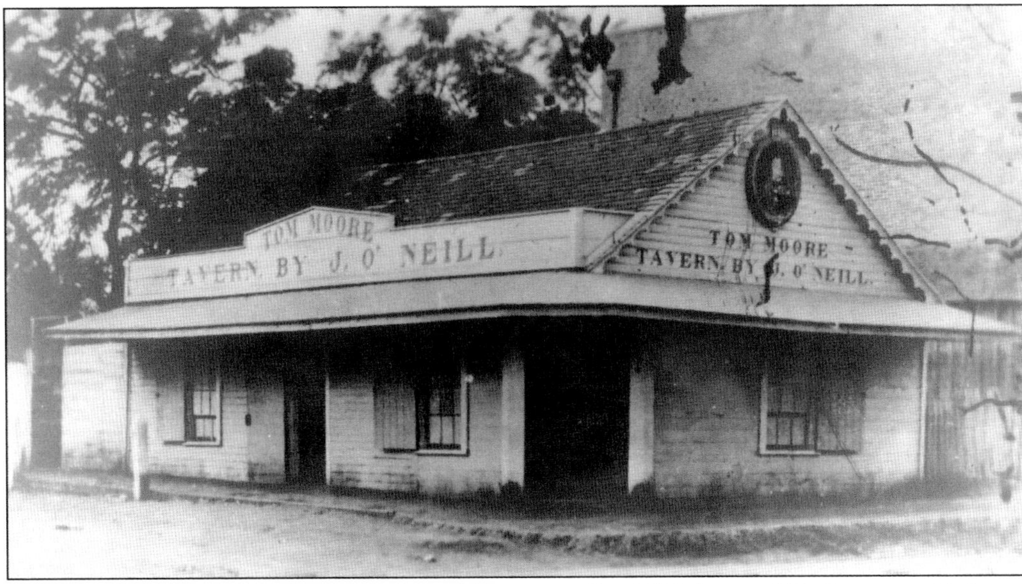

TOM MOORE TAVERN, KING AND FORT, 1865. Proprietor Jim O'Neil named his liquor establishment after his hero, Sir Thomas More, the English counselor who refused King Henry's 1584 separation from the Catholic Church. (Curiously, O'Neil misspelled More's name.) From the 1820s through the 1870s, during the times of the sandalwood trade and the whaling industry, there were perhaps hundreds of ships per year in the port whose sailors frequented these liquor establishments. Think of the numbers of sailors with shore leave. (HSA.)

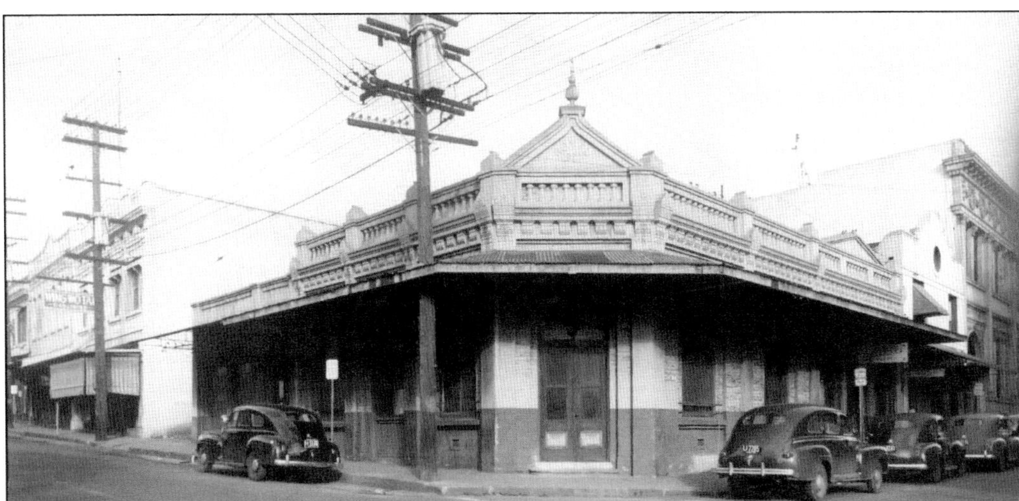

ROYAL SALOON. During the whaling period, the royal government simply looked the other way as sailors patronized saloons and taverns along Nuuanu Avenue. By 1862, the government had sufficiently disengaged itself from missionary influence to realize that legalization of liquor (and sale of liquor permits) could be a significant source of government revenue. Walter C. Peacock, a local barkeeper and businessman, acquired a saloon on this site and erected this new building in 1890. (Bishop Museum.)

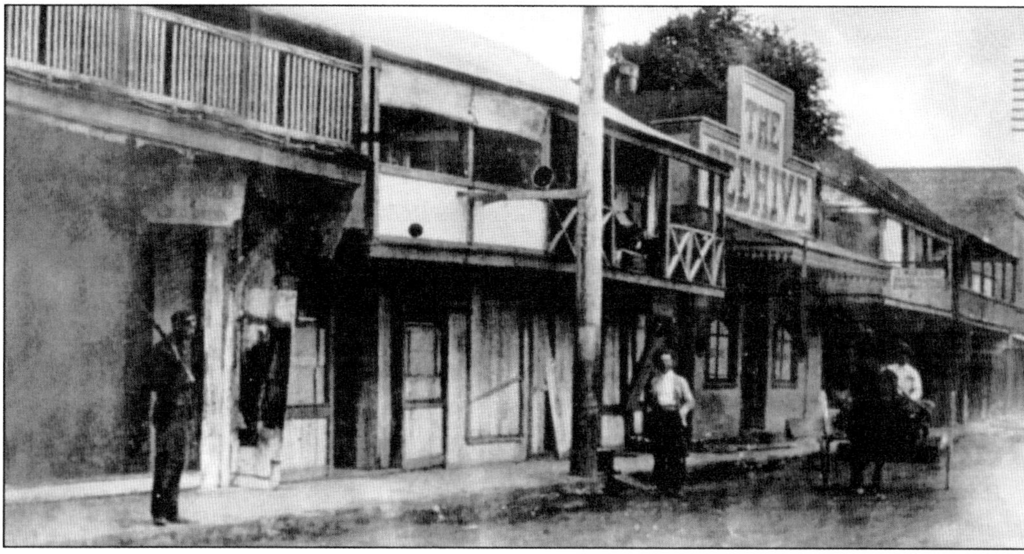

THE BEEHIVE, c. 1900. By its name, this saloon must have been abuzz with patrons. The establishment was operated by H. Vierra and had a false facade with a huge sign relative to the other bars or grog shops on the street. Notice this entire Nuuanu block has second stories that overhang the sidewalk. In 1900, many urban streets were still unpaved. (Palama Settlement.)

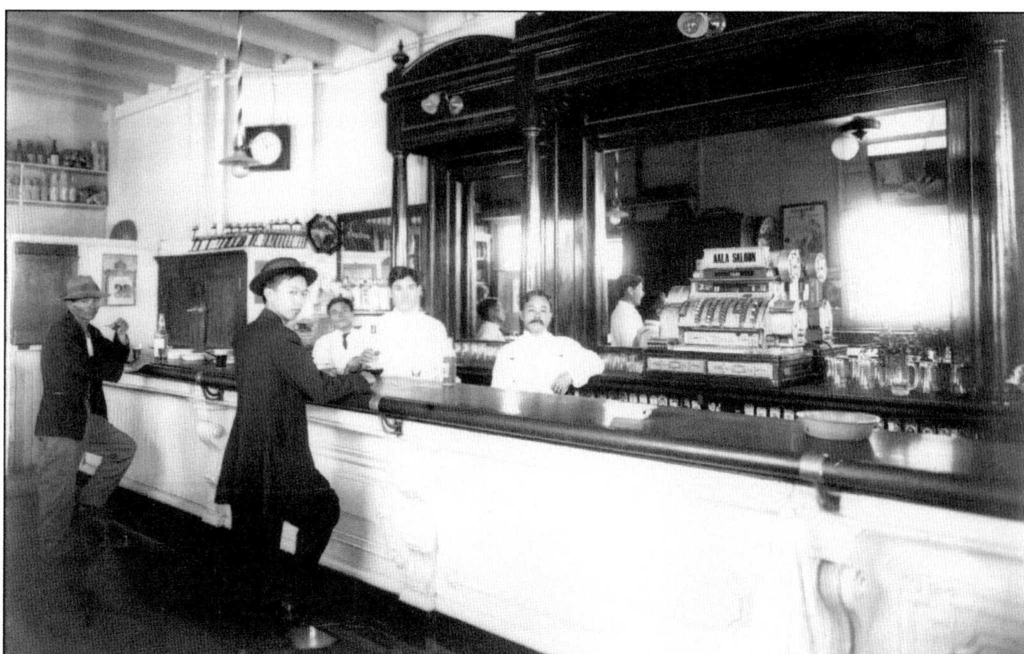

AALA SALOON, NEAR AALA AND BERETANIA STREETS, c. 1915. The Japantown neighborhood of Aala, though heavily beholden to Japanese trade goods, was also strongly influenced by American establishments. Following the 1900 Chinatown fire, at the time of this photograph, there had been a large influx of people into Aala. The dress and posture of the patrons and the interior decor of the bar are clearly early-20th-century American. (Photograph by On Char; Bishop Museum.)

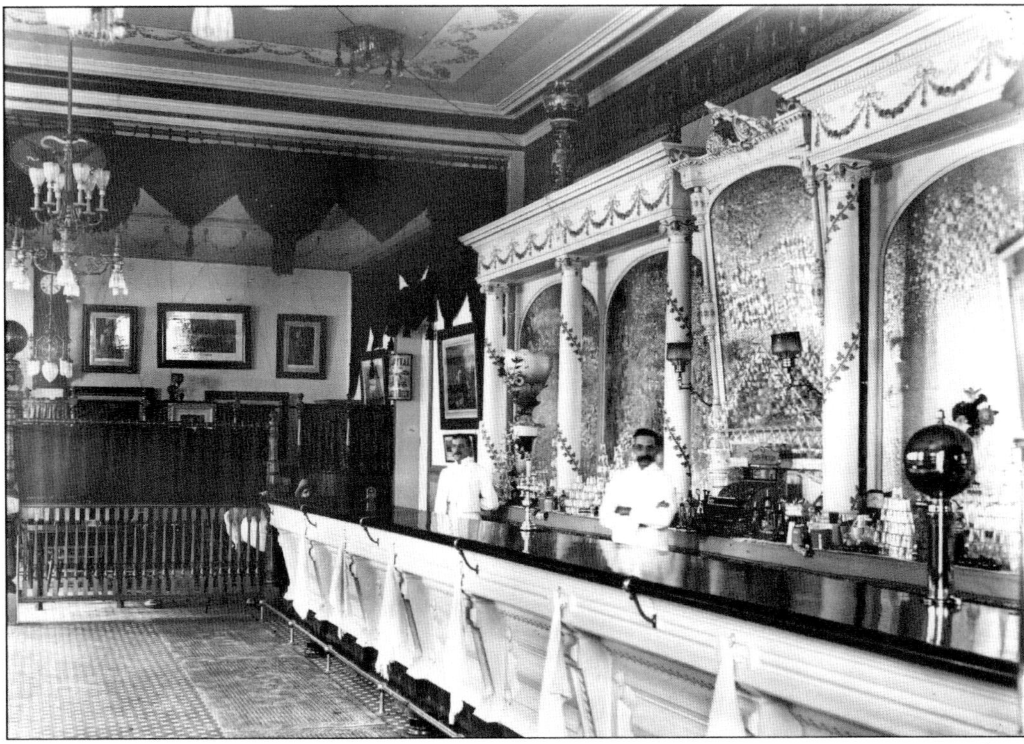

HOFFMAN'S SALOON, NUUANU AND HOTEL STREETS. This high-end saloon, with its ornate decor and partitioned area for private business meetings, was competing for the "best" patrons, though it is unlikely that women frequented such bars in the early 20th century. Towels hanging under the bar and spittoons on the floor mirror mainland establishments. L.H. Dee was the proprietor. (Bishop Museum.)

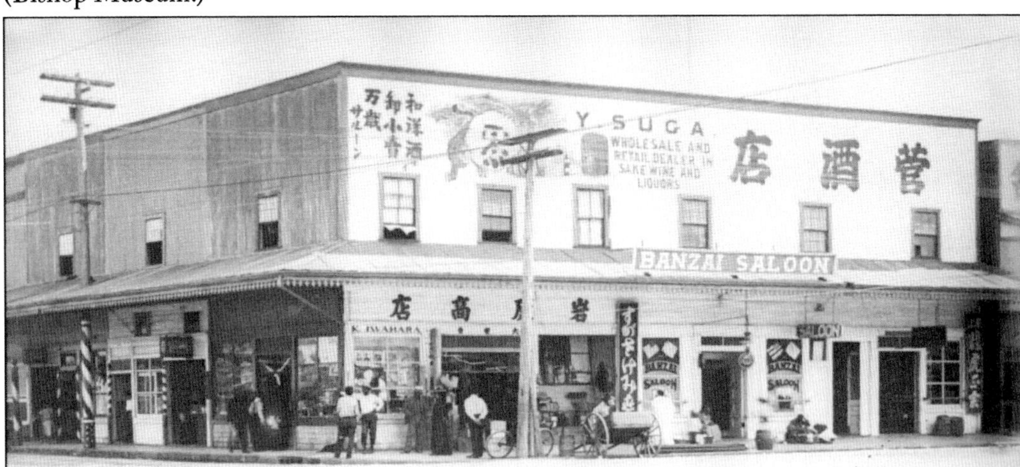

BANZAI SALOON, JUNE 1911. Like the Ginza and Chuo Rengo, Aala Rengo was a retail association catering to a mostly Japanese clientele. Aala Rengo was located in the block bounded by Iwilei, King, and Awa Streets makai of Aala Park and close to the Oahu Railroad and Land Company's Honolulu Station. This allowed Aala Rengo's Banzai Saloon to service patrons arriving in town, waiting out the spouse's shopping activities, or having one last one before the long train ride back home. (Uyeda Collection.)

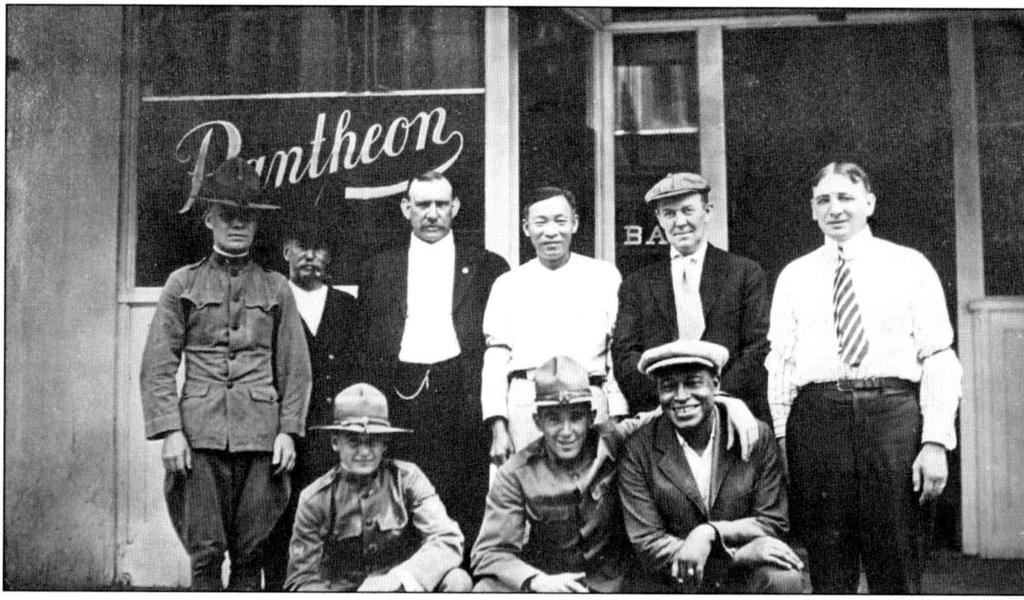

PANTHEON SALOON, 1918. Joseph Silva's Pantheon, the oldest continually operated saloon, originated in 1883 and included a traditional large wooden bar that had made the trip around Cape Horn. The saloon occupied three different locations over time, including the building shown here, erected in 1911 at 1129 Nuuanu Avenue. Bars such as the Pantheon welcomed all. It was a custom for men, no matter what their occupations, to wear jackets and hats or caps. The men in shirtsleeves with garters are the bartenders. (Bishop Museum.)

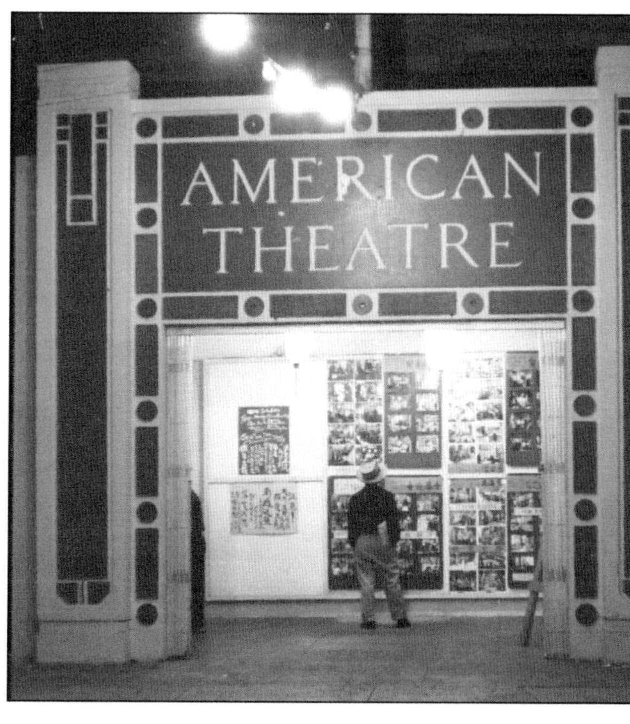

POLITICS AND AMERICAN THEATRE, c. 1955. At the present location of the Maunakea Marketplace on Hotel Street, the American Theatre was the site of a December 14, 1903 speech by Chinese nationalist Dr. Sun Yat Sen advocating the armed overthrow of the Manchu government. Sun, who came to Hawaii six times, was educated and raised funds for his revolutionary efforts here. This image shows the theater's decline to peepshow-parlor status by the 1950s. (Photograph from Laurence Hata Collection, Bishop Museum.)

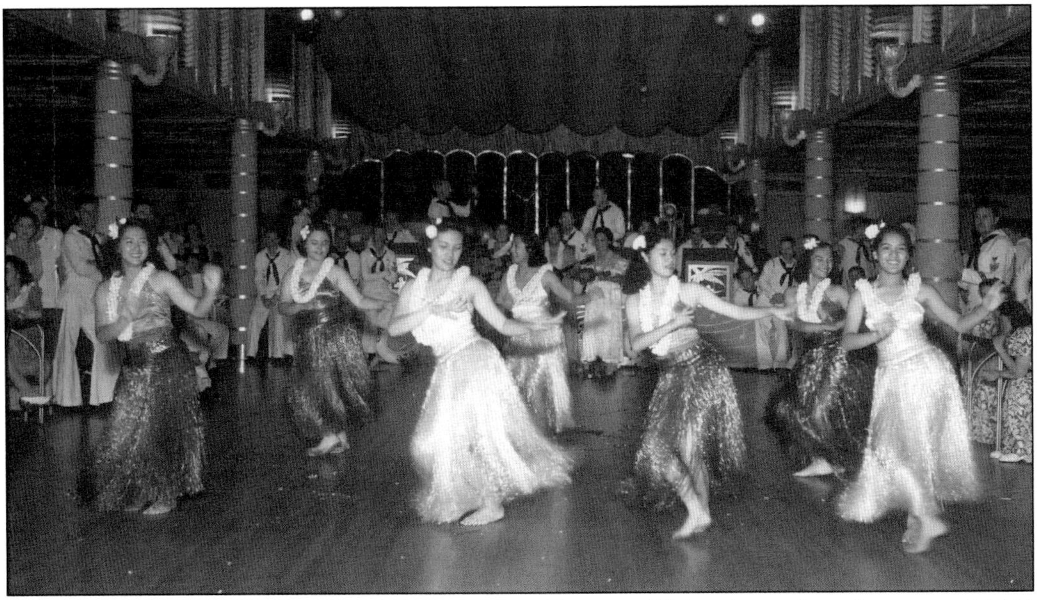

FLOOR SHOW AT ALEXANDER YOUNG HOTEL ROOF GARDEN. This gaiety takes place around 1941 and before World War II, though the war is looming in the near future. Note that the dancers wear cellophane "grass" skirts and dance on a spacious wooden dance floor. The decor of the room is contemporary art deco. The view from the roof at sunset, minus the high-rises of today, must have been spectacular. The crowd of sailors has no idea how close to war they really are. (Photograph by Tai Sing Loo; Bishop Museum.)

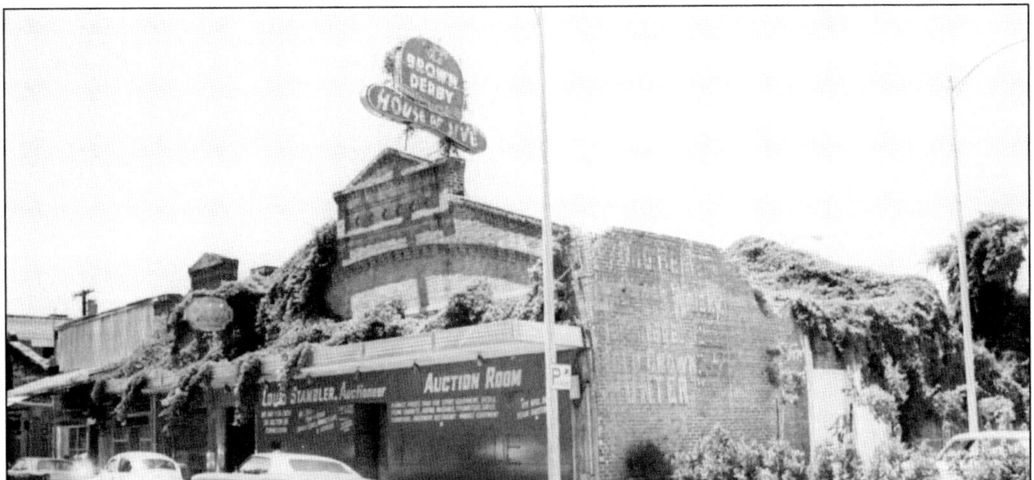

SWINGTIME IN HONOLULU, THE BROWN DERBY. Jazz was at its hottest between 1947 and 1959, with music in clubs such as the Blue Note, Gibson's Bar, Two Jacks, Tradewinds, Swing Club, Playroom, and the Brown Derby (at 1166 Nuuanu Avenue). Note the "House of Jive" is covered with an aggressive vegetative covering. "Are you hip to the jive?" (SHPD.)

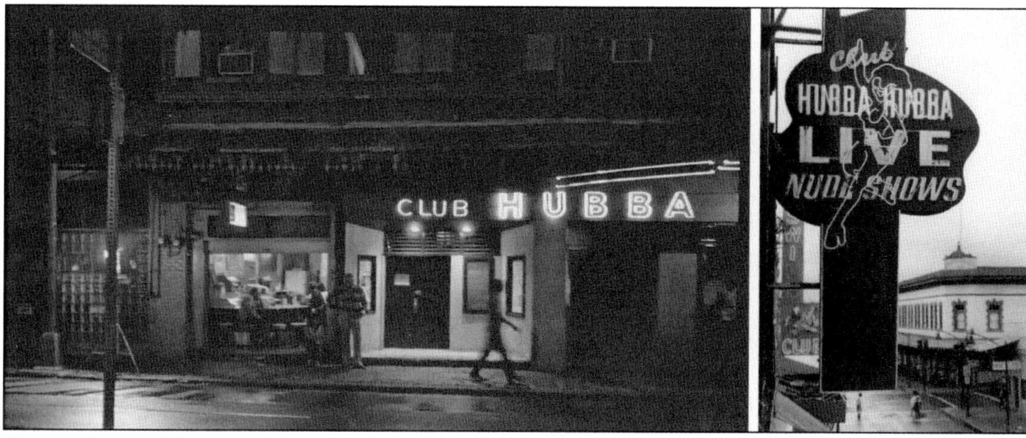

CLUB HUBBA HUBBA. A survivor of the 1900 fire, this redbrick building had a nondescript mercantile life selling general merchandise and photographs until 1947. The year Café Hubba Hubba opened, it became one of the most noted jazz, burlesque, and later strip-show venues in the area. The name changed slightly to Club Hubba Hubba in 1953, featuring "Bozo" Shigemura's neon sign advertising "LIVE nude shows" with a superimposed high-heeled dancing woman. (Photographs by William Lowe and Kristina Larssen.)

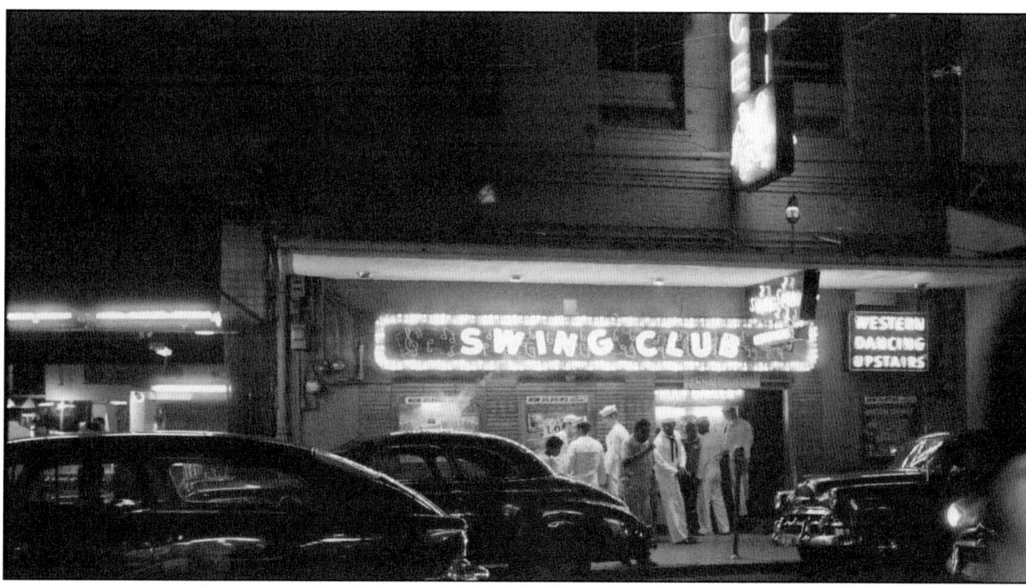

THE SWING CLUB. "It don't mean a thing if it ain't got that swing" on Hotel Street. The Swing Club opened at the end of the jazz heyday but remained in operation for 45 years. It had lots of neon inside and western dancing upstairs. The club mirrored the economic situation of Chinatown, featuring live music during the 1950s and 1960s. As the area became more rundown, it gradually featured pornographic films instead of live music, and strippers became the live entertainment. (Photograph from Laurence Hata Collection, Bishop Museum.)

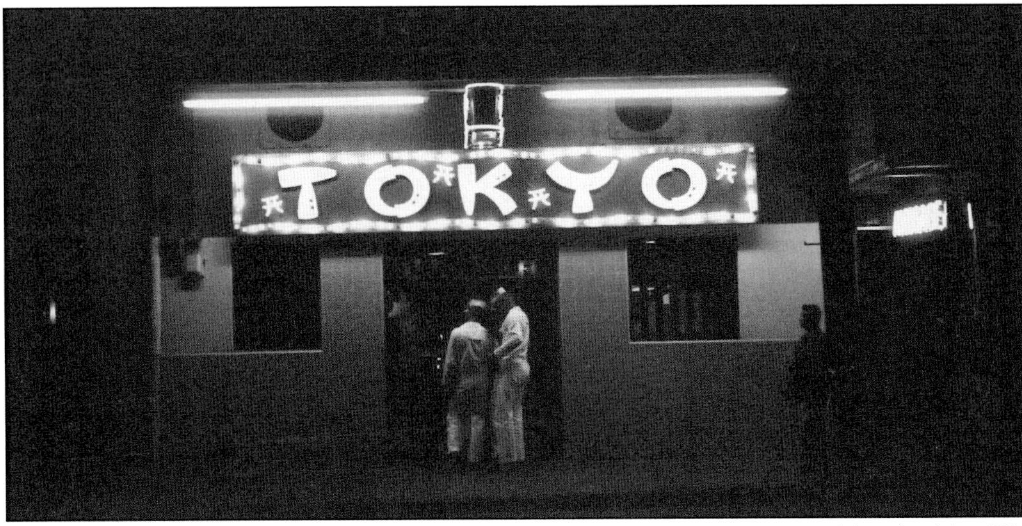

THE TOKYO BAR. The Hotel Street Tokyo Bar also appealed to military and locals alike. The Tokyo lettering approximates Asian calligraphy-style brushstrokes, and the repeated character on the neon sign has no Japanese meaning but vaguely looks like a *torii* (Japanese gate) motif. The sign suggests an exotic "oriental" flavor. (Photograph from Laurence Hata Collection, Bishop Museum.)

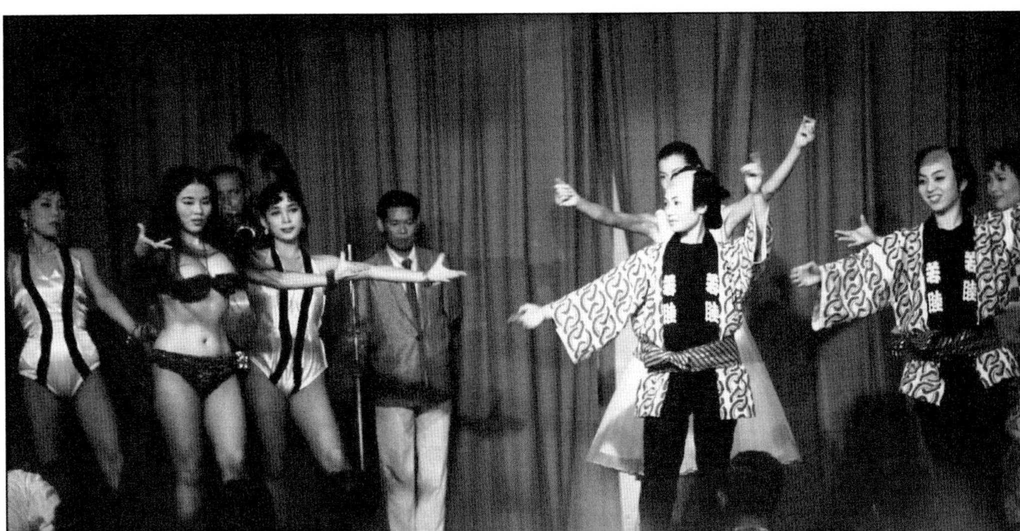

NIGHTCLUB FINALE, 1958. The Wakamutsu Troupe at this unknown nightspot is likely a Japanese group of professional dancers touring Hawaii. The costuming suggests Japanese folk-Kabuki or rural-dance styles. And, as if not to count any type of entertainment out, other women performers wear starched-petticoat dresses and bikinis. These theatricals were in the style of the Maunakea Street's Asahi Theatre folk-Kabuki, political-themed *shibai* (drama advocating better wages for sugar workers), and early-20th-century vaudeville. (Photograph from Laurence Hata Collection, Bishop Museum.)

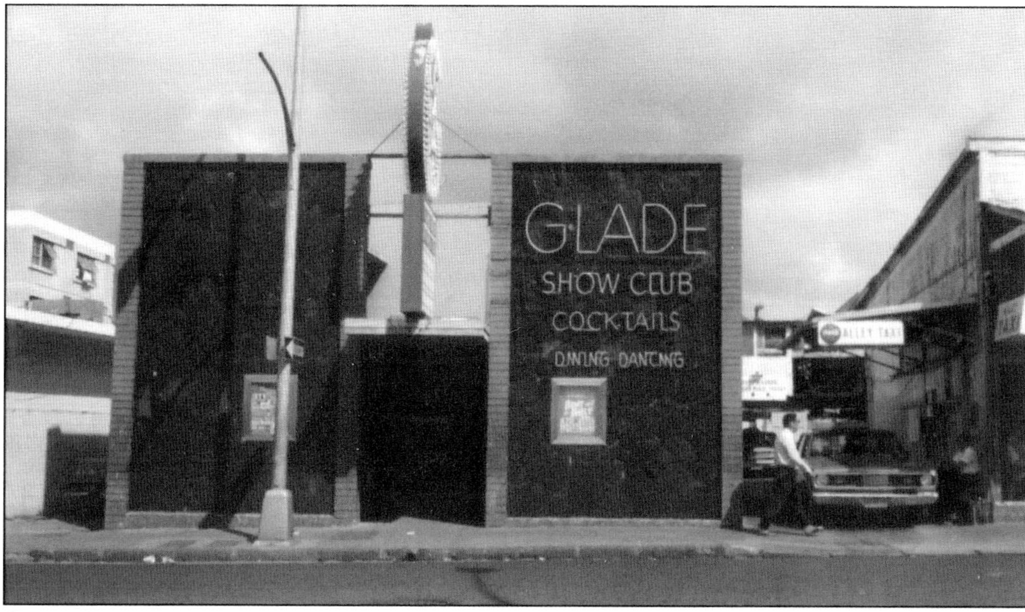

GLADE SHOW CLUB. Founded by local landlord Attilio "Tilly" Leonardi to bring in more business into the area, "The Glades" featured live music, floorshows, and drag shows. The club brought in busloads of tourists for early shows and locals for late shows between opening in 1964 and closure in 1981. Well-known *mahu* (gay or transsexual) performers on its multitiered stage included Prince Hanalei, Brandy Lee, and Macie Willliams. (SHPD.)

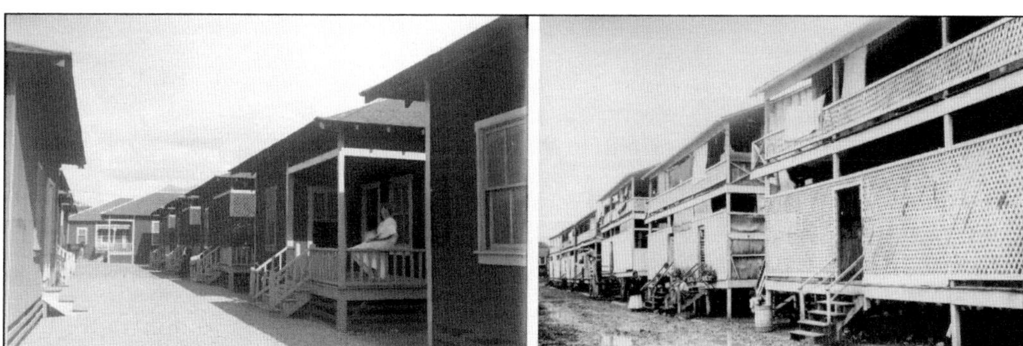

IWILEI PLEASURE PALACES, 1912 (LEFT) AND 1911 (RIGHT). In the early years of the 20th century, Iwilei was a flourishing red-light district until it was forced to close in 1917. Women had to produce weekly sanitary inspection certificates. It was a restricted area surrounded by a high wooden fence with no liquor establishments within. As much as "righteous" townsfolk worked to shut down the red-light district, they failed to understand that Iwilei ironically pumped lots of military and plantation-worker money through the women into Honolulu Town. (Photographs by Ray J. Baker; Bishop Museum and HHS.)

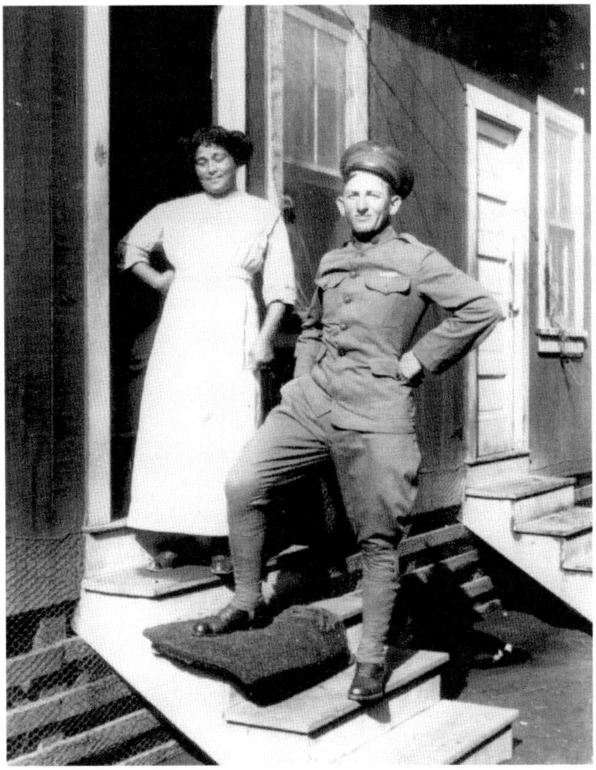

An Iwilei Prostitute and Friend, 1911. This photograph closely resembles a passage from "Rain," a short story by W. Somerset Maugham published in 1921: "Men wandered about, looking at the women who sat at their windows, reading or sewing, for the most part taking no notice of the passers-by; and like the women they were of all nationalities. There were Americans . . . somberly drunk, and soldiers from the regiments, white and black, quartered on the island; there were Japanese, walking in twos and threes; Hawaiians, Chinese in long robes, and Filipinos in preposterous hats. They were silent and as it were oppressed. Desire is sad." (HHS.)

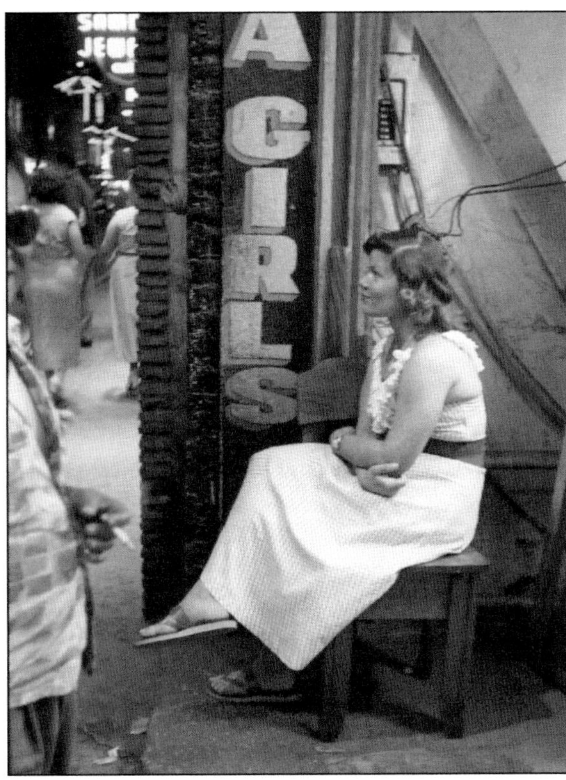

Chinatown Red Light District. Houses of prostitution ("boogie houses") spread from Iwilei to Chinatown before World War II. Although illegal, they made an unofficial agreement with the police to restrict themselves Ewa of Fort and makai of Kukui after the Senator and Ambassador "hotels" proved too close to the Nuuanu YMCA and the Harris Memorial Church. The girls were medically examined weekly and required to live in the houses, with curfew at 10:30 p.m. (Photograph from Laurence Hata Collection, Bishop Museum.)

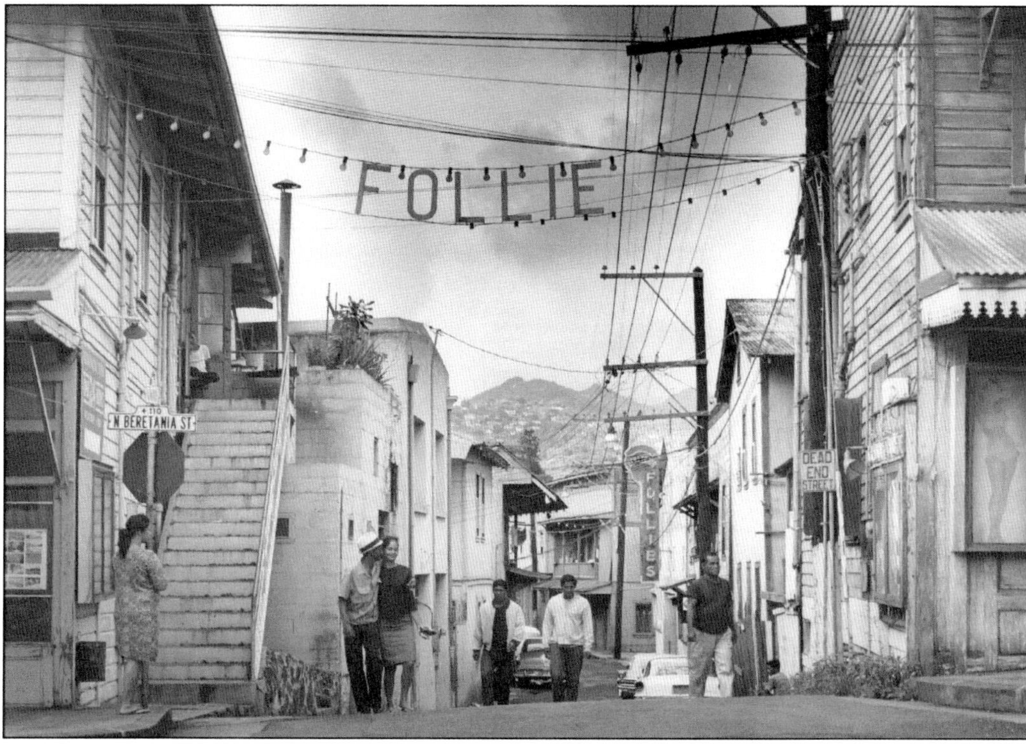

Burlesque at the Beretania Follies. Hawaii's pioneer burlesque house was the Beretania Theater, located at 1229 Kamanuwai Lane and mauka of Beretania, near the location of the first and second Kamakapili Church. It was a congested, narrow road where substandard buildings had been erected following the 1900 Chinatown fire. The Follies in this photograph had seen better days—the *s* is missing from the Follies street sign. This street was also known as Tin Pan Alley. (Photograph by Francis Haar; UHL–JCC.)

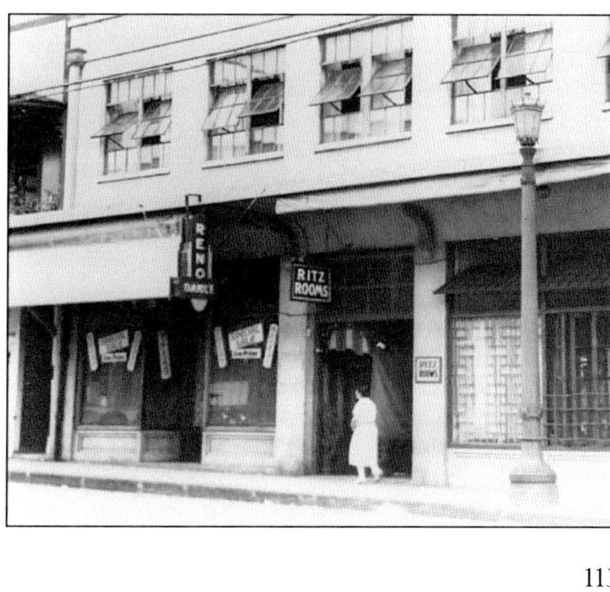

The Reno Dance Hall (First Floor); the Ritz Rooms (Second Floor). Buildings often had dance halls below and rooms upstairs. This brothel, owned by Chun Lai Shee, had a landlady, Helen Burton, and three girls who "worked" the premises. As the number of clients overwhelmed the limited number of girls available, a four-step mass production of services was employed. Boys would "climb the stairs," undress, wait, be "serviced," and clean up. The houses were closed in 1944 after a public tiff between a madam and the police. (USAMH.)

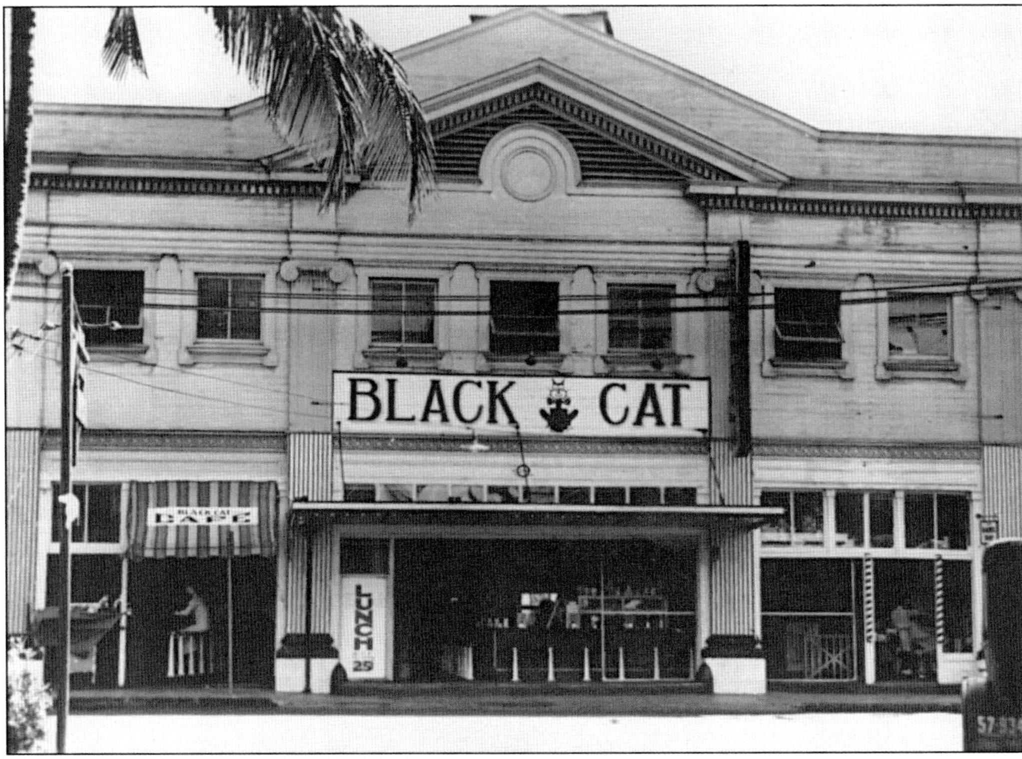

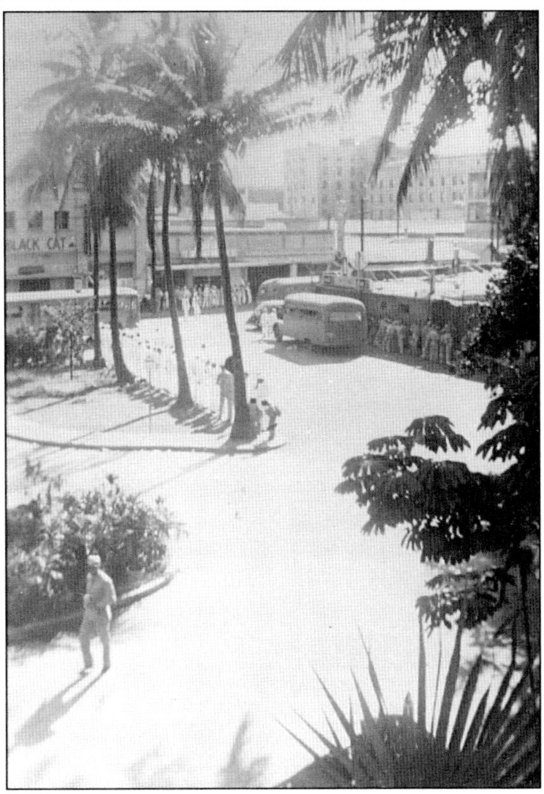

THE BLACK CAT. The Black Cat Café at the corner of Hotel and Richards was across from the Armed Forces YMCA. Its welcoming sign looked very much like the popular *Krazy Kat* cartoon. For servicemen with limited income, the friendly Black Cat's food was ideal. Prices were rock bottom: the menu in 1941 listed hotcakes for 10¢, hamburgers for 15¢, a half fried chicken with bacon for 60¢, and a porterhouse steak with mushrooms for $1. The café was open 24 hours, and the meals were especially generous for men ravenous from late night carousing on Hotel Street. Men could play slot machines or pose for souvenir photographs with "hula girls." In the 1930 photograph at left, servicemen are lined up waiting for buses to take them back to their bases—or possibly to eat more at the Black Cat. (Both, USAMH.)

Six

Unnatural Disasters

Hawaii's central location and long-term isolation in the North Pacific, combined with the town's unsurpassed and welcoming harbor, guaranteed that Honolulu would be the door through which most diseases entered. Scourges included measles, smallpox, and plague, resulting in mass deaths. In the 1850s, open carts collected the dead for burial in large, now unmarked cemeteries near the old Kakaako Fire Station on South Street.

Honolulu was initially developed on high ground near the waterfront. Unfortunately, streams often backed up, resulting in flooding in Chinatown, Aala, Kapalama, Kakaako, and Kewalo. For example, on February 28, 1935, a huge freak storm rained six inches in town with an additional 17 inches mauka, which raced downhill. Compounding that, "Some residents, who had never seen hailstones, refused at first to touch them, not knowing whether they are cold or hot," reported the *Frederick* (Maryland) *News* on March 3, 1935. The introduction of mosquitoes and the existence of untilled fields and untended *loi* (due to a declining population) were an unhealthy mix. Efforts to ease the devastating floods and the unchecked pestilence included the construction of a narrow Pauoa Stream channel to encourage flushing action, the erection of walls along Nuuanu Stream, and the filling of lowland areas such as Aala and Kewalo.

The original wooden compact town and waterfront fueled major fires on land in 1886 and 1900 and periodically among docked ships. Water pressure for firefighting was limited. It was no wonder that the first building and zoning codes in the city related to density, construction materials, and the prevention of fires.

Disposal of solid waste was always a challenge. Kewalo became famous for burning piles of rubbish whose smoke could be seen for miles before municipal incinerators ("crematoriums") were constructed. Periodic community trash collections (like recycling campaigns today) were so voluminous that even the present site of the federal building across from Iolani Palace was pressed into service as a burn site.

Sewage removal was also a problem. Cesspools poisoned the ground, while privies emptied directly into Nuuanu Stream or could simply overflow. The initial sewer system, the Kakaako Sewage Pumping Station of 1900, was followed by further initiatives in the 1920s and 1950s that were meant to handle population growth.

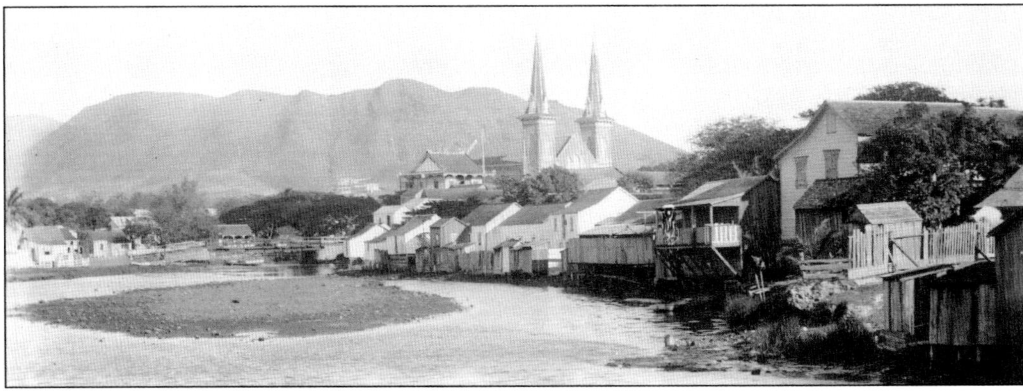

NUUANU STREAM BEFORE CHANNELIZATION AND NUUANU STREAM FLOOD. Above, in the distance are the twin spires of the second Kaumakapili Church on Beretania and the Punchbowl Crater beyond. Before 1900, Nuuanu Stream was very shallow and was unable to sweep out waste. Infrastructure such as storm drains, stream channelization, and sewers did not exist. As the town grew, the stream became a health hazard. Note outhouses perched over the edge of the water and a central "island" of alluvial deposits. As a result, when heavy rains pushed down Pauoa, Puehuehu, and Nuuanu Streams, privies built over the water were carried away, and roads and buildings flooded. Below, Kaumakapili Church is overcome by a flood near River and Beretania. (Both photographs by Frank Davey; Bishop Museum.)

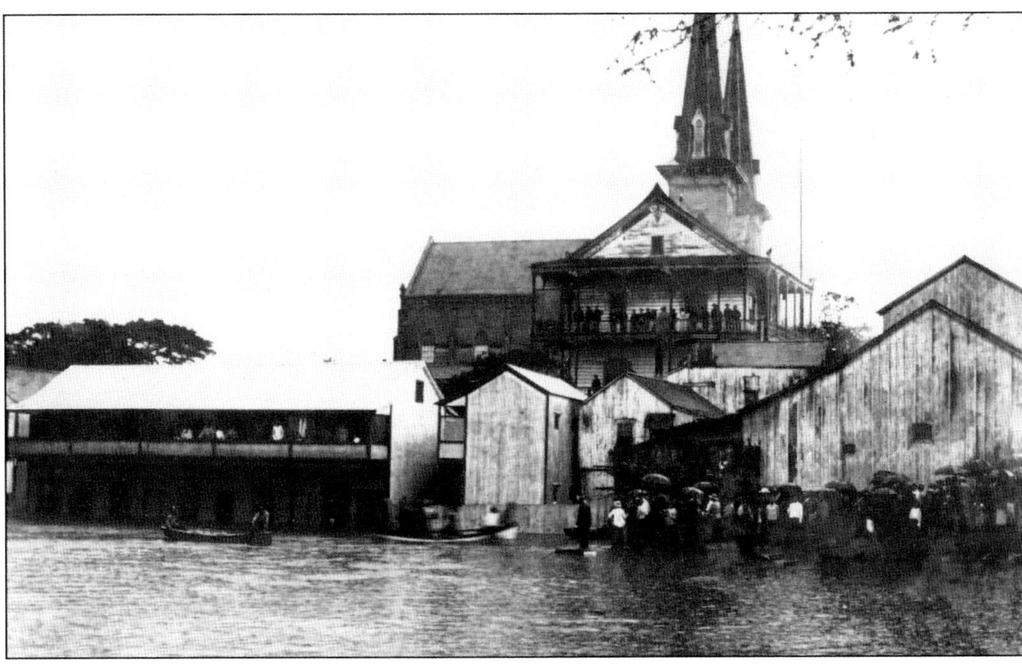

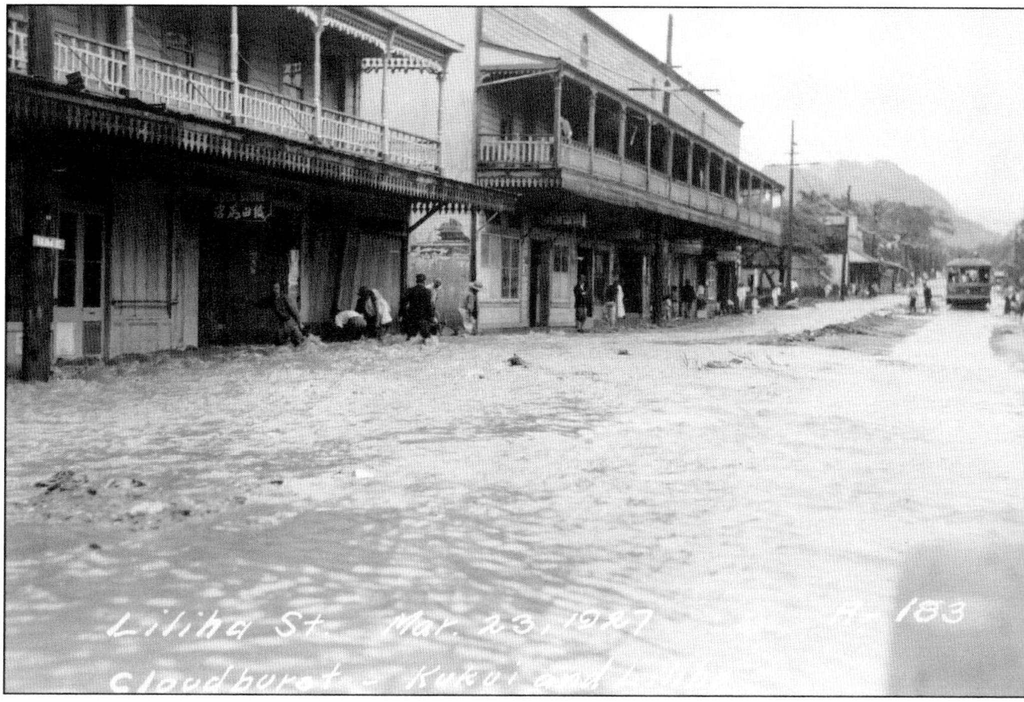

FLOOD ON LILIHA (LOOKING MAUKA) NEAR KUKUI, 1927. Over 2,000 acres of Honolulu are actually reclaimed (filled-in) land. Honolulu struggled to finance and build massive stream channelization and storm drain systems that would provide drainage protection for the above filled lands. Without these projects, stores and homes faced water damage and floating waste from overflowing dump pits. Note the streetcar making its way mauka to escape the worst of the flood caused by a recent cloudburst. (Bishop Museum.)

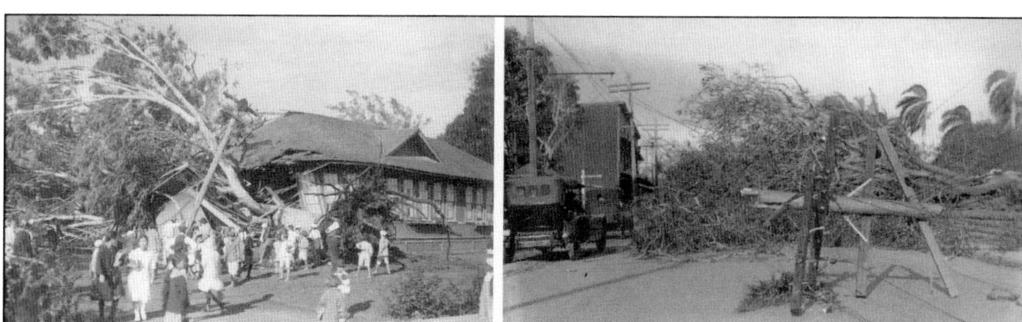

STORMS. As happens today, high winds and rain were capable of inflicting substantial damage. In 1916 or 1917, students and neighbors have come to view damage to a classroom at St. Andrew's Priory (left). The size of this uprooted tree can be judged by the height of the two students examining the roots in the center of the photograph. Toppled trees and telephone pole also impeded traffic (right). (EC and HSA.)

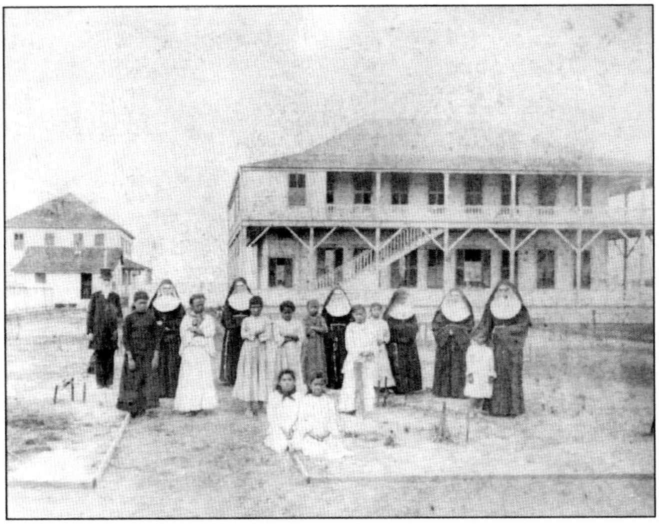

Kakaako Leper Hospital, 1886. In 1881, a hospital for those in the initial stages of leprosy was opened at the present intersection of Coral and Ala Moana. Mother Marianne Cope and six other Catholic sisters took over management in 1883. Shown above are the sisters and Kakaako patients with Prime Minister Walter Murray Gibson. The Kakaako Hospital facilities were removed to Kalihi Kai around 1889 due to flooding by high tides at the Kakaako site. (HSA.)

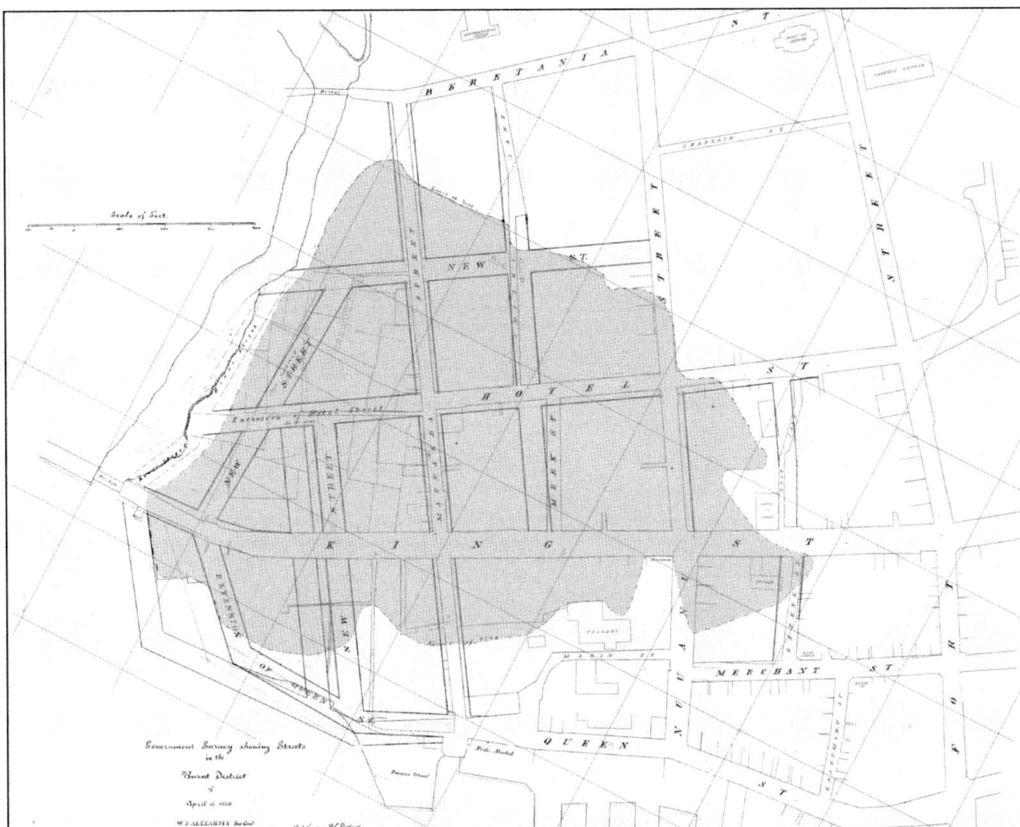

Burnt District, April 18, 1886. Originating near the corner of Hotel and Smith, the 1886 fire destroyed much of the town Ewa of Nuuanu, but had repercussions over an even wider area. The government responded to the debacle by reorganizing roads to improve access. Hotel, King, Nuuanu, and Maunakea were widened. Queen, Bethel, and Smith were straightened and extended, and Pauahi, River, and Kekaulike Streets were further developed. (Government Survey Original Registered Title Map 1141.)

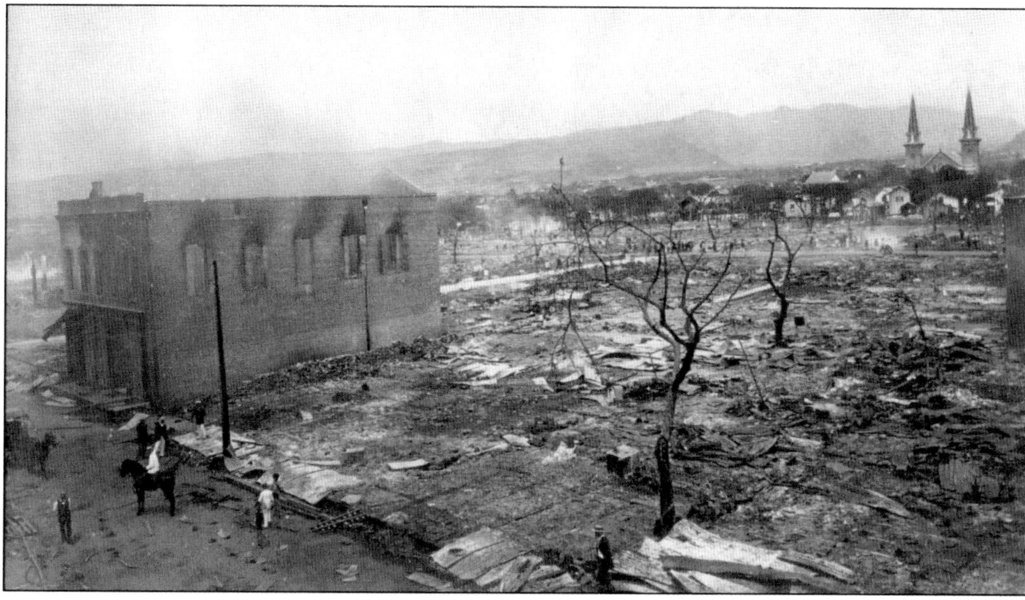

1886 BURNED LANDSCAPE. After completing their plantation labor contracts, many immigrants resettled in what became Chinatown. Here, they hoped to obtain more remunerative professions. The quick spread of the 1886 fire prevented many from saving their possessions. When they were allowed to return, the spectacle of denuded chimneys and buildings must have been very discouraging. The determination of these people to rebuild was a testimony to their character. In the lower left, horse tracks are visible in the soot. (HSA.)

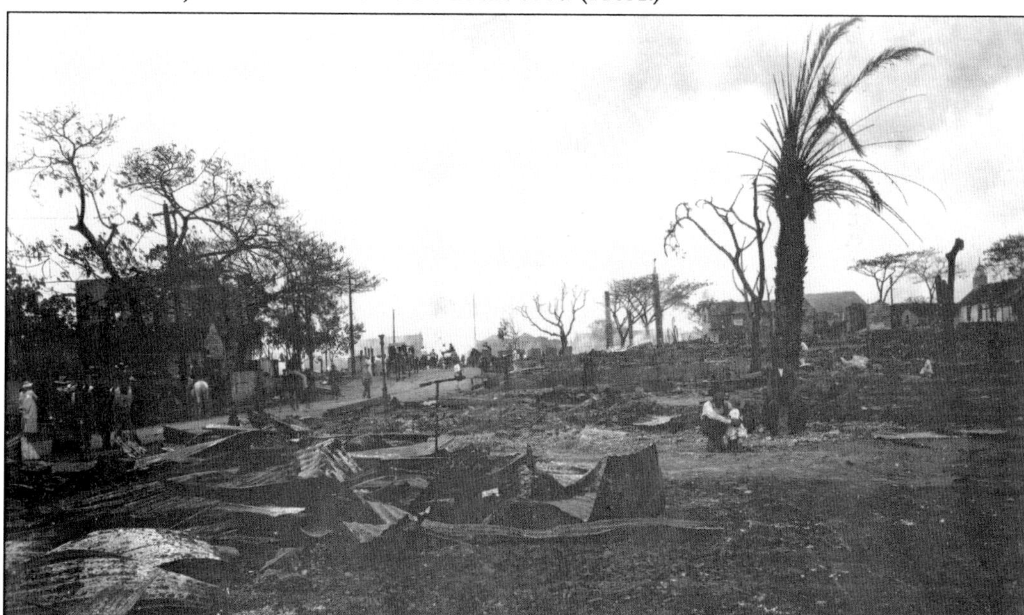

1886 FIRE. The gaping hole left by the fire in the heart of the city can be understood by the empty foreground contrasting with the buildings in the distance. Construction techniques and property layouts can also be discerned by the remains of trees in the centers of the blocks, where gardens and courtyards had remained hidden from the street. The twisted remains of *totan* (corrugated tin) roofing once covered single-wall wooden buildings. (HSA.)

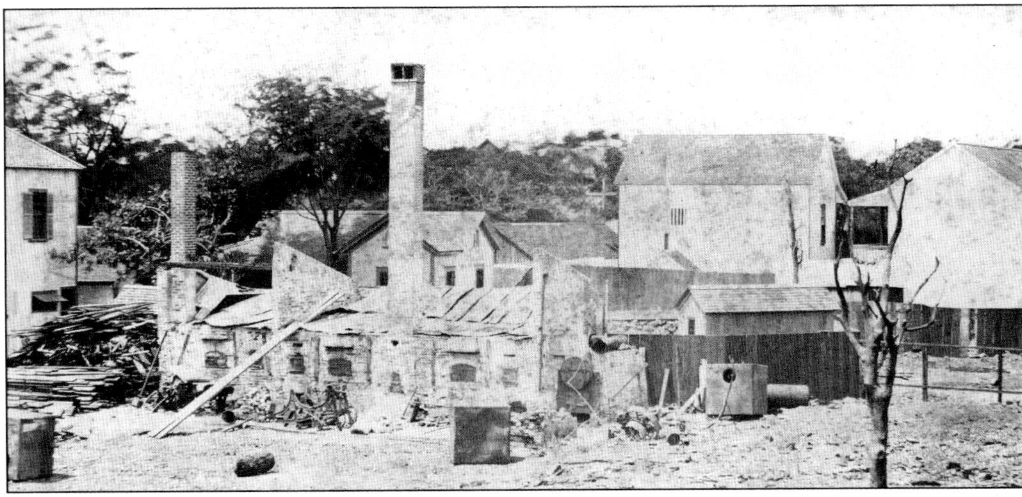

RUINS OF LOVE'S BAKERY, 1886. A native of Glasgow, Scotland, Robert Love arrived in Honolulu in 1851 and established his bakery on the Ewa side of Nuuanu Avenue in 1853. The bulk of his business originally came from purchasing spoiled bread from ships, re-baking it, and then selling it back as hardtack (hard biscuits). Love's Bakery succumbed to the conflagration, leaving only the ovens standing. (HSA.)

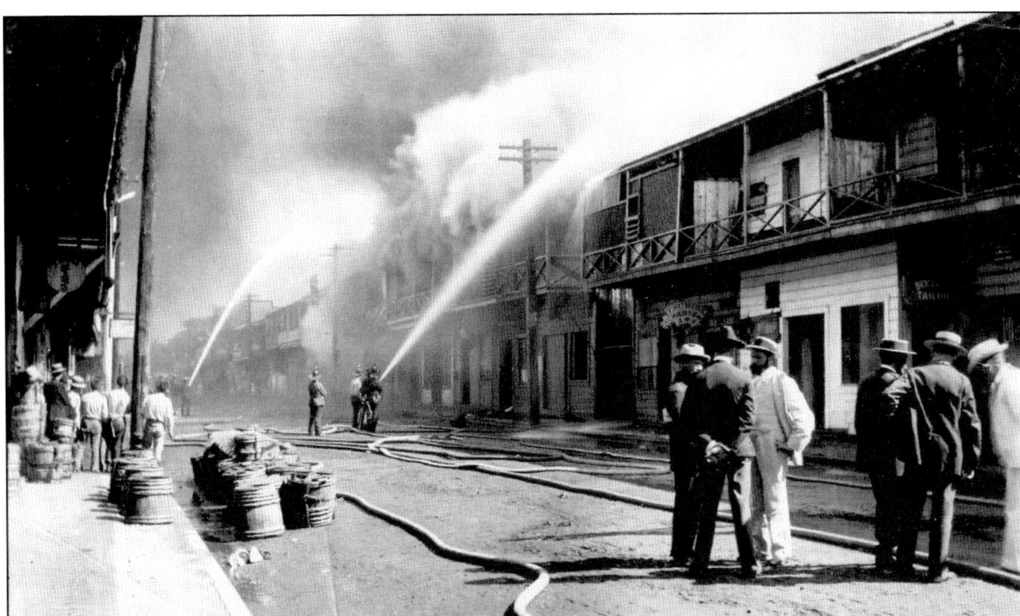

CONFERENCE, 1900. The Board of Health Doctors—Clifford Wood, Francis Day, and Nathaniel Emerson—took control of Honolulu government in 1899 when You Chong, an employee of the Wing Wo Tai Company on Nuuanu, died of "pestis." The doctors quarantined the area between Kukui, Nuuanu, and Marin, the harbor, and Nuuanu Stream and decided to burn any buildings within that were suspected of containing the plague. (HHS.)

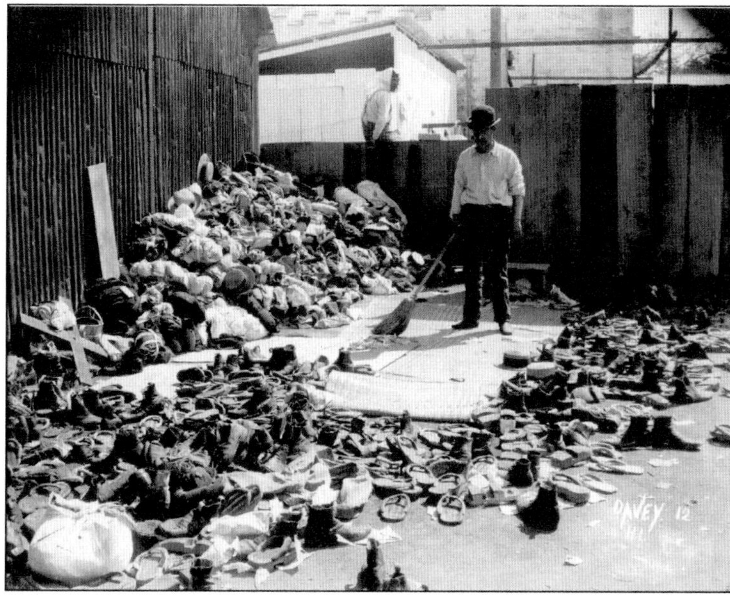

PLAGUE CONTROL. Prior to the conflagration, the government had conducted controlled burning of buildings and personal possessions of those living near suspected pestis. This photograph illustrates clothing, boots, and *zori* (Japanese slippers) left behind, probably by those required to take antiseptic baths. (HHS.)

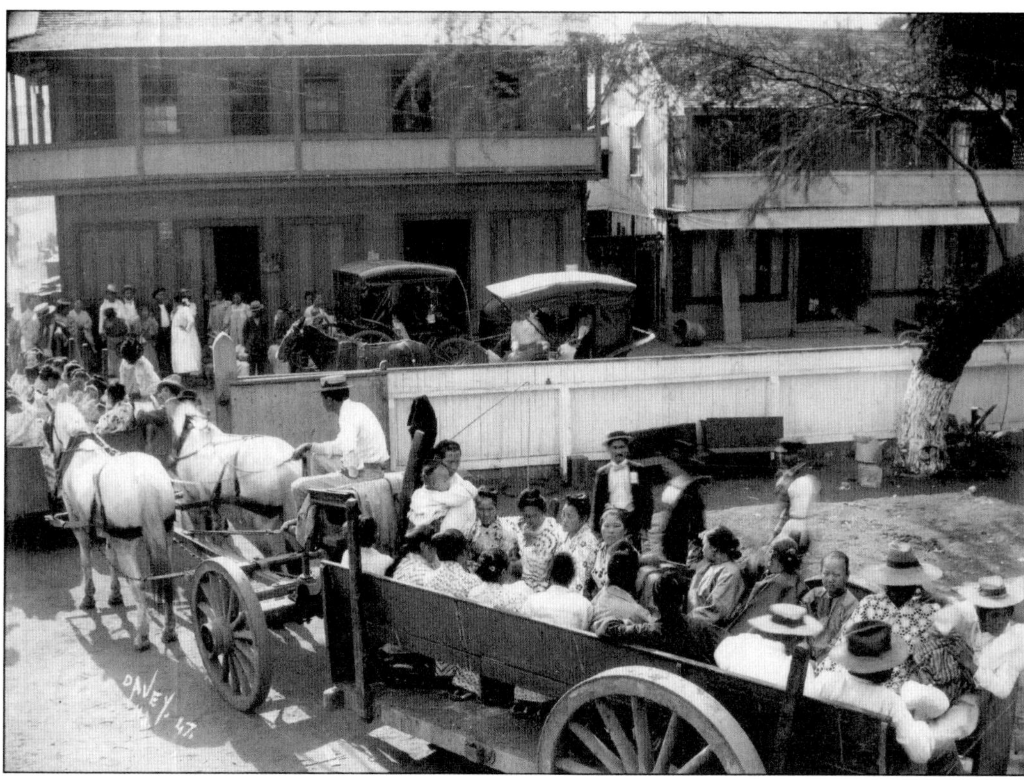

EVACUATION. Movement of people out of the quarantine/fire area was under strict supervision (note the three men in the center). Here, cross-traffic is stopped as refugees sequestered in wagons leave the infected area in a caravan. The women in this wagon are wearing Japanese, Chinese, and Hawaiian dress. (HHS.)

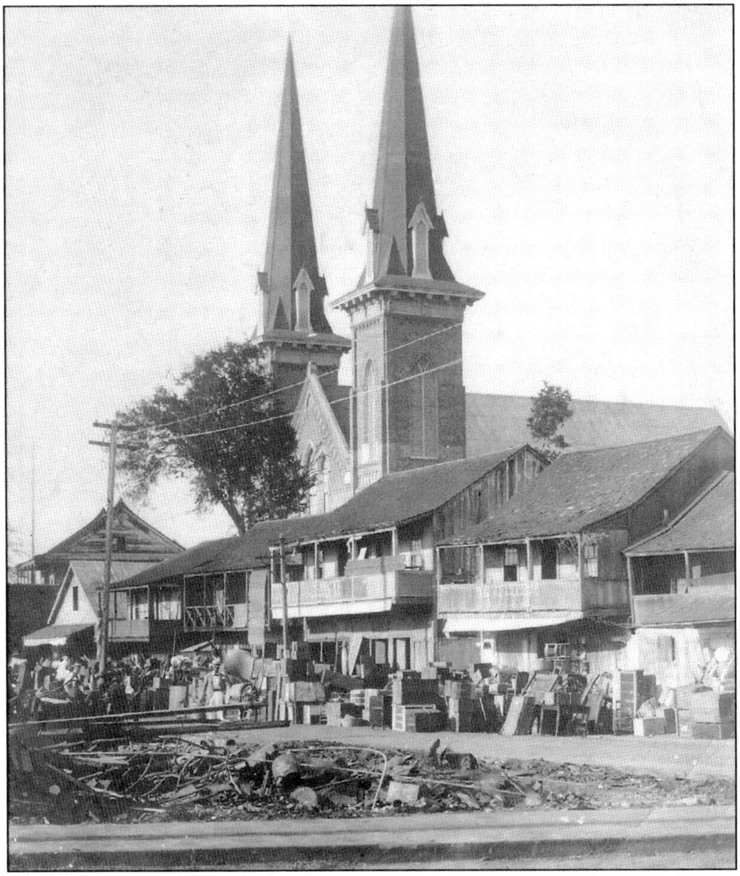

CROWDED CONDITIONS AROUND KAUMAKAPILI CHURCH, 1900. The lessons offered by the 1886 fire were not well learned. Note the wood construction, closeness of buildings, narrowness of Beretania Street, and overhangs above the sidewalk. Occupants of buildings adjacent to Kaumakapili Church evacuated their belongings in advance of a planned burn. Such a burn Diamond Head of the church in January 1900 turned to tragedy as the wind picked up and changed direction, sending sparks toward the church and ultimately consuming everything shown in this image. (HSA.)

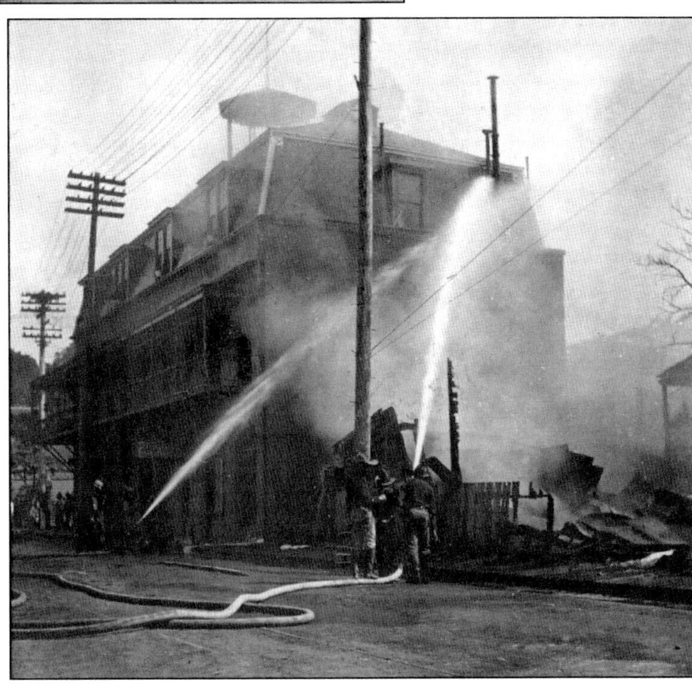

BURNING BUILDINGS OUTSIDE CHINATOWN, 1900. Contrary to popular belief, buildings were also deliberately torched outside of Chinatown in the government's attempt to control the spread of bubonic plague. In the photograph, the mauka-Diamond Head corner of Merchant and Alakea has been burned while firemen seek to prevent the Occidental Hotel (makai-Diamond Head corner of King and Alakea) from burning also. (HSA.)

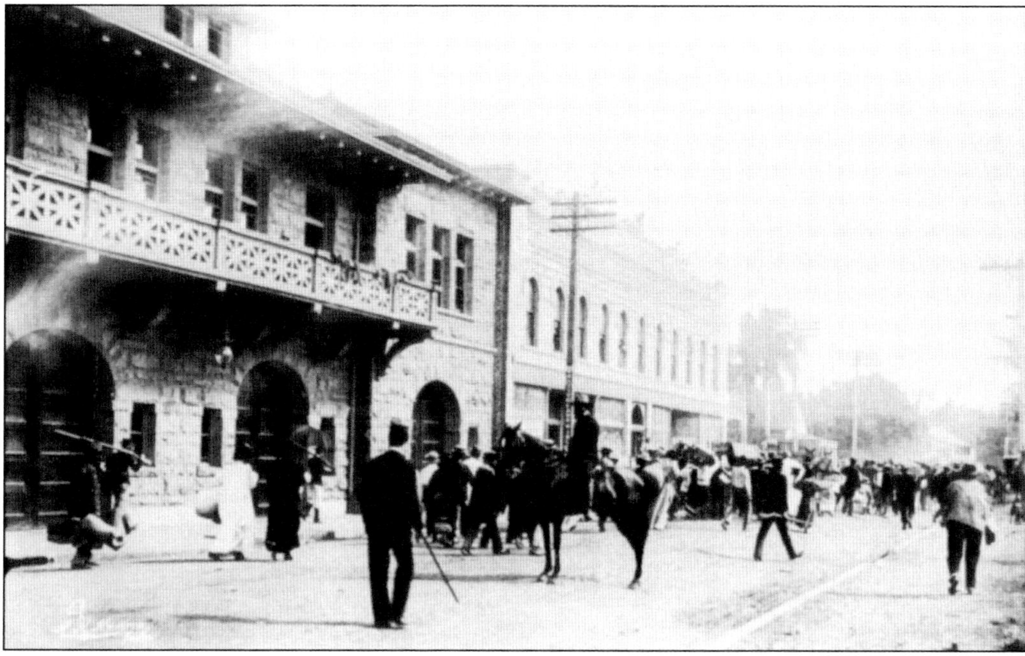

FIRE EVACUEES FLEE PAST THE FIRE STATION. Here, police direct refugees from the 1900 fire, sending them Diamond Head on Beretania toward an encampment at Kawaiahao Church. Ironically, they are in front of the bluestone 1897 Central Fire Station, at Fort and Beretania Streets, designed by Clinton B. Ripley and C.W. Dickey. The building was later torn down and replaced by the present C.W. Dickey Building in 1934. (PS.)

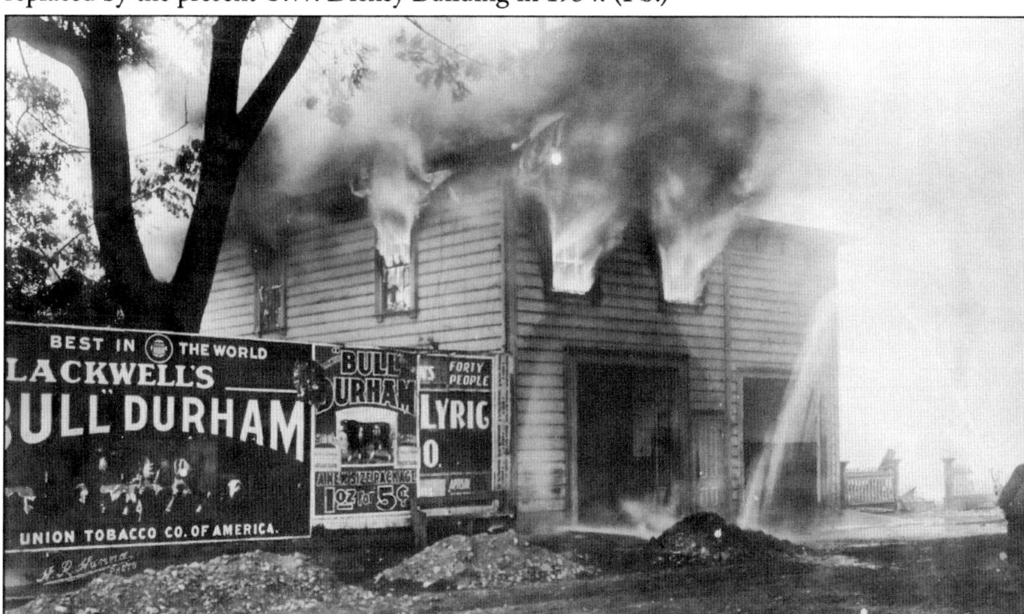

FATE OF WOODEN BUILDINGS, 1900 FIRE. What appears to be a warehouse building burns, with the windows blown out, feeding the interior fire and leading to a roof collapse before the bottom level was consumed. A fireman on the extreme right, utilizing what little water pressure was available, does his best to control the conflagration. (PS.)

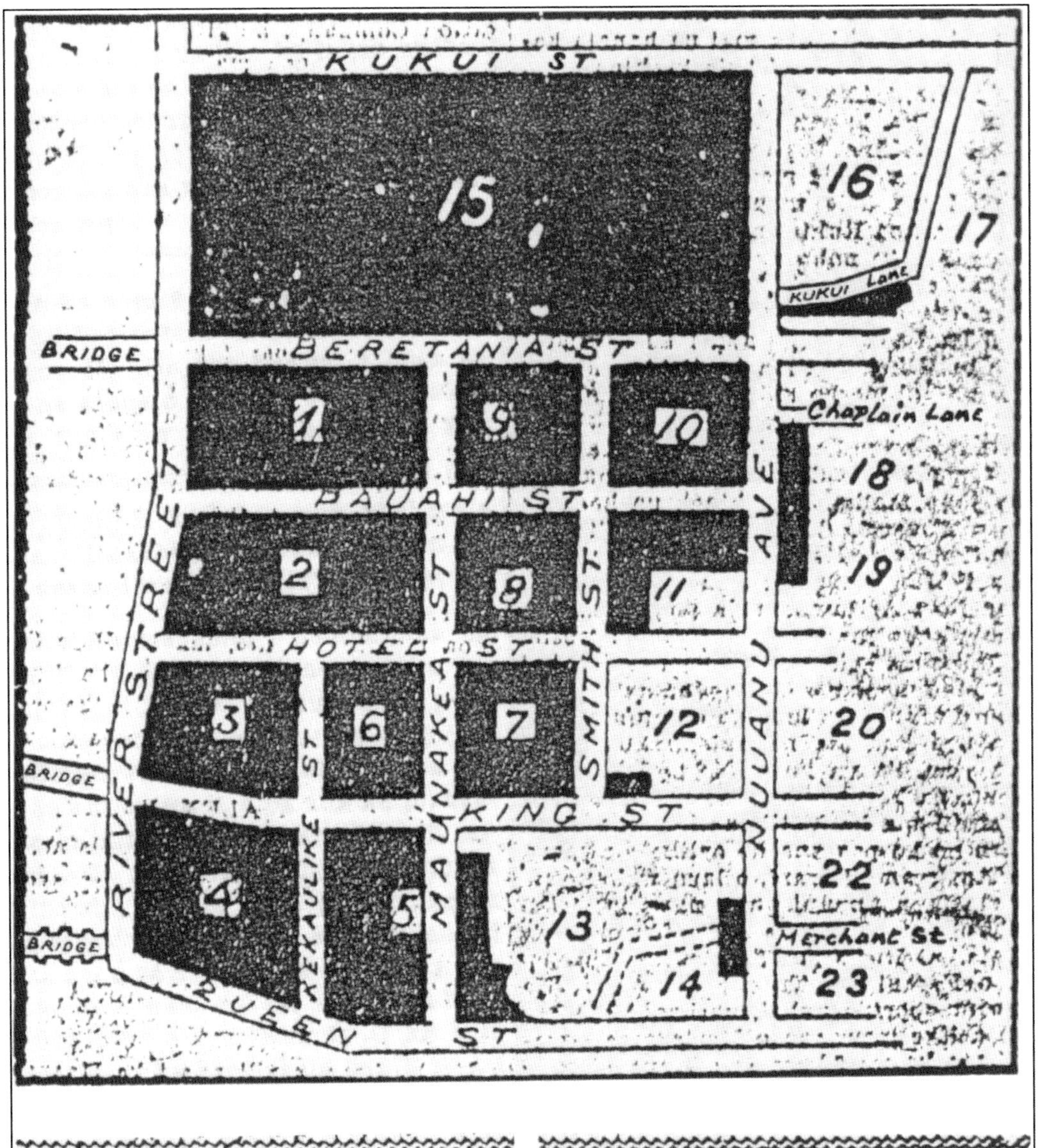

BURNT DISTRICT 1900. Although the streets had been widened and straightened after the 1886 conflagration, such streets were not effective enough firebreaks in an environment of predominately densely packed wooden structures and poor water pressure. After this second massive fire in 14 years, owners were required by law to build using only noncombustible brick and stone. (*Kuokoa*.)

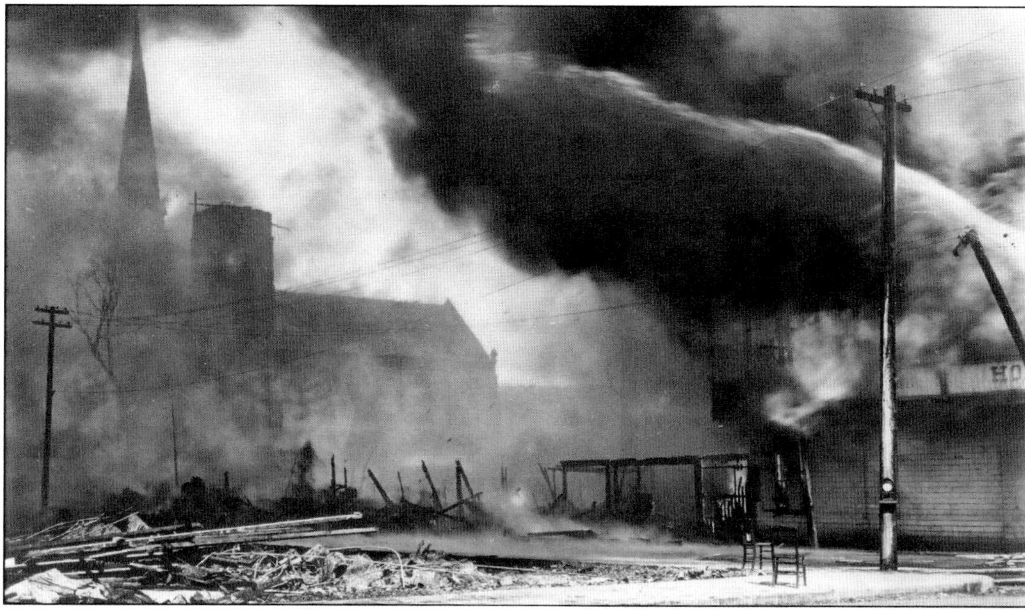

SPREAD OF 1900 FIRE, KAUMAKAPILI. As the fire moved in the Ewa direction, the stream of water from a fire department hose could be seen on the right trying to prevent another building from burning. In the left background the Diamond Head steeple of Kaumakapili was consumed, while the Ewa steeple soon suffered a similar fate. A change in wind direction and speed turned a planned controlled burn into a conflagration that overwhelmed the fire department. (PS.)

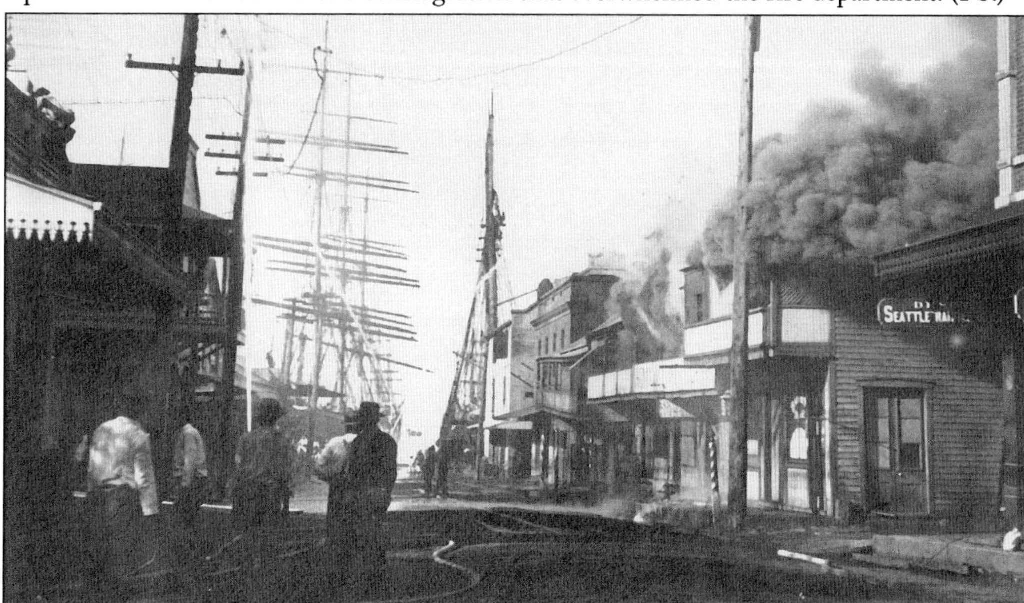

HONOLULU TOWN'S WORST NIGHTMARE. As Chinatown burned on January 20, 1900, the flames get close to the harbor. Two masted wooden ships can be seen makai dangerously nearby the burning buildings on Nuuanu between King and Merchant. The real threat was that this might give the flames new routes back into the city, and that the tightly packed ships would also burn, making fire control even more difficult and covering the harbor bottom with ruined hulks. (HSA.)

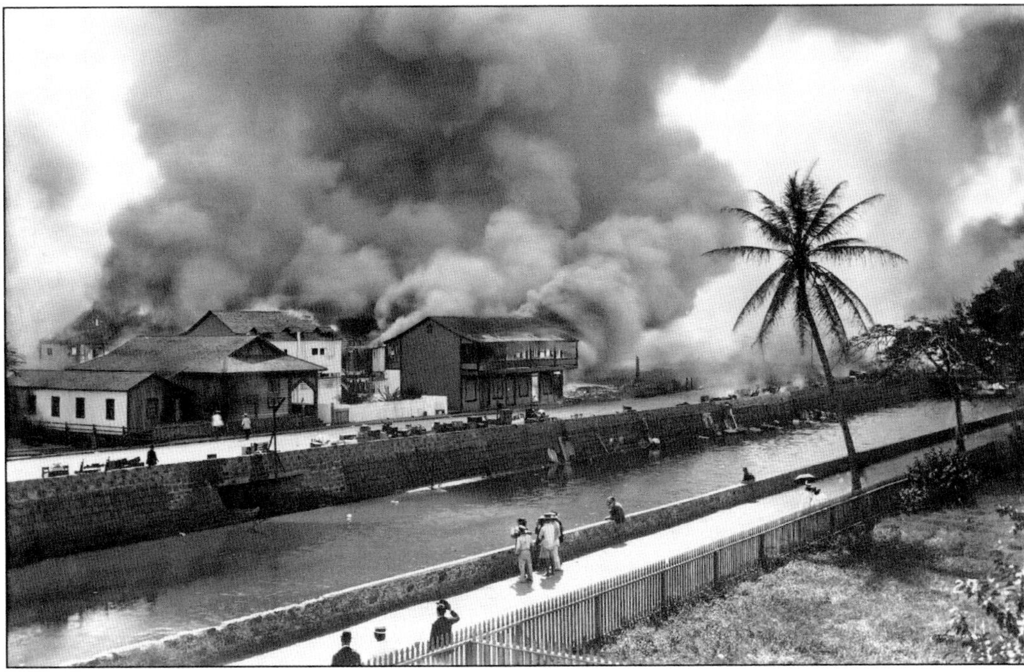

1900 FIRE STOPPED BY NUUANU STREAM. Personal belongings and business goods can be seen stacked beside the Nuuanu Stream channel's Diamond Head wall in an attempt by Chinatown residents to save their property. Pushcarts and hand trucks have been lowered into the stream to further safeguard them against the fire. Kaumakapili Church is engulfed in smoke. Meanwhile, the conflagration continues extending makai toward the waterfront where close-packed ships and coal stocks also present a severe fire hazard. (Photograph by Brother Bertram; HSA.)

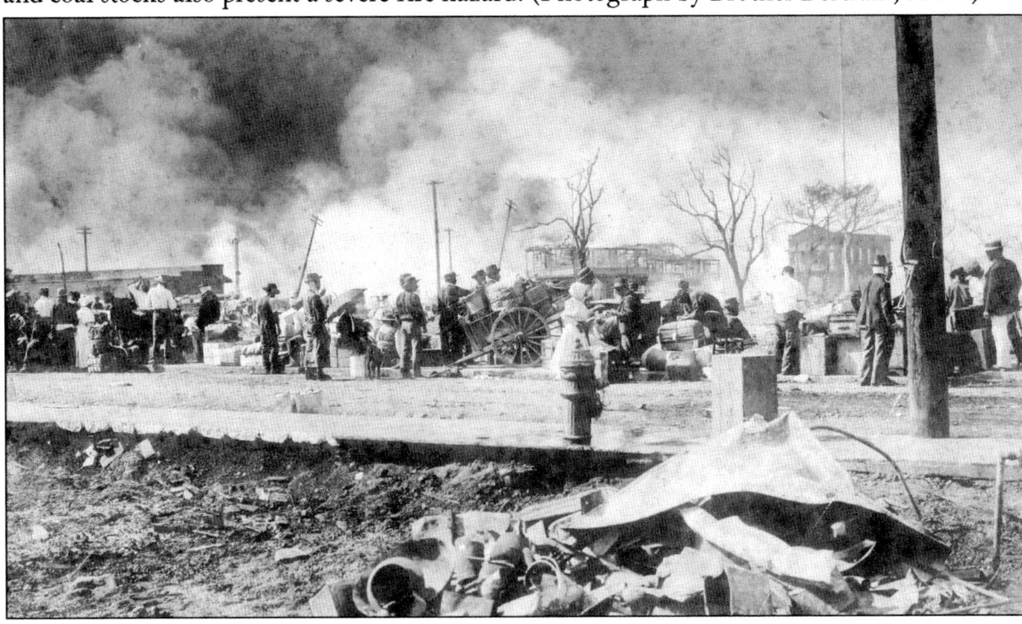

DISBELIEF. Victims of the fire of 1900 watch the advance of the flames and smoke from areas already consumed. Some had managed to save a few possessions, while others just sit and watch the surreal scene (note chair on the right). (HSA.)

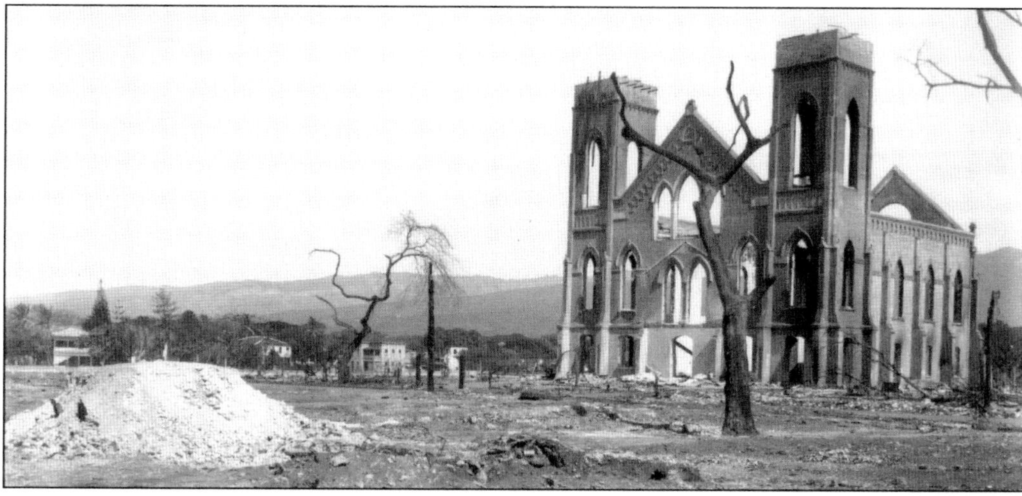

KAUMAKAPILI CHURCH SHELL, 1900. It is clear from this close-up view of the ruin of Kaumakapili Church that it once dominated its neighborhood. However, because this was the second major fire in two decades (combined with continued fears of disease), the government promulgated policies that dispersed the population. Kaumakapili Church would follow its parishioners to Austin Lane makai of the Palama Fire Station before locating at King and Palama Streets. (Photograph by Brother Bertram; HSA.)

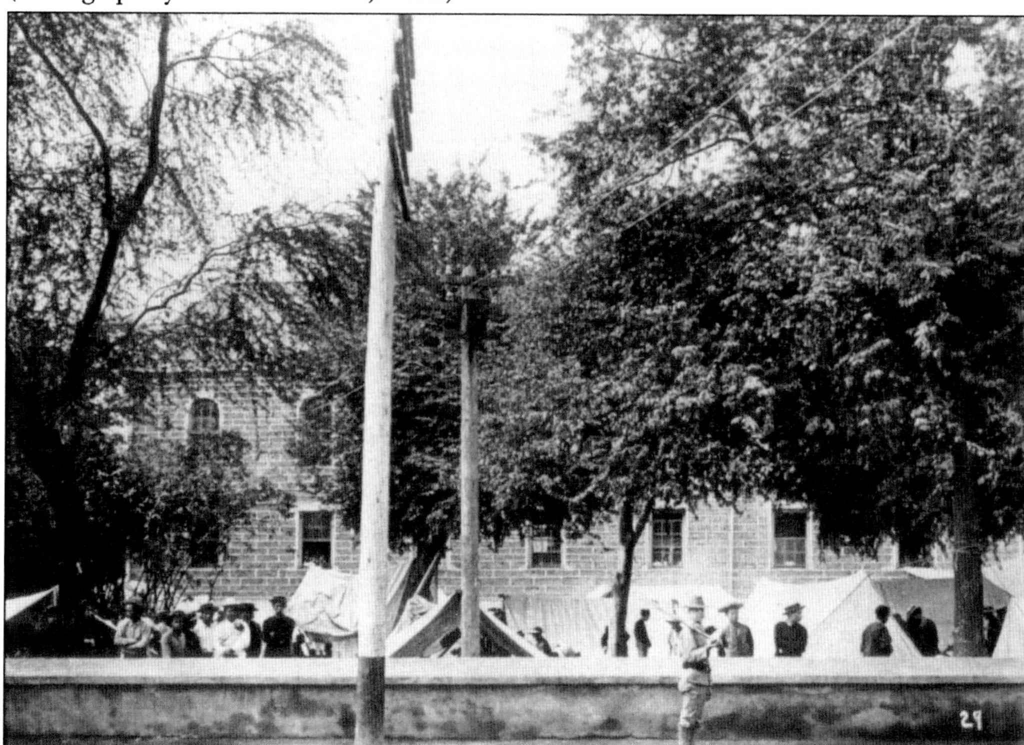

REFUGE, 1900. Monitored by soldiers, victims of the 1900 fire remain under quarantine even after reaching the grounds of Kawaiahao Church. This view looking makai shows the refugees at the site of today's fountain just makai of South King. Kawaiahao Church still has such a low wall along the street. (PS.)